PHILOSC ...NGUAGE

This book offers readers a collection of 50 short chapter entries on topics in the philosophy of language. Each entry addresses a paradox, a longstanding puzzle, or a major theme that has emerged in the field from the last 150 years, tracing overlap with issues in philosophy of mind, cognitive science, ethics, political philosophy, and literature. Each of the 50 entries is written as a piece that can stand on its own, though useful connections to other entries are mentioned throughout the text. Readers can open the book and start with almost any of the entries, following themes of greatest interest to them. Each entry includes recommendations for further reading on the topic.

Philosophy of Language: 50 Puzzles, Paradoxes, and Thought Experiments is useful as a standalone textbook, or can be supplemented by additional readings that instructors choose. The accessible style makes it suitable for introductory level through intermediate undergraduate courses, as well as for independent learners, or even as a reference for more advanced students and researchers.

Key Features:

- Uses a problem-centered approach to philosophy of language (rather than author- or theory-centered) making the text more inviting to first-time students of the subject.
- Offers stand-alone chapters, allowing students to quickly understand an issue and giving instructors flexibility in assigning readings to match the themes of the course.
- Provides up-to-date recommended readings at the end of each chapter, or about 500 sources in total, amounting to an extensive review of the literature on each topic.

Michael P. Wolf is Professor of Philosophy at Washington and Jefferson College. He writes on topics in philosophy of language, epistemology, and metaethics. His published works include *The Normative and the Natural* (2016) with Jeremy Koons, and numerous articles in journals such as *Philosophical Studies*, *Pacific Philosophical Quarterly*, and *Philosophical Investigations*.

PUZZLES, PARADOXES, AND THOUGHT EXPERIMENTS IN PHILOSOPHY

Imaginative cases – or what might be called puzzles, paradoxes, and other thought experiments – play a central role in philosophy. This series offers students and researchers a wide range of such imaginative cases, with each volume devoted fifty such cases in a major subfield of philosophy. Every book in the series includes: some initial background information on each case, a clear and detailed description of the case, and an explanation of the issue(s) to which the case is relevant. Key responses to the case and suggested readings lists are also included.

Recently Published Volumes:

EPISTEMOLOGY
KEVIN McCAIN

PHILOSOPHY OF LANGUAGE
MICHAEL P. WOLF

FREE WILL AND HUMAN AGENCY
GARRETT PENDERGRAFT

AESTHETICS
MICHEL-ANTOINE XHIGNESSE

Forthcoming Volumes:

ETHICS
SARAH STROUD AND DANIEL MUÑOZ

PHILOSOPHY OF MIND
TORIN ALTER, AMY KIND, AND CHASE B. WRENN

BIOETHICS
SEAN AAS, COLLIN O'NEIL, AND CHIARA LEPORA

METAPHYSICS
SAM COWLING, WESLEY D. CRAY, AND KELLY TROGDON

For a full list of published volumes in **Puzzles, Paradoxes, and Thought Experiments in Philosophy**, please visit www.routledge.com/Puzzles,Paradoxes,andThoughtExperimentsinPhilosophy/book-series/PPTEP

PHILOSOPHY OF LANGUAGE: 50 PUZZLES, PARADOXES, AND THOUGHT EXPERIMENTS

Michael P. Wolf

NEW YORK AND LONDON

Designed cover image: © Getty Images

First published 2023
by Routledge
605 Third Avenue, New York, NY 10158

and by Routledge
4 Park Square, Milton Park, Abingdon, Oxon, OX14 4RN

Routledge is an imprint of the Taylor & Francis Group, an informa business

ISBN: 978-1-032-02386-1 (hbk)
ISBN: 978-1-032-02385-4 (pbk)
ISBN: 978-1-003-18316-7 (ebk)

DOI: 10.4324/9781003183167

Typeset in Bembo
by Apex CoVantage, LLC

For my parents,
Anne and Daniel

CONTENTS

PREFACE

This is a book about language. Each of its entries tackles a paradox, puzzle, problem, or theme from the study of language, but each one is intended to be a window into some feature of the larger topography of natural language as a whole. While each of these essays discusses the work of some notable philosophers, each one is first and foremost a look at what some part of a language means, or how we make use of it. They are arranged loosely around some major themes, but it would be possible to read them in any order you like and start with whichever entries sound interesting.

The book begins – following this preface – with a longer general background essay, which is significantly longer. That background essay introduces several technical concepts that play a part in almost all of the entries that follow. I'd encourage you to read it first and return to it later whenever those concepts play an important role in another entry that you're reading. Each section of entries also has a brief background entry to help orient your reading in more specific ways. To help you draw further connections between all these ideas, each one directs you to other entries where there are useful intersections of topics. Each one also includes about a dozen recommended readings on the topics, and briefly describes how they fit into the landscape of the topic.

There are a few other things I should say about this book. A few years ago, my friend Chauncey Maher said that I needed to write a book on the philosophy of language. He said this in such flattering, Michael-Padraic-Wolf-affirming terms that I assumed he was going to hit me up for a ride to the airport later, but it all appears to have been sincere. A couple years later, Andy Beck from Routledge told me that he had read some of my work and thought I should write a book on the philosophy of language. At that point, with two exceptionally smart people making the same case, how could I refuse? My thanks to both of them for their encouragement in taking on such a project.

I want to thank Elizabeth Weimer for serving as my editorial assistant for much of the work done on this book. Let me also thank Washington and Jefferson College for recognizing the value of her work and supporting our efforts. I also got a great deal of useful advice and feedback from Helen Daly, Kate Vanier, Sam Stewart, and Jocelyn Waite.

My special thanks to Jocelyn Waite for talking me down from various ledges, commiserating all the miseries, and vilifying sundry foes on the way to completing this project.

GENERAL INTRODUCTION

This volume, devoted to the ways in which philosophers have sought to understand language, presents 50 problems in the discipline for those new to its study. While the entries can be used as an introduction to philosophy of language, they can also serve as a gateway or supplement to the study of knowledge, metaphysics, ethics, and other fields within philosophy.

Philosophical efforts to come to grips with language and its links to thought stretch back thousands of years. Confucian philosophers of ancient China stressed precise use of language to avoid confusion and disorder, and scholars devoted a great deal of attention to methods for achieving such clarity. (A "rectification" or "right ordering" of the language, as it was put.) Mohist scholars in China would respond with accounts that emphasized the role of language in logic and reasoning. Grammarians of Sanskrit sacred texts in what we now call India took matters of interpretation, meaning, and the transmission of belief via language to be urgent philosophical concerns, worthy of systematic investigation in their own right.

In the Western tradition, language was long of merely peripheral concern to philosophers, with questions about thought considered to be more fundamental to our understanding of ourselves. At the beginning of the 20th century, language became a field of its own in

DOI: 10.4324/9781003183167-1

Western philosophy. Several factors played into this shift. There had been considerable development of logical tools and methods, making deeper, more illuminating analysis possible. Mathematics in the West had been in tumult for decades, as revolutionary ideas from Georg Cantor had upended orthodox theories and sparked interest in defining terms and the foundations of mathematics. The natural sciences were also in an especially fruitful period, with the advent of quantum mechanics and relativistic mechanics suggesting great leaps forward. Inspired by these changes and the work of Gottlob Frege, Bertrand Russell, and Ludwig Wittgenstein in particular, many English- and German-speaking philosophers took a new interest in language.

Taking their cues from mathematics and the natural sciences, philosophers working in this vein strove for greater precision and circumscription in their work. Rather than grand books purporting to explain everything, the dominant form of written philosophy in Western intellectual circles became short journal articles devoted to careful analysis of narrowly defined problems. This set of concerns, approaches, and methods came to be known as *analytic philosophy*, and it has been the predominant style of philosophy in the English-speaking world for much of the last century. Though there are disputes about just who is an analytic philosopher, that label could be applied to a large majority of the philosophers and texts referenced in this book.

With this in mind, let me offer a few notes about the entries in this book. Entries on single subjects are grouped together by topic, though these groupings are relatively loose. Most of the entries can be understood on their own, without the need to read others beforehand. There is always some overlap in the material, in that taking up theoretical commitments always entails further consequences, and answers to theoretical questions invariably invite further theoretical questions. Where this overlap seems especially important, I have noted it by suggesting further entries to read. Each entry also includes a set of recommended readings, discussed briefly in a "Responses" section. In some entries, I simply point you to recommended readings when additional discussion would make the entry too long. Wherever possible, I have opted for recent and readily accessible sources. Where I do mention older texts, many are in the public domain and readily available online.

Each entry is presented as a "case study," in a manner appropriate for its place in a book series on puzzles, paradoxes, and thought experiments. Puzzles and thought experiments have a prominent place in the philosophical fields of ethics and the theory of knowledge. In articles on knowledge, it's common to find fictional scenarios in which something strange happens, and we then consider whether someone's belief still counts as knowledge. That sort of framing device is less common in the philosophy of language. More articles simply take a "Here's three weird sentences!" approach and dive into the details. As these entries are intended as introductions to these problems, I have in many cases added framing to illustrate some motivations for considering them.

There are also a number of concepts and terms that are used in very specific ways among philosophers of language, some of which will occur in almost every entry in this book. Rather than explain them quickly (and poorly) in each entry, let me define them here.

SENTENCES AND PROPOSITIONS

Philosophers and linguists draw a distinction between sentences and propositions. Sentences are well-formed strings of words in some language. That could be a natural language like English or American Sign Language, or a formal language like the systems of predicate logic that students learn in undergraduate philosophy courses. For all but a few entries in this book, you can assume that we're talking about sentences in natural languages. Thus, 'Gregg gave a book to Hanna!' is an English sentence; 'to book a! gave Gregg Hanna' is assuredly not. Nor would countless other random combinations of symbols be. This example is a statement in the indicative mood, as grammarians would say. We could also have well-formed sentences that were questions, commands, and many other sorts.

The examples thus far have been exclusively English sentences, and Modern English sentences at that. We might imagine saying "the same thing" with different sentences from a variety of different languages (with a few rough phonetic guides):

Modern English: The cat sat on the mat.
Old English: Se catte on maette saet.

German:	Die Katze saß auf der Matte.
Swahili:	Paka aliketi juu ya mkeka.
Turkish:	Kedi matın üstüne oturdu. [*kay-dee maw-tin oo-stin-ah oh-tor-da*]
Hebrew:	המחצלת על יושב החתול. [*Ha chaTOOL yoSHAv al hamachTZELet*]
Arabic:	جلست القطة على السجادة [*Jalasat Al kita fee Al bisaat*]
Hindi:	बिल्ली चटाई पर बैठ गई।[*Billee chaTaee par baiTh gayee*]
Korean:	그 고양이는 매트 위에 앉았다 [*Geugoyang-i-neun mae-teu wee-eh ahn-jaht-da*][1]

These sentences are certainly not the same in a letter-by-letter, word-by-word sense. Yet there is some sense in which they all say "the same thing" in their respective languages.

That common content, whatever theoretical account we give of it, is what we will call a "proposition." Sentences that state facts (like those above) can be said to express propositions, and we would expect every well-formed sentence that presents itself as a statement of fact to express some proposition. The same sentence might express different propositions on different occasions if some of the terms in the sentence are sensitive to features of the context of their use. For instance, 'I am here' contains the pronoun 'I' whose designation depends on who uses the sentence on any given occasion, and the adverb 'here,' which depends on the place in which it is used. Questions, commands, and the other sorts I mentioned earlier don't exactly express propositions in this sense; 'What time is it?' doesn't express any proposition about what time it is, for instance. So sometimes logicians and semanticists will use the term 'sentence' only for those sentences that do purport to state facts – and thus express propositions – and leave the rest to linguists and grammarians. However, we can generally understand the function of those other types of sentences in relation to such proposition-expressing sentences. 'What time is it?' poses a question that may be answered by a statement of various different proposition-expressing sentences – e.g., 'It's 3:17 PM.'

Some philosophers have explained propositions in terms of abstract, non-physical entities, while others have suggested states of affairs, sets of possible worlds, or other combinations of concrete entities. Still others have suggested that meaning is bound up with the use we make of a language, so an account of propositions should reflect that.

Deciding which, if any, of these approaches to adopt lies beyond the scope of this text, but any one of them will preserve this distinction between sentences and propositions.

SYNTAX AND SEMANTICS

When we address a sentence's semantic content, we're considering what people would colloquially call its meaning, or the meanings of its parts. There are many different accounts of meaning, as we will see, so this is just a rough first pass at a philosophically contentious subject. However, most philosophers of language would include properties such as the truth of a sentence and the reference of any words in it to be among its semantic properties.

We can also examine what makes sentences well-formed, interpretable strings of words. These formal properties are the syntax of a sentence. While few people explicitly know the grammar rules of the languages they use well enough to articulate what makes for good or bad syntax, most can still recognize better and worse versions:

(1)   Jeremy and I had pizza while we talked about philosophy.
(2)   While we had pizza, I and Jeremy, about philosophy we talked.
(3)   I philosophy while. and pizza Jeremy about talked had we

Most English speakers will have no difficulty interpreting the first sentence here. The second will sound confused, but some of its clauses might still be read (possibly in Yoda's voice). The third example is just a jumble of words and would not be recognizable as a sentence at all. Different natural languages will manage and distinguish their syntactical categories in various ways. In English, the simplest declarative sentences will start with the subject of the sentence (such as a name, or 'Jeremy and I' in (1)), follow that with a verb, then move on to any other clauses. Word order is especially important in English syntax. In other natural languages, there are far more ways in which nouns and verbs may be *inflected* – modified, such as by adding a prefix or suffix – to make syntactical distinctions. With more such markers, word order will be less important in a language's syntax.

While there are important distinctions to be drawn between syntactic and semantic features of sentences, readers should be careful not to think of them as wholly independent of one another. And the syntactic form of a sentence tells us how to interpret the meaning of a whole that would not be possible by looking at the meanings of its parts in isolation. For instance:

(4)   Flynn loves Liz.
(5)   Liz loves Flynn.

These sentences include the same words, presumably referring to the same people, but the sentences have very different semantic contents because different names occupy the subject position. Flynn does the lovin' in the first sentence, while Liz does it in the second. Neither name names someone differently but changes in their arrangement lead us to a different statement.

PRAGMATICS AND SPEECH ACTS

We can also distinguish between the meaning of a sentence in all the various ways mentioned so far and the different ways it might be used by speakers for various purposes. A well-worn illustration involves the English sentence 'The door is open.' We can account for its syntax and semantics as described above, but a language user might take very different actions with it even as its meaning remains the same. Someone might use that sentence to report that the door is open, but also to indirectly command someone to close the door, or (with a little stage-setting) as a dramatic metaphor of encouragement. ("Kate, if you want great things, you have to walk through the doors that life opens up for you. And Kate, right now, *the door is open!*") The goals and purposes to which the use of this sentence is directed in a context are essential to understanding it fully. These different uses that a sentence might be put to are the focus of the field of pragmatics within the philosophy of language.

Pragmatics as a field is less uniform and systematic than syntax or semantics. There are an enormous number of different ends that we might undertake with a language, and few philosophers argue that theoretical accounts of them will exhibit a tidy, simple order. One feature of natural languages that is often lumped in under pragmatics that might permit greater systematic treatment is the context-sensitivity of certain expressions. Use of expressions like pronouns ('I,' 'you,' etc.) requires attention to the context of that use, not just a fixed account of their meaning. But the ways in which they change with context will be systematic – we fix the reference of 'I' by noting who uses the expression in a given utterance. Whether there are further pragmatic implications in using such expressions will be the subject of several entries that follow.

Some philosophers of language have offered accounts that stressed various categories of actions users of a language can undertake. We can call these *speech acts*. A systematic taxonomy of possible speech acts might be a goal of philosophers interested in this question, though not all attempt to offer one. Asserting some sentence as true would be one such speech act, but consider some others:

(6)   I confer upon you the degree of Bachelor of Arts in philosophy.
(7)   We'll call him Michael.
(8)   Drop and give me 20!
(9)   Never gonna give you up, never gonna let you down.

The phrasing in (6) is something you might hear at a graduation ceremony said by a dean or president, but it is not an assertion. The dean or president is acting to officially change the status of someone by saying this, not asserting that they already have a degree. A sentence like (7) might be said by a new parent, but they are not making a *prediction*. In that case, they introduce a name to themselves and other language users, setting a precedent and licensing everyone to use it. Sentence (8) might be shouted by a coach as a *command*, and someone saying (9) is *promising* these things to their audience. In some cases, a speech act type may have distinct terms or phrases associated with it that explicitly invoke the type they perform: 'I confer upon . . .', 'I promise that . . .'.

Different accounts postulate different categories of speech acts, with many varieties within each category. Speech act theorists don't generally purport to offer a complete list of all possible act types, as there is no *a priori* framework from which the categories and types are derived. Instead, we tend to find them where people's interests are consistent and urgent enough that developing and reinforcing distinctive parts of a language is worth the effort of introducing and reinforcing them.

LOGIC AND PARADOX

To say that there is a "logic" to some use of language is to say that there is some order to it that we follow to reason about a subject, and that we might make that order explicit as a set of rules. In this broad sense, there are many different types of logic: inductive, deductive, abductive; C.S. Peirce wrote extensively on scientific methods and reasoning, consistently calling them "logic." When most philosophers of language have talked of "logic," they have historically been using that as shorthand for deductive logic, and we'll follow that practice in this book.

Deductive logic will be familiar to anyone who has taken a logic course, and even those who haven't will have done some deductive reasoning in a mathematics course. Systems of deductive logic allow us to characterize, catalog, and test arguments based on their form alone. The relevant sense of form in this case is how the premises assumed in an argument relate pieces of information to one another, and then relate all of them to the information in a conclusion. If the form of an argument is deductively valid, then its form guarantees with certainty that if its premises are true, then its conclusion is true as well. Obviously, this is a very powerful tool in understanding good reasoning. However, there are infinitely many arguments we could make in any natural language, with only a small portion of them deductively valid, and we have no hope of checking all of them one at a time. Systems of deductive logic strip away the conceptual details of real arguments to concentrate on the formal relations between pieces of information. When I teach logic, I compare this to the move from arithmetic to algebra.

To get a sense of this, consider two arguments:

(A)	All dogs are mammals.	(B)	All whales have tails.
	This is a dog.		This is a whale.
	This is a mammal.		This has a tail.

The first two sentences in each of these arguments are premises – i.e., assumptions that purportedly lead to our conclusion, the third sentence. The underlining separates premises from conclusion. (For the moment, imagine that I'm pointing to something to indicate what 'This' designates in each argument.)

You might have reservations about these premises. "What if a whale lost its tail?" Could happen I suppose, but in doing deductive logic, we want to get away from specific questions like that to concentrate on logical form. For now, just assume that the premises in (A) and (B) are true. If so, is there any way that the conclusions in each argument could be false? No, they couldn't. The form of the argument *guarantees* that. Even if one of those premises turned out to be false – we have misjudged the biology of dogs, or the fate of whale tails – the form itself would not be what misled us. If you look again at those arguments, you can see that I've chosen examples that very closely parallel one another. They are about different subjects but they are very similar in form. If (A) is good, then (B) must be as well. Spotting these kinds of formal similarities is the stuff of an introductory logic class, and this is one of the most common argument forms. We could write it out schematically (C), and then translate it into the symbolic form used in the predicate calculus:

(C)   All As are Bs.   (D) $(\forall x)(Ax \rightarrow Bx)$
       <u>This is an A.</u>   <u>Aa</u>
       This is a B.   Ba

Deductive logic became central to projects in analytic philosophy of language from its historical outset. Frege and Russell, the two authors most responsible for the early development of analytic philosophy, were both mathematicians before being corrupted by philosophy. In some cases, they sought to analyze arguments like the (A)-(D) above, but more importantly, they found the formal language developed (like (D)) especially useful in analyzing the meanings of sentences in natural languages. While I have written the entries in this book in a way that does not require extensive knowledge of deductive logic, I would recommend a course (or more) on it to any reader who wishes to dive more deeply into this field.

We can use some of these logical notions to spell out the idea of a paradox more precisely. People often speak of a "paradox" when they encounter surprising results, or tension between their interests. "Americans have more access to information than ever, yet they have become increasingly dogmatic in their views. What a paradox!" That's surprising if true, but it's not a paradox in the strict sense that philosophers use the term. A paradox is a sentence (or small set of sentences) that, despite being plausible and perhaps even apparently true, entails a contradiction. The plausibility and apparent truth matter here; it's not difficult to produce a sentence that entails a contradiction, but we dismiss most of them out of hand:

(10)   Michael P. Wolf has type O+ blood and Michael P. Wolf does not have type O+ blood.

This entails a contradiction, but we can say that it is false. Problem solved. To give readers a hint of what's to come in entries #16–20, take the sentence:

(11)   This sentence is false.

If this sentence is true, then it must be false (since that's what it states). Contradiction! If it is false, then it must be true. Contradiction!

A paradox might not seem that important on its own. The difficulty arises when we realize that the systems of deductive logic described here would be upended by a genuine paradox. As we'll see, one contradiction in the types of logic traditionally adopted by Western philosophers would be enough to upend the truth or falsity of every sentence in the entire language and render every possible argument worthless. So, addressing paradoxes, either by explaining them away or revising our understanding of logic, is a subject of great concern to philosophers of language.

NOTE

1.   Thanks here to Al Nasser Al-Mahrouqi, Bob East, Hanna Kim, Vered Margalit, Lauryn Mayer, Anupama Shanmuganathan, and Anne Wolf for help on these translations.

PART I

BIG PICTURE QUESTIONS

INTRODUCTION

This first section includes entries on the biggest topic in the philosophy of language: what are languages, and how do they come to exist in the first place? If we think of 'language' first and foremost as the sort of complex system of sounds and signs that characterizes how we communicate, there are several thousand spoken actively at present though a large majority of the world's population speaks one of just a few dozen of those as their first language. The interesting philosophical questions involve what structural features (if any) seem to be necessary for any natural language we might come to use, and why natural languages must have them. Entry #1 discusses some responses to these questions.

Entry #2 addresses a challenge to the priority we assign to natural languages. Many philosophers have argued that natural languages are so irregular and vague that they cannot serve as the basis for philosophy, science, and other theoretical projects. Some have argued that we could radically revise our languages to correct these failures with the help of logic. The philosophical question then becomes whether the objects of our study should be natural languages as we already find them, or the ideal languages that might replace them.

Another assumption that readers may bring to the table is that the languages we speak serve as a neutral representational medium; this

DOI: 10.4324/9781003183167-3

allows us to describe the world in many ways, and we tailor our beliefs and claims to the world as we find it. Entry #3 poses a challenge to this. In some cross-cultural linguistic studies, evidence suggests that natural languages differ so deeply that what is said or thought in one language cannot be said or thought in another. In the most radical interpretations of these findings, it has been suggested that users of some natural languages "live in a different world" than those of us speaking, say, English. On these radical interpretations, natural language is the framework that makes belief and perception possible, and a radically different framework can only produce a radically different worldview.

In entry #4, we look at the role of conventions in the emergence of natural languages. Most features of natural languages don't appear to have any kind of natural necessity to them. The appropriate ways of using a natural language appear to be matters of convention – standards introduced by users of those languages and sustained by their agreement. A puzzle presents itself: if conventions underwrite the language, but users must interact and agree to establish those conventions, then how could they have begun interacting with one another to jump-start a language in the first place?

'I AM NO TREE! I AM AN ENT!'

Background: There is little dispute that humans are a language-using species and that our facility with them is of special philosophical, biological, and psychological significance. However, this takes for granted what counts as a language. There are numerous ways of using symbols for different purposes and many ways in which organisms interact in order to transfer information. Establishing precise criteria is challenging but a prime example of philosophical inquiry.

What is a language, and when can we say that we're using one? These are two questions that would seem should be within our grasp, given that we frequently engage in linguistic behavior during our waking lives, and probably a little bit in our dream lives as well. Suppose we start by proposing some conditions that would be part of any definition. When I have taught this subject in the past, one of the first responses that I often get is that languages are *spoken*. Many are, of course, but they can also be written. We could imagine a language that was never spoken aloud, and exchanges with it only took place in written form. There are very good examples of languages that are never spoken: sign languages. Sign languages are not just systems of gestures to stand in for the words of another language; they are languages in their own right, with all the structural complexity and

DOI: 10.4324/9781003183167-4

expressive possibilities of spoken languages. Those who sign in American Sign Language (ASL) are using a distinct language, not simply gesturing English words.

There are also systems that we call languages that are never spoken, nor signed, nor really expressed between people using the language. Here, I have in mind the kinds of formal languages that are used in computer programming. If I write a piece of code in JavaScript or C++, I might *show* it to someone else (such as a professor in a programming class), but I'm not saying those things to that person. I'm not telling them to alphabetize a list, or change the color of a pixel, or whatever else my app might do. That sort of language allows me to give instructions to particular types of machines that then complete tasks, but they are not really my partners in conversation. So here, we might note a couple of conditions. The sorts of languages that we were implicitly thinking about in the opening of this entry are what we call *natural languages*, which are used and shared *in communication* with other users of those languages. English would be a natural language in this sense, as would ASL, and all other spoken, written, and signed languages that communities share to communicate with one another. (Programming and other artificial languages are philosophically interesting, but they're not our concern for the moment.)

As a first pass, let me suggest that communication with a natural language can take place only when some token of it (a spoken or written sentence, a signed word, etc.) is met by a fellow speaker of the language. That condition deserves some attention. A quick thought experiment will help here. Botanists have known for some time that certain types of plants – particularly some species of trees and fungi – form large networks with fellow members of their species and pass information between members of those networks. Some fungi can also form mycorrhizas, or mutual symbiotic associations with other plants, which are themselves bound up with larger networks of interaction that allow them all to adapt to shifting environmental conditions to adapt more favorably. Plants in some networks have been observed sending chemical signals to fellow members in response to elevated levels of toxins at the ground level and insect infestations. Those chemical signals then prompted responses that increased the plants' resistance. (Recent work in this field is reviewed in Gorzalek *et al.* (2015).) There are more esoteric versions of this sort of "tree talk" hypothesis, but biologists generally accept that there is a degree of interaction here that merits serious consideration. In mycorrhizas and "tree talk," we have organisms passing information amongst themselves, with the effect of optimizing responses to shared threats to the network. That sounds like it meets the rough notion of communication I gave earlier. If biologists could discover how the means by which those signals were passed and the conditions to which they responded were correlated, could that, in principle, be a natural language?

RESPONSES

One way to address this is to say that these networks of organisms don't have a natural language because they lack the types of thought that we have, and that using a natural language is possible only for creatures with the capacity for such types of thought. The simple electrochemical signals transferred back and forth between organisms in these networks don't appear to have any grammar at all – just signals that promote a response. So, there is little evidence for assigning those signals *meaning*, as opposed to causal efficacy alone. (When a cue ball strikes an eight-ball on a pool table, it is not saying, "Go in the side pocket!" even if it makes that happen.) Other organisms might communicate, signaling back and forth in ways that influence each other's behavior, but not in ways that reflect a richer set of conceptual capacities that genuine language would require. Many who would reject "tree talk" out of hand would do so because they take it that plants don't think and are not conscious. I would agree, though making a definitive case for this point is trickier than it seems, given how slippery "thought" turns out to be as a category. Maher (2017) takes a thorough look at this question and is worth reading even if one is convinced that plants are not language users. (For more contentious discussions, see entry #42 for a review of non-human animals and their capacities for language.)

If we take thought to be a necessary condition for using a language, we must still ask what sort of relation language bears to thought. John Locke (1689/1975) claimed that words were "signs for ideas." By "ideas" he meant to suggest anything that might present itself before our mind – any type of thought, as we might now say. Locke did mean that to be a very inward-looking conception of the sign in this case. The words in a natural language have their meaning in virtue of their signifying some internal state of us. Sharing it with others would be a helpful byproduct of this, but spoken words simply serve as overt, external tokens that we exchange with one another, based on an immediate grasp of our own thoughts. This framework continued to develop among Western philosophers into the 20th century. Following the work of H.P. Grice (1957/1989), many philosophers took up a notion of "speaker meaning," or a more subjective, mental grasp of some content that found public expression in words and sentences whose meanings were set by convention (though with an eye towards the thoughts they were to express). Linguistic communication on this sort of view amounts to speakers trying to get their audience to believe something by getting the audience to take the speaker's intention as a reason for belief. Words would thus not simply designate things, as in Locke's original view, but also be used by speakers to change the contents of others' minds as well.

Locke's take on signs was resolutely empiricist – he treated the mind as a blank slate that would accrue experiences, sort through them to note affinities, and gradually construct conceptual distinctions. That approach came under greater scrutiny over time, and many philosophers, linguists, and psychologists turned to models that posited innate linguistic capacities in humans. Psycholinguists like Chomsky (1980) and Fodor (1975) proposed models in which human brains were biologically disposed to develop knowledge of the grammar of natural languages with minimal external stimulation early in their lives. People would be born primed to exercise an internal "language of thought," that processed different sorts of information generated in different regions of their brains, much like programs run on a computer. (For more on this, see entries #12, 41–42.)

Another approach would be to say that languages are fundamentally symbolic systems that signify (as in Locke's approach), but that what they signify is not solely mental states. Words might be taken to be signifiers of all types of things, including things outside the mind, and languages would thus be systems by which those signifiers could be arranged with the help of a variety of logical operators to state facts and describe the world. John Stuart Mill (1849/1975), for instance, took the role of names to consist primarily in their denotation of something and took them as fundamental to an account of language. In elaborating what things might be named, Mill went on to include qualities, attributes, and other relations. These "abstract names" then appear in predicates, by which we say that something has that property, or belongs to the class of things that do. Further extensions of this approach would be necessary for other sorts of linguistic moves, (e.g., questions, commands, fictions, jokes), but this general approach has been widely adopted in linguistics and philosophy in the West. It served as a starting point (though one often rejected or amended) for the analytic philosophy described in entries #5–10. And while it has been influential among Western philosophers, there have been similar views at work in other parts of the world for much longer. Ganeri (2006) describes the work of several schools of Indian philosophy as "realist" theories of meaning, on which "the meaning of an expression is the external object for which it stands" (9), very much in the same spirit as Mill's account 1,000 years before he wrote it, with similar (much-disputed) provisions for the denotation of properties that particular referents might then have.

There has been a growing wariness among Western philosophers about looking inwards to account for meaning. Semantic externalists such as Burge (1979) have demonstrated that many categories of expressions in natural languages cannot be grounded in our thinking of them, but rather must be grounded in objects and properties external to our thoughts. As Hilary Putnam pithily put it, "'meanings' just ain't in the head" for many things we say. This turn towards the external coincided with a turn towards the practical. Philosophers like J.L Austin (1962) began to consider not just the representational dimensions of language – describing things, stating facts, etc. – but also the wide range of different actions that could be undertaken with it. We do state facts by our use of a language, but we also promise, command, condemn, excuse, plead, and do many other things with it as well. This suggested that fixed, conventional meanings for words and sentences were at most part of our story about language and must be coupled with a deeply pragmatic account of the use that we make of it with one another. This would suggest a more profoundly social conception of language, rooted in culture and shared practices, and this was an approach adopted by Wittgenstein (1958) in his later works. Wittgenstein's work had a profound influence on 20th century philosophy (see entries #11–15 for more on this). This trend also extended to scientists working in evolutionary and developmental psychology, who came to place greater emphasis on social and cooperative dimensions of cognition. Tomasello (2008) makes a case for this as the source of humans' distinctive linguistic abilities (see entry #45 for more).

RECOMMENDED READINGS

Austin, J. 1962. *How to Do Things with Words*. Oxford: Oxford University Press.

Burge, T. 1979. "Individualism and the Mental." *Midwest Studies in Philosophy* 4: 73–122.

Chomsky, N. 1980. "Language and Unconscious Knowledge." In *Rules and Representations*, 217–290. New York: Columbia University Press.

Fodor, J. 1975. *The Language of Thought*. Cambridge: Harvard University Press.

Ganeri, J. 2006. *Artha: Meaning (Foundations of Philosophy in India)*. New York: Oxford University Press.

Gorzalek, M., A. Asay, B. Pickles, and S. Simard. 2015. "Inter-Plant Communication Through Mycorrhizal Netowrks Mediates Complex Adaptive Behaviour in Plant Communities." *AoB Plants* 7 (plv050).

Grice, H. 1957/1989. "Meaning." In *Studies in the Way of Words*, 214–223. Cambridge: Harvard University Press.

Locke, J. 1689/1975. "Of Words." In *An Essay Concerning Human Understanding*, edited by P. Nidditch. Oxford: Clarendon Press.

Maher, C. 2017. *Plant Minds: A Philosophical Defense*. New York: Routledge Pub.

Mill, J.S. 1849/1975. "Book I: Of Names and Propositions." In *A System of Logic (Collected Works of John Stuart Mill, vol. 7)*, edited by J. Robson. London: Routledge and Kegan Paul.

Tomasello, M. 2008. *Origins of Human Communication*. Cambridge, MA: The MIT Press.

Wittgesntein, L. 1958. *The Blue and Brown Books*. New York: Harper Torchbooks.

IDEAL LANGUAGE OR ORDINARY LANGUAGES?

Background: In entry #1, we considered the wide variety of things that might count as languages, and what the minimal necessary conditions for one might be. Theoretical languages such as those used in science and mathematics suggest it would be possible to develop more refined versions of natural languages, which presents a methodological question: is the role of philosophical inquiry into language to describe it as it stands, or to develop the best version of it for our purposes?

By the 1920s, what is now known as analytic philosophy had picked up steam and was beginning to predominate among philosophers in British and some German and Austrian universities. Work on the foundations of mathematics in the late 19th century had spurred revolutionary new work in logic. Those new logical methods had led many of those philosophers to a new interest in language and hopes that the right sort of analysis would resolve previously intractable problems in metaphysics, epistemology, and ethics. Among a group of Austrian philosophers who came to be known as logical positivists, this interest in language, coupled with an ambitious program in the philosophy of science, suggested an almost complete revision of Western philosophy.

DOI: 10.4324/9781003183167-5

The logical positivists drew inspiration for these ambitious projects from the ideas of Ludwig Wittgenstein. His early work culminated in *Tractatus Logico-Philosophicus*, a dense, austere book analyzing the nature of language and its implications for the very possibility of philosophy. However, over time, Wittgenstein began to doubt the prospect of perfecting a language that his early work had implied. Interpreting Wittgenstein is an industry unto itself, but it is fair to say that as time went on, Wittgenstein took a dim view of the kind of grand analytic projects that he had inspired.

Thus, a clash of outlooks was simmering when Wittgenstein first met Rudolf Carnap and Moritz Schlick, two prominent logical positivists, in 1927. Carnap's account includes an oddly confrontational moment:

> Schlick unfortunately mentioned that I was interested in the problem of an international language like Esperanto. As I had expected, Wittgenstein was definitely opposed to this idea. But I was surprised by the vehemence of his emotions. A language which had not "grown organically" seemed to him not only useless but despicable.
>
> (1963, p. 25)

Wittgenstein was not known for his congeniality, but what was agitating him here? If Esperanto is not familiar to you, it is a constructed language, developed in the late 19th century by L.L. Zamenhof. To call it "constructed" is to say that it arose not out of the interactions among a community of speakers, but entirely by Zamenhof's design. He took vocabulary and grammatical features from several European languages, explicitly directing how each part was to be used. In doing so, he left out many irregularities that natural languages have, in hopes of avoiding confusion and allowing speakers to learn quickly. There are many fragmentary constructed languages developed for movies and books (e.g., Valyrian from *Game of Thrones*), but Esperanto is one of the few with sufficient resources for fluent conversation. Yet it remains a curiosity. To anyone who speaks a language well, everything in Esperanto sounds stilted and artificial, almost like a lifeless parody of a language. Carnap's enthusiasm for this was appalling to Wittgenstein. To him, it would have been like seeing your friends with their new baby and learning that they were raising it to speak only Klingon.[1]

Who had a hold of a better philosophical insight here, though? While I doubt philosophy will be done in Esperanto any time soon, Carnap's interest reflects an ambition in Western philosophy that runs back at least to Plato, and a dismal view of natural language that often accompanies it. Plato took philosophy as the search for certain types of eternal truths that ordinary understanding does not provide. One can't have these kinds of conversations for long without running into ambiguities that arise from the language we use. Deep grammatical ambiguities abound, often in ways that only considerable training in logic can lay bare. The ways in which we ordinarily speak about topics of philosophical importance are so full of ambiguities that they often appear as impediments to resolving problems, frustrating our efforts. Even the most modest philosophers will often take themselves to be *refining* our everyday language to shed light on important distinctions, but some have gone even further. Some Western philosophers have gone so far as to suggest that everyday language is past the point of repair, and that we should develop a new, ideal language in which to communicate.

Gottfried Leibniz suggested such an ideal language in several of his writings. He thought progress in philosophy and science would eventually require a formal calculus of reasoning – a "*characteristica universalis*" as he called it – with each distinct, well-defined concept being given a distinct symbol, and formal rules for using and manipulating them. The symbols would thus resemble pictograms more than words, and the entire language would resemble algebra more than English sentences. Leibniz never developed this idea in detail, though his reflections on the idea would have considerable influence on later generations of logicians. (See Cohen (1954) for an historical review of Leibniz's remarks.). One admirer of Leibniz's idea was Gottlob Frege, who developed many of the important ideas in contemporary logic in the 1870s. He invoked Leibniz's *characteristica* in introducing his own *Begriffsschrift* ("concept script"), though his aspirations were somewhat more circumscribed. Rather than a constructed formal language for all knowledge, Frege offered one only to capture logical inference. From this idealized refinement of logical language, stripped of its ambiguities and wearing its logical structure on its face, we get the first-order logic familiar to many philosophy students from logic courses. This was just one facet of the ideal language that Leibniz had hoped for, but Frege's hopes remained ambitious:

> [E]ven if this great aim cannot be achieved at the first attempt, one need not despair of a slow, step by step approach. If a problem in its full generality appears insoluble, it has to be limited provisionally; it can then, perhaps, be dealt with by advancing gradually.
>
> (50)

This hope for ideal philosophical languages to supersede ordinary language for theoretical purposes left an impact on analytic philosophers like Carnap and Schlick, for whom the integration of physics was a priority. They saw the language of physical theory as the fundamental form of science, and one imbued with all the precision of mathematics and logic. The reduction of the laws and vocabularies of all empirical theories to the laws and vocabularies of physics (and then to strictly logical truths and statements about sense-data, depending on which logical positivists you asked) would tame ordinary language into an impeccably clear tool for philosophical work. Ordinary language was something for philosophy to overcome in this way; an ideal language would be our proper philosophical goal.

RESPONSES

By the mid-20th century, defenders of everyday usage were mounting a counteroffensive, with Wittgenstein as their leading light. During the 1930s and 40s, he had extended stays at Cambridge, during which he taught an unorthodox series of seminars calling much of the prevailing philosophy of language of the day (including, arguably, his earlier work) into question. Whereas philosophers of language since Frege had been analyzing the logical and semantic features of languages, hoping to uncover the ideal conceptual architecture beneath it, Wittgenstein came to see natural languages as patchworks of overlapping practices aiming at diverse outcomes. This suggests that the apparent ambiguities we find in many parts of our languages don't generally emerge out of carelessness or stupidity among non-specialists, but rather that they reflect a great many overlapping purposes to which they may be put. And this complemented an even more radical theme in his later work: the efforts of philosophers to craft an ideal version of natural languages, or replace them altogether, are themselves distortions of our understanding. Good philosophy should clarify matters but leave our world as it was when we began; bad philosophy saddles us with misguided expectations and problems, cloaking them in sophisticated jargon. (See Wittgenstein's (1958).)

A cohort of "ordinary language" philosophers descended from Wittgenstein's seminars (though this term came along later). What this loose collection of philosophers shared with Wittgenstein was an emphasis on the actual use speakers made of terms, particularly those of apparent philosophical interest. Thus, Malcolm (1942, 1951) attempts to show that skeptical objections in epistemology can get no traction because theoretical assumptions drive them, but these assumptions are not reflected in common usage of 'know' and similar terms. John Wisdom (1996) challenged the tradition of philosophical doubts that we know the contents of one another's minds, arguing that the doubts arose from the methods of Cartesian philosophy, not from the understanding of knowledge and thought that guide ordinary usage. H.L.A. Hart (1949) looks at ordinary judgments of people's rights and suggests that they display a distinctive ascriptive quality that philosophers had neglected in favor of more esoteric concerns. Ordinary language philosophers were not necessarily objecting to the use of more technical jargon for certain purposes, but to passing off some terms that emerged from academic philosophical discourse as ordinary language. If the epistemologists' term 'know' or 'justification' implied greatly elevated standards, that in itself might not be objectionable. But casting those as the terms that most speakers use, and insisting that they meet unfamiliar demands, was a misuse of language.

The emphasis on use would also inspire much of the thinking that led to the speech act theory of Austin, Grice, and many others. These views are discussed in greater detail in entries #28–31, so I will refer readers there, rather than rehearse them here. The piecemeal, descriptive character of much of ordinary language's work gave way to more formal approaches to meaning, coupled with more formal approaches to the practical effects of speech acts. Ordinary language philosophy seemed too facile to more theory-minded philosophers of language. But the spirit of opposition to philosophical idealization and turning to non-academic practices and speakers has reemerged in recent decades in the form of "experimental philosophy." This approach incorporates techniques from the social sciences to examine the overlapping territory between academic and non-academic language, especially where philosophers appeal to purported pre-theoretic intuitions among ordinary speakers that then do explanatory work in philosophical debates. There are scant grounds to say what most people's pre-theoretical intuitions *are*, much less whether they would support such philosophical moves. Experimental philosophy attempts to bridge this gap in an empirical fashion, often at the cost of assumptions critical to more traditional philosophical arguments. Important studies in this vein have examined moral responsibility (Roskie and Nichols 2008) and knowledge ascription (Machery, *et al*. 2015). Hansen (2020) connects such projects with the legacy of ordinary language philosophy, and how they may be reconciled with more contemporary experimental methods.

NOTE

1.　Apologies to any offended *Star Trek* enthusiasts.

RECOMMENDED READINGS

MAJOR WORKS

Cohen, C. 1954. "On the Project of a Universal Character." *Mind* 63 (249): 49–63.

Frege, G. 1879/1997. "Begriffschrift (Preface and Part 1)." In *The Frege Reader*, edited by M. Beaney, 47–78. Oxford: Blackwell.

Wisdom, J. 1996. *Other Minds*. Berkeley: University of California Press.

Wittgesntein, L. 1958. *The Blue and Brown Books*. New York: Harper Torchbooks.

RESPONSES

Carnap, R. 1963. "Intellectual Biography." In *The Philosophy of Rudolf Carnap*, edited by A. Schlipp, 3–43. LaSalle: Open Court.

Hansen, N. 2020. "'Nobody Would Really Talk That Way!'; the Critical Project in Contemporary Ordinary Language Philosophy." *Synthèse* 197: 2433–2464.

Hart, H. 1949. "The Ascription of Resonsibility and Rights." *Proceedings of the Aristotelian Society* 49: 171–194.

Machery, E., S. Sitch, D. Rose, A. Chatterjee, K. Karasawa, N. Strunicher, and S. Sirker. 2015. "Gettier Across Cultures." *Nous* 51 (3): 645–664.

Malcolm, N. 1942. "Moore and Ordinary Language." In *The Philosophy of G.E. Moore (Vol. IV of the Library of Living Philosophers)*, edited by A. Schlipp, 345–368. Evanston: Northwestern Univeristy Press.

Malcolm, N. 1951. "Philosophy for Philosophers." *Philosophical Review* 60: 329–340.

Roskie, A., and S. Nichols. 2008. "Bringing Moral Responsibility Down to Earth." *The Journal of Philosophy* 105 (7): 371–388.

THE SAPIR-WHORF HYPOTHESIS

Background: One assumption common to many accounts of meaning and language is that natural languages represent the world for us in our thoughts. But there is considerable empirical evidence that the languages we speak can influence our thinking in subtle ways, by reinforcing some associations and discouraging others.

In Ted Chiang's science-fiction novella *The Story of Your Life*, Earth is visited by an alien species called the Heptapods, who seek contact and communication. Different groups around the world work to translate the aliens' language, and the story follows a linguist as she deciphers the grammar and learns to speak with the Heptapods. Chiang's novella was highly praised, and was soon adapted into the film *Arrival*. Part of what distinguishes the novella and the film from most science fiction is the central focus on the scientific study of language, as opposed to physics or biology. Both the film and the book make scientific inquiry central to the narrative. Characters are driven by an urge to understand what is unfamiliar, and scientific methods reveal new ways of understanding and imagining the possibilities of their world. Chiang dove into a study of linguistics before completing the novella, so many of the details in the story are rooted in actual accounts from the scientific literature. (The film does perpetuate the myth that mid-level

DOI: 10.4324/9781003183167-6

professors work in spacious, well-furnished offices with immaculately arranged bookshelves and uncluttered desks. That part is drawn purely from the realm of fantasy.)

Without giving away *too* many spoilers, the novella and film are largely concerned with determinism – the view that nothing about your life is really open to chance or choice; even what appear to be your free choices are set in place by forces outside you, working together like clockwork toward your eventual fate. That is fodder for philosophical consideration, though for a book other than this one. More importantly for us, the key to the characters' realization of this is largely linguistic. By learning a different type of language, the characters come to think about and perceive their world in radically different ways. Providing humans with those ways of thinking about and perceiving their world is an important goal in the Heptapods' making contact.

The suggestion that a language provides us with a sort of lens through which we think and perceive has a long history in Western philosophy, as does the idea that different groups of people might have very different lenses and thus "live in different worlds," even when they are right beside each other. Note that this is a view about groups of people, not individual people. In some cases, we do talk about linguistic features that belong to individual people; linguists will call this an *idiolect*. The idea we're entertaining here doesn't concern those sorts of differences; it concerns the ways that the shared framework of a language shapes the ways in which speakers understand and perceive the world. Different people may use parts of that framework in different ways, but the fact that they can speak to one another would suggest that the language as a whole is still available to all of them. The framework that a language provides enables us to think and perceive in certain ways, and thereby empowers us. But if a language has such features, it must typically do so by excluding other ways of speaking, thinking, and perceiving. We might expect speakers of very different languages to have very different "lenses" by which they engage with the world and one another.

Contemporary versions of this idea drew inspiration from the work of Edward Sapir and Benjamin Whorf, and people sometimes speak of the "Sapir-Whorf hypothesis." This is a bit misleading; Sapir and Whorf never collaborated. (Sapir was also devoted to field work, while Whorf wrote more philosophical works. I'll focus on Whorf here.) Their views were informed by work taking shape in field linguistics and anthropology during the 1920s. Whorf was particularly interested in the grammatical intricacies of Native American languages. Several of his most noted works addressed the Hopi, Nootka, and Shawnee languages. He noted that most European languages allowed for kinds of abstraction about objects and numbers that would be alien to Hopi speakers. His most famous examples from Hopi concerned tenses. Tenses are different forms that verbs can take, indicating the time at which something takes place. For instance, and English sentence that begins with "I work at . . ." or "I'm working at . . ." indicates that something is being done in the present; a sentence that begins with "I worked at . . ." indicates that it happened in the past.

In English, speakers are accustomed to speaking in the past, present, and future tenses. There are more exotic variations, like past perfect ('I had written . . .') or future progressive ('I will be travelling next week . . .'), along with several others. We also sometimes use verbs in an infinitive tense, which avoids giving any temporal specification at all ('The dude abides'). But the categorical division between past, present, and future when we do indicate time is characteristic of English verbs, as well as most other Indo-European languages. Hopi does not have that sort of formal structure in its verbs. Instead, Whorf claimed, it has "reportive" and "expective" assertions. A reportive assertion reported some event or circumstance (somewhat like our past and present tenses), while expective assertions indicated that the speaker expected something to be so (somewhat like our future tense).[1] In both cases, an ordering of things in time as we have with tenses of English verbs was simply not part of the verbs themselves. Moreover, Whorf claimed that this was not a deficit of the Hopi language. There were still ways in which temporal distinctions could be made, but they had a distinct structure that was supported by a very different conceptual framework.

Whorf's suggestion seems bold, and it always sparks the imagination of students when I introduce it. However, it also suffers a bit from its radical quality. People often hear it, get intrigued by, and then exaggerate it. "Whorf said the Hopi have no concept of time!!" Whorf never said that, only that English and Hopi conceptions of time could not be mapped onto one another. (Though he probably

did misunderstand the Hopi conception of time.) Whorf did make
some grand pronouncements, though:

> [E]very language is a vast pattern-system, different from others, in
> which are culturally ordained the forms and categories by which the
> personality not only communicates but also analyzes nature, notices
> or neglects types of relationship and phenomena, channels his rea-
> soning, and builds the house of his consciousness.
>
> (1952, p. 252)

A strong version of Sapir and Whorf's idea would be *linguistic determinism*: the view that our capacities for thought and perception are
wholly determined by the structure of the language we speak. The
first language we learn is especially important, on this view. A weaker
version of this would be *linguistic relativism*: the view that our capacities for thought are profoundly and primarily shaped by the structure
of the language we speak. Both versions assume that the structure
of our thought and perception are not innate or universal among
humans. If linguistic determinism is true, then our capacities to think
and perceive are like clay, waiting to be molded into some shape by
the language we learn and the culture that embodies it. If linguistic
relativism is true, there may be some features of our thought and perception that are innate, but even those will be shaped, to some degree,
by our language. The consensus view among philosophers and linguists has been that linguistic determinism is not supported by empirical evidence. There may still be a viable form of linguistic relativism,
as will see in the Responses section.

Let me give you a thought experiment drawn from the work of
Donald Davidson (1974/2006). Davidson was no fan of Whorf, nor
of the very idea of different languages forming different "conceptual schemes" by which we might engage the world. Davidson noted
that for all the differences Whorf suggested there were between Hopi
and English, he still gave perfectly good English translations of Hopi
sentences. If we could translate the sentences in another language to
some in our own, then what the sentences said and what we thought
in saying them couldn't be all that different, so linguistic relativism was
wrong. And if we couldn't translate what others were saying into our
own language, then we had no reason to say that they were thinking

or speaking a language at all. Imagine some aliens landed here, started making complex noises at one another, and sharing in apparently coordinated behavior. But now imagine we never successfully translated any part of this into our own languages. (What if the linguist in Chiang's story had *failed completely*?) What should we conclude? How different could something be from the "lenses" of our language and still seem like a language at all?

RESPONSES

As the above descriptions might suggest, the fiercest opponents of both versions of the Sapir-Whorf hypothesis have been linguists and cognitive scientists who say that most of our capacity to think is innate in us. Linguists like Noam Chomsky and cognitive scientists like Steven Pinker (1994) hold the view that our capacities for thought and language are hardwired into our brains from birth; they will develop of their own accord, just as our organs do, and are simply waiting for a little stimulus from the world to switch on. They point to the universality of many basic features of thought across different communities, despite all the apparent cultural differences, as evidence for this. Each language does have its quirks and peculiarities, Chomsky and Pinker might say, but they also all have first, second, and third person, nouns, verbs, questions, and a host of other fundamental linguistic features. (They could say similar things about psychological structures, too.) While the surface-level features of our languages and cultures may look wildly different, Chomsky and Pinker might say, they are very much the same under the hood.

There have not been many defenders of linguistic determinism in recent decades. Linguistic relativism has had periods of occasional revival, though. Linguist George Lakoff (1987) has spoken favorably of some of Whorf's writings, and of the prospects for linguistic relativism in general. While Whorf's studies themselves had various flaws, Lakoff sees them as opening new approaches that are better supported by later studies. Much of Lakoff's work concerns conceptual metaphors, which are attempts to understand one idea (or domain of ideas) in terms of another. A conceptual metaphor like "The temperature is falling" mixes quantities with spatial directions; "Argument is war" mixes abstract ideas about linguistic behavior with concrete physical experiences one might have. Having these conceptual metaphors become common in our language may then change how we conceive of ourselves and our behavior —counterparts in an argument must be *destroyed* or *defeated*, as enemies in war. What is implicit in our cognition can thus be shaped from the outside in by the language around us. (See McWhorter 2014 for responses.)

NOTE

1. Whorf (1939/1952, pp. 143–145).

RECOMMENDED READINGS

MAJOR WORKS

Davidson, D. 1974/2006. "On the Very Idea of a Conceptual Scheme." In *The Essential Davidson*, edited by D. Davidson, 196–208. New York: Oxford University Press.

Whorf, B.L. 1939/1952. "The Relation of Habitual Thought and Behavior to Language." In *Language, Thought, and Reality*, edited by B.L. Whorf and J.B. Carroll, 134–159. Boston, MA: The MIT Press.

Whorf, B.L. 1941/1956. "Language, Mind, and Reality." In *Language, Thought, and Reality*, edited by B.L. Whorf and J.B. Carroll, 246–270. Cambridge, MA: The MIT Press.

RESPONSES

Chiang, T. 2002. "Story of Your Life." In *Stories of Your Life and Others*, edited by T. Chiang, 91–146. New York: Vintage Books.

Lakoff, G. 1987. *Women, Fire and Dangerous Things*. Chicago: University of Chicago Press.

McWhorter, J. 2014. *The Language Hoax*. New York: Oxford University Press.

Pinker, S. 1994. *The Language Instinct: How the Mind Creates Language*. New York: Harper Collins.

CONVENTIONS

Background: There is little doubt that conventions play an important role in natural languages, but there is disagreement about how much of a language could be conventional, and whether coming to consensus on conventions could explain the origins of natural languages. How the first languages could emerge when we seem to need linguistic interaction to establish such conventions posed a challenge for any philosopher seeking to explain natural languages as the products of our interaction.

It has been suggested that natural languages are fundamentally constituted by social conventions. That we use just the words we do in the ways that we do does not reflect a deeper order to the world, but rather a collection of shared norms that have coalesced over time. If this were so, there might still be standards of correctness for the use we make of different parts of the language, and we might enforce them very strictly. But conventions are social and historical artifacts, and for any one a community might adopt, we can readily imagine alternatives. Such conventions may shift over time, even if they lie deep in a language's grammar.

All of this may sound familiar enough, and for many philosophers of language, it is uncontroversial to suggest that convention plays a role in natural language. However, there is also a tension lurking in

DOI: 10.4324/9781003183167-7

these assumptions. On the one hand, there is often an appeal to convention as an explanation for the primordial origins of language: past generations of speakers agreed on ways of using words, and contemporary conventions descend from those. Yet this leaves us to ask how that emergence of convention first takes place, and this suggests a puzzle. We could address this in several ways, but let me propose that we think of the puzzle at hand as involving commitment to three claims:

(A)   Natural language emerges by virtue of linguistic communities adopting conventions.
(B)   Social conventions are settled by consensus among the members of a linguistic community.
(C)   The process of establishing consensus among the members of a linguistic community on anything requires a shared language that allows agreement, disagreement, and negotiation over details.

To accept (A) and (B) makes (C) problematic, because (C) would imply that speakers must share a language to settle on the conventions that constitute that language. But (B) and (C) seem clearly true of conventions, which casts doubt on (A). Arguments in this spirit have been made by numerous authors, but one noteworthy for our discussion is Quine (1936), who offered a similar argument tailored to logical truths. (And, as Armstrong (2016) notes, Quine directly influenced Lewis and Davidson, whom we will discuss shortly.)

Can there be a primordial role for convention? Lewis (1969, 1975) approached this problem by noting that there are two, apparently divergent, conceptions of a language. One answer to this would be that a language should be understood formally, as a function that maps strings of sounds, marks, and signs to meanings. Meanings, in his view, are something that "when combined with factual information . . . yields a truth-value" (1975, p. 3). Lewis's influential version of this formal project made sets of possible worlds central to this answer. A language in this sense is a formal, abstract semantic system, to be articulated within a framework that resembles logic or mathematics. Another answer takes language to be a social phenomenon rooted in the sounds, marks, and signs that people make to one another, and this approach focuses on the role that language plays in rational interactions and the coordination of action. This second conception of language presumes the existence of and extensive appeal to social conventions. Lewis characterizes conventions as regularities in social behavior that almost everyone conforms to and believes others conform to, and in which this near universality gives each agent a reason to maintain their conformity and to prefer that others do so. Any such regularity will be only one possibility among many. They are arbitrary in this sense, even if there are historical details that explain their predominance.

What can we make of these different conceptions? Many philosophers have discarded one or the other, either developing idealized versions of languages that better fit formal methods, or denying that there can be a formal account of something so deeply organic and mercurial. (See entry #2.) What Lewis seeks instead is a synthesis of the two conceptions. Speakers of a language in the second sense use a language in the first, and the convention by which they do so can be determined in terms of truthfulness and trust. It will be a convention that speakers try never to utter untrue sentences when they speak to others, and that they trust others to be truthful when forming beliefs in light of what they say. Speakers who trust other speakers to speak truthfully can both conform to the linguistic forms of others' sounds, etc., and take their beliefs and reasons on as their own. Thus, their emergence may be the product of efforts to solve problems in which they must jointly agree on a course of action, while their continuing shared interests will sustain the conventions as they give added weight to precedent in similar scenarios. A community of speakers shares a language in the formal sense when its conventions about which signs to use and how to converge on some version of the sort of mapping function described earlier. Natural language may thus be wholly conventional.

RESPONSES

Part of the innovation in Lewis's response was the use of game-theoretical approaches to explain linguistic convention (more extensively in (1969)), particularly its initial emergence. Conventions were to be solutions to coordination problems in which agents with coinciding interests jointly choose between alternatives and must make those choices by anticipating the moves and intentions of others. Ascribing intentions on this view need only account for others' observed behavior, and might be done pre-linguistically, serving as a ground for linguistic conventions. While this proved influential, it also drew detractors. Favereau (2008) describes Lewis's game-theoretical innovations in accessible detail, noting how these have influenced researchers in the social sciences, and how that subsequent work reflects back on Lewis. Gilbert (2008) sees a mismatch between the public character of conventions and the "individualism" of Lewis's view, as she called it. Convention requires a "holistic" view on which conventions are held collectively by groups, rather than individually by their members. Kölbel (1998) argues that actual linguistic interaction is filled with deceit, cageyness, insincerity, and a wealth of other regularities in people's behavior that fall well short of truthfulness, and that an account of the primordial origins of linguistic convention must explain why truthfulness and not one of these other regularities takes hold. However, he remains sympathetic to Lewis's approach and offers an amended account in hopes of addressing this.

Hawthorne (1990) notes that the regularities of trust and truthfulness are supposed to determine the language that a community uses, but any natural language contains indefinitely many sentences, indefinitely many of which are longer than anyone could ever say, sign, etc. We use only a finite fragment of a language in this sense. With finite evidence, communities would be left to choose among indefinitely many candidates for the language that they are speaking, undermining Lewis's effort to pin an account of meaning on convention. Jackman (1998) notes that Lewis's account runs afoul of semantic externalist objections from Kripke and Putnam (see entries #46 and 48). However, he thinks that these difficulties may be overcome if we loosen the requirement that speakers use *exactly* the same language (down to the most precise formal details) for communication. We may instead adopt a view on which they share many of the same *particular* practices (i.e., actual, present ones) and impose more modest rational constraints on conventions.

Millikan (1998) criticizes Lewis's account of convention, both on grounds that his account suggests a complexity to conventions that is often not present, and that conditions he takes to be essential to conventions are not so. Conformity to a convention may be quite weak – few people wear green every St. Patrick's Day, for instance – yet it remains a convention, contrary to Lewis's emphasis on regularity. Millikan also suggests that conventions should not generally be understood prescriptively as governing behavior; a rule such as "wear green on St. Patrick's Day" describes a convention, rather than prescribing behavior. In place of Lewis's appeals to truthfulness and trust, Millikan emphasizes reproduction and the weight of precedent. Conventions are reproduced in that they don't perpetuate themselves (we must instruct others about them), but also in that they don't arise from some natural superiority over alternative behaviors. Their appearance is due to our behavior, not an intrinsic advantage that they convey. The weight of precedent, rather than any rational grounds, creates the inertia by which conventions endure. Where Lewis looked to rational choices and game theory to account for convention, Millikan seeks a much more naturalistic path that runs through biology instead.

Davidson (1984, 1986/2001) criticized Lewis's appeals to convention, in large part because he felt that making it central to an account of natural languages was a disservice to their freewheeling, innovative qualities. Speakers generate new expressions and novel uses of existing ones all the time. They do this in familiar ways via literary devices like metaphor, but also in irregular everyday ways such as malapropisms. In such cases, language users may communicate and interpret one another, but by means that conventions would not provide or that might even run afoul of them. Davidson's more radical, dynamic approach to interpretation came to be known as "triangulation": two language users communicating and interpreting one another, the world they share, and an ongoing series of adjustments on each user's part to adjust their representational states and those they ascribe to the other user as their interaction unfolds. Rather than a stock of fixed conventions to deploy, as Lewis suggested, language users would have a *prior theory* by which they were initially prepared to interpret others and produce their own utterances, and a *passing theory* by which they would adjust to unanticipated aspects of new interactions (1986/2001, pp. 101–104). Speakers never have identical prior and passing theories, but they need not. Davidson's account of triangulation does not build in the same expectations of cooperation and coordination that Lewis's account does, nor does it presume that the means of interpretation must endure, as Lewis's conventions would.

Davidson went so far as to assert that there are *no languages* – "no learnable common core of consistent behaviour, no shared grammar or rules, no portable interpreting machine set to grind out the meaning of an arbitrary utterance" (1986/2001, p. 107). Davidson is not suggesting that there is no difference between, say, English and French, but that no such language is a fixed, eternal body of knowledge residing in the mind of every competent speaker. Davidson acknowledges that there are linguistic conventions, but they play an instrumental role rather than a constitutive one. Language users may know of them and use them in their prior theories in interpreting others, but they are not essential components in our production and interpretation of speech, signs, etc. They are thus like defensive alignments in basketball or football: usefully repeatable ways of playing the game, but not fundamental to the game itself. Armstrong (2016) offers an extended exegesis of Lewis's and Davidson's views on convention, particularly Davidson's work that is critical of Lewis's account. He, like many others, winds up critical of Davidson's triangulation account. Doubts about triangulation were perhaps driven by the fact that Davidson claimed it as a solution to so many philosophical problems, from underpinning all of semantics to refuting skepticism. More positive readings of his work can be found in Myers and Verheggen (2016) and Goldberg (2009), both of whom attempt to serve that account by offering more rigorous, systematic development of numerous threads in Davidson's original work.

RECOMMENDED READINGS

MAJOR WORKS

Lewis, D. 1969. *Convention*. Cambridge: Harvard University Press.

Lewis, D. 1975. "Languages and Language." In *Language, Mind and Knowledge: Minnesota Studies in the Philosophy of Science*, edited by K. Gunderson, vol. 7, 3–35. Minneapolis: University of Minnesota Press.

Davidson, D. 1986/2001. "A Nice Derangement of Epitaphs." In *Truth, Language, and History*, 89–107. Oxford: Clarendon Press.

RESPONSES

Armstrong, J. 2016. "Coordiantion, Triangulation, and Language Use." *Inquiry* 59 (1): 80–112.

Davidson, D. 1984. "Communication and Convention." *Synthèse* 59 (1): 3–17.

Favereau, O. 2008. "The Unconventional, but Conventionalist, Legacy of Lewis's 'Convention'." *Topoi* 27 (1–2): 115–126.

Gilbert, M. 2008. "Social Convention Revisited." *Topoi* 1–2: 5–16.

Goldberg, N. 2009. "Triangulation, Untranslatability, and Reconciliation." *Philoso-phia* 37 (2): 261–280.

Hawthorne, J. 1990. "A Note on 'Languages and Language'." *Australasian Journal of Philosophy* 68 (1): 116–118.

Jackman, H. 1998. "Convention and Language." *Synthèse* 117 (3): 295–312.

Kölbel, M. 1998. "Language, Lust and Lies." *Inquiry* 41 (3): 301–315.

Millikan, R.G. 1998. "Language Conventions Made Simple." *Journal of Philosophy* 95 (4): 161–180.

Myers, R., and C. Verheggen. 2016. *Donald Davidson's Triangulation Argument: A Philosophical Inquiry*. New York: Routledge.

Quine, W. 1936. "Truth by Convention." In *Philosophical Essays for Alfred North Whitehead*, 90–124. New York: Longmans, Green & Co.

PART II

EARLY ANALYTIC PHILOSOPHY AND PRAGMATISM

INTRODUCTION

The entries in this section address several themes and problems that were at the fore of many Western philosophers' minds at the end of the 19th and early 20th centuries. To a degree, this section thus serves as historical background for many ideas that will reappear in other entries. Entries #5 and #6 are particularly historically important in this way. In #5, I introduce Frege's distinction between the sense and the reference of an expression, and in #6, we encounter Russell's analysis of the phrase 'the present King of France.' Those texts would introduce methods for the analysis of the logical forms of sentences and expressions, revealing structural features of their meanings that would have previously been understood entirely in terms of signifying. (Note that there is no present King of France; that phrase signifies nothing. How could it be meaningful if meaning were only signifying things?) Logic had long been a tool for analyzing arguments; what Frege and Russell proposed was an analysis of language itself – pruning it down to its most fundamental element, and then systematically examining the structures by which those elements combined to sustain the whole. This would prove so influential that much of the philosophy written in Western academic institutions in the 20th century followed suit and came to be known as "analytic philosophy."

DOI: 10.4324/9781003183167-9

When most contemporary Western philosophers hear "philosophy of language," it is work from the analytic tradition that they think of first.

During the same period, there was a new school of thought taking root in American universities known as "pragmatism." Philosophers such as William James, Charles Sanders Peirce, and John Dewey proposed a radically different approach to the whole of philosophy. Western philosophers since Plato had aspired to discover eternal truths about the world through abstraction and reflection on their own concepts. The pragmatists rejected these methodological starting points, insisting that concepts and beliefs were to be analyzed and judged in terms of their practical importance. We come to a clear understanding of what we believe and what we should believe by analyzing matters in terms of pragmatic significance: what difference does it make to use one concept rather than another(?); how would our actions be guided and how well would our interests be satisfied by holding one belief rather than another(?). Entries #9 and #10 address the work of W.V.O. Quine, whose work incorporates elements of both the analytic and pragmatist traditions.

5

FREGE ON SENSE AND REFERENCE

Background: Leading into the 20th century, most Western philosophers took linguistic meaning to be fundamentally a matter of designation. Words would mean something by designating it. This has the unexpected consequence that all the expressions that designate the same things have the same meaning, even though it makes a difference to our thought which words we use. Given that language has traditionally been construed as an outward manifestation of thought, this presents a problem of "cognitive significance" — what difference it makes to our thought to say one thing rather than another.

Allow me to make a bold statement:

(1)   Farrokh Bulsara is Farrokh Bulsara.

Shocking! Enlightening! It was insights like this that led you to choose this book, I know.

This is not a very bold statement, of course. I'd be willing to bet that most of those who read this won't know someone named Farrokh Bulsara, and no one comes to mind when you read that sentence. I would be willing to bet that even if you don't know anyone named 'Farrokh Bulsara' (as most won't), and don't know who I'm referring

DOI: 10.4324/9781003183167-10

to here, you will still be willing to accept the truth of (1). Why? Just about everyone who reads this has an intuitive grasp of what logicians call the law of identity: roughly, every individual thing is identical to itself. You know this, and you read (1) as a statement of one such consequence of this law.

Implicit in this example is another feature of your linguistic competence. You know, implicitly at least, that 'is' and other conjugations of the verb 'to be' sometimes function like an equal sign does in mathematics – in (1), the person named on the left is being equated or identified with the person named on the right. Note that this is not to say that the person named on the left is very much *like* the person named on the right. There's *just one person*, who is being mentioned by name twice. The law of identity makes accepting this trivial. There is nothing informative or interesting about being told that something is itself. But what about identity statements that are informative?

(2)   Farrokh Bulsara is Freddie Mercury.

This is true. Farrokh Bulsara took up the name 'Freddie Mercury' when he started performing professionally. Music and film are full of examples like this. Jay-Z is Shawn Corey Carter. Lady Gaga is Stefani Joanne Angelina Germanotta. You know some of these, and others may be genuinely informative when you hear them. They may be informative in an even more surprising way. Suppose you went to high school in New York with Stefani Germanotta. You remember her as Stefani, that student who's always down in the theater department. Years later, you see a Lady Gaga video and become a fan. Still years after that, you flip through your high school yearbook and say, "Wait. Lady Gaga is Stefani Germanotta!" The person you knew by one name turns out to be the same person you now know by another name. We learn similar informative identities all the time. In one famous example, 'Hesperus' and 'Phosphorus' (or 'the evening star' and 'the morning star') name the same object. The morning star ('Phosphorus') is the last celestial object (aside from the moon) that can be seen as daylight takes over the sky, and the evening star ('Hesperus') is the first one that can typically be seen as daylight recedes in the evening. It turns out that Hesperus is Phosphorus; both names refer to the planet Venus. These names were widely used in Europe since the ancient Greeks, and the discovery of their identity was genuinely informative.

What does all this tell us about language? For Western philosophers at the tail end of the 19th century, this posed a rather serious problem. The prevailing view in Western philosophy for centuries, even among philosophers who agreed about little else, was that we should understand linguistic meaning as a type of signification. Words mean what they mean by virtue of signifying or referring to something. 'Michael Padraic Wolf' signifies me; your name signifies you; 'green' signifies a color (or perhaps a range of similar colors); 'xenon hexafluoride' signifies a type of molecule, and so on. Other expressions may play logical roles in connecting these signifying terms to one another, but this signifying role is fundamental to meaning. But if this is true, then these two sentences say exactly the same thing:

(1)   Farrokh Bulsara is Farrokh Bulsara.
(2)   Farrokh Bulsara is Freddie Mercury.

If they say the same thing, then believing or reading one should be no different than believing or reading the other. They should have the same "cognitive significance" as it was sometimes put. But they do differ. That's why (1) is trivial, even if you don't know who Bulsara is, and (2) is informative. You learn something from (2) that you don't learn from (1).

At this critical moment, German logician Gottlob Frege (1892b/1997) stepped in. Noting the problem at hand here, he suggested that "signs" (names, words, expressions) had a two-part structure. On the one hand, there would be a reference for that sign. So, my name signifies me, this person, as we discussed above. But a sign does so by *presenting* the referent to us in a particular fashion, and the mode in which it presents this to us could be called the "sense" of that sign. Different signs would have different senses, but they might have the same referent. Two proper names like 'Farrokh Bulsara' and 'Freddie Mercury' have different senses (they present something to us in different ways), but they have the same reference (that particular person). More complex signs like definite descriptions would have senses, too, and those different senses might lead us to the same reference. 'The first prime number greater than 55' and 'the largest odd number less than 60' have different senses, but they both lead us to the number 59. It would also be possible for a sign to have a definite sense but have no referent at all. 'Michael Padraic Wolf's older sister' has a sense, but no reference. (I have no older siblings, and no sisters.) I know how the senses of the words guide me, and I know what such a thing would be, even if I know that no such thing exists.

Our characterization of Frege's notion of sense is very broad here, but this is faithful to his original presentation of the point. Formulating this notion more precisely would remain a challenge for years to come, and it is an implicit part of many of the other entries in this book. It will be tempting here to think of the sense of a sign as something psychological, or an "internal idea" as Frege put it. This is not what he is suggesting, however. Our personal grasp on something psychological is too "subjective," he said, and a sense must be "common property of many [people's ideas] and therefore not a part of a mode of the individual mind" (p. 154). My personal idea of the sense of an expression may include unclear parts or errors – e.g., if, when I hear 'Freddie Mercury,' I think 'that guy from Led Zeppelin,' when in fact he's performed with Queen. An idea may also have personal feelings or associations attached to it. If you mention the street on which I grew up, I flash back to a variety of memories, many of them with various shades of joy, sadness, etc. But it would be wrong to suggest that the name of that street should have all those personal associations loaded into its sense when others use it.

So, proper names would have a sense that determines their reference. Different names have different senses but might have the same reference. Complex phrases like 'the largest odd number less than 60' have a sense (which may be analyzed as the product of words that they include), and that sense will determine a reference for them. Suppose we ask what the sense and reference of an entire declarative sentence might be. A declarative sentence purports to tell us some circumstance is the case, so long as we're asserting it (rather than treating it as fiction, or a joke, for instance). Such a sentence may be true or false, and when we interpret the sentence, it is determining one of those two truth values for it that concerns us, much like determining which referent a sense leads us to for a name.

Here, we come to a crucial point in Frege's account. We grasp the sense of a proper name when we know what, if anything, it stands for. We grasp the sense of a sentence when we know which truth value it points toward. That is, we know the meaning of a sentence when we know the conditions under which it is true. This doctrine has been enormously influential in the philosophy of language and forms the backbone of many contemporary accounts. Frege's work also had the effect of marking territory for philosophy in a novel way. The referents of our words might be subjects for the physical sciences and biology, but senses were objects in the realm of logic, unfit for the kind of empirical study done in science. Instead, they required the kind of investigation and theoretical development that were suited to the more ideal, abstract nature of concepts that logicians and mathematicians conduct. They required *analysis* of a distinctively philosophical sort. The work of those who followed Frege's lead (particularly English-speaking philosophers), came to be known as "analytic philosophy." Much of the work covered in this book either fits into analytic philosophy or responds to some element of it.

RESPONSES

Frege's views on sense, reference, and truth conditions in accounts of meaning dominated work in the philosophy of language in the first half of the 20th century and shaped the work of Bertrand Russell and the early work of Ludwig Wittgenstein. Wittgenstein's later work would diverge significantly from Frege's emphasis on truth and logical analysis, focusing instead on the practical dimensions of language and sparking efforts to articulate meaning in terms of usage. Wittgenstein's later work is discussed in entries #11–15, and some of those ideas echo those of the American pragmatists, whose early figures are discussed in entries #7–8.

Analytic philosophers following Frege's lead would also put great stock in the notion of an *analytic truth*. (The term predates analytic philosophy by about 200 years.) A sentence like 'All bachelors are unmarried, eligible males' would be true solely in virtue of the meanings of its expressions, and so its truth might be revealed by analysis independent of any empirical investigation. Statements of the meanings of expressions would be analytic truths on this view, and so they had increasingly important theoretical roles to philosophers of language. In 1948, W.V.O. Quine would challenge the very idea of analytic truth, and in so doing, throw the central assumptions behind Frege's account into question. Quine's seminal work on this subject, *Two Dogmas of Empiricism*, is discussed in entry #9.

Somewhat less directly, Frege's work on the senses of proper names spurred discussions that culminates in what have been called "cluster concept" accounts of names and kind terms. On such accounts, the sense of a proper name like 'Freddie Mercury' might be analyzed and articulated by a cluster of descriptions, all or most of which are true of the referent – e.g., 'born in Zanzibar, wrote "Bohemian Rhapsody," etc.' Such views have come under sustained attack since the 1970s, largely inspired by the work of Saul Kripke and Hilary Putnam. Those accounts are discussed in entries #46–50.

RECOMMENDED READINGS

MAJOR WORKS

Frege, G. 1892a/1997. "Comments on Sinn and Bedeutung." In *The Frege Reader*, edited by M. Beaney, 172–180. Cambridge: Basil Blackwell.

Frege, G. 1892b/1997. "On Sinn and Bedeutung." In *The Frege Reader*, edited by M. Beaney, 151–171. Cambridge: Basil Blackwell.

Textor, M. 2010. *Routledge Philosophy Guidebook to Frege on Sense and Reference*. New York: Routledge.

RESPONSES

Dummett, M. 1981. *The Interpretation of Frege's Philosophy*. Cambridge: Harvard University Press.

Heck, R., and R. May. 2008. "Frege's Contribution to Philosophy of Language." In *The Oxford Handbook of Philosophy of Language*, edited by E. Lepore and B. Smith, 1–29. Oxford: Oxford University Press.

Kremer, M. 2010. "Sense and Reference: The Origins and Development of the Distinction." In *The Cambridge Companion to Frege*, edited by M. Potter and T. Ricketts, 220–292. Cambridge: Cambridge University Press.

McDowell, J. 1998. "On the Sense and Reference of a Proper Name." In *Meaning, Knowledge, and Reality*, 171–198. Cambridge: Harvard University Press.

Soames, S. 2014. "Critical Challenges." In *The Analytic Tradition in Philosophy*, 60–130. Princeton: Princeton University Press.

Taschek, W. 2010. "On Sense and Reference: A Critical Reception." In *The Cambridge Companion to Frege*, edited by M. Potter and T. Ricketts, 293–341. Cambridge: Cambridge University Press.

Wiggins, D. 2017. "Meaning and Truth-Conditions: From Frege's Grand Design to Davidson's." In *A Companion to the Philosophy of Language*, edited by B. Hale, C. Wright, and A. Miller, 2nd ed., 27–48. New York: Wiley-Blackwell.

6

RUSSELL ON 'THE PRESENT KING OF FRANCE'

Background: Frege's work was little read for years after it first appeared, but his ideas found a supporter in Bertrand Russell. As a fellow mathematician-turned-philosopher, he saw more clearly than most the promise in Frege's approach. He would take the project of logical analysis in new directions, analyzing non-referring expressions in ways not initially available to Frege.

Frege's work drew little attention initially but was later promoted by Bertrand Russell at a time when Russell was perhaps the most famous and respected philosopher in the English-speaking world. One significant challenge to this account was the status and significance of non-referring names and descriptions. Truth had become central to accounts of meaning, but sentences including non-referring expressions could not apparently have truth values. (What would make them true?) Still, such sentences often don't seem meaningless, so Russell offered a novel analysis of one class of expressions – definite descriptions – with an eye toward general accounts of meaning. Russell's account becomes very technical, but he frames it with three puzzles that we can readily grasp.[1] Consider:

(1)   The present King of France is bald.
(2)   Cormac McCarthy is the author of *The Road*.

DOI: 10.4324/9781003183167-11

(3)   Gregg believes that Cormac McCarthy is Cormac McCarthy.
(4)   Gregg believes that Cormac McCarthy is the author of *The Road*.
(5)   There is no largest prime number.

Puzzle#1: France no longer has a monarchy, so there is no present King of France. Is (1) true or false? (Does either answer imply that there's such a person?)

Puzzle#2: Imagine that Gregg does not read much and does not remember authors' names very well. In that case, (3) might be true and (4) might be false. Assume that for the moment. But (2) is true, so even if they have different senses, 'Cormac McCarthy' and 'the author of *The Road*' should have the same reference. Given that we have substituted an expression with the same reference into (3) to get (4), those two sentences should have the same truth value. So how can they differ?

Puzzle#3: (5) is true, but 'largest prime number' is an expression without a reference, and presumably the sentence cannot be true (or false). Yet it is. How?

Russell distinguished what he called "logically proper names" from "denoting phrases." Denoting phrases purport to denote something, but do so by matching an article with some noun or description; so, 'a man,' 'some man,' 'every man,' 'the largest prime number,' to name a few. Russell boldly stated, "denoting phrases never have any meaning in themselves, but that every proposition in whose verbal expression they occur has a meaning" (1905, p. 480).

That should sound strange at first. If these phrases have no meaning of their own, but the propositions in which they occur do, then do the propositions give them meaning somehow? Are they just idly tagging along? Think of them as incomplete and waiting to be matched with other items to make a complete proposition. If I said to you, "The tallest person in the room . . ." and then trailed off, you might feel like I'd started to say something, and expect me to finish. (*What about* this tallest person?) Russell's view was that parts of propositions like these did not have a self-contained meaning that they brought to a proposition; instead, they functioned along with other parts to compose what is being said. The meaning expressed by a sentence was not simply the addition of meaningful words to one another, but a logically complex interweaving of them. "[A] denoting phrase is essentially *part* of a sentence, and does not, like most single words, have any significance on its own account" (1905, p. 488)

The key was to give a logical analysis of the propositions in which these phrases occur. Russell begins that account with variables and propositional functions. The notion of a variable should be familiar from algebra. We often write equations like '$x + 3 = 7$' and solve for x. But we also sometimes leave it entirely open what a variable stands for to capture some important relation or function that might be filled in many ways. When we state the Pythagorean theorem as '$a^2 + b^2 = c^2$,' this spells out something true of all right triangles and can be filled with infinitely many values; in that theorem, 'a' is not *secretly* 7 or 12 or any other number, waiting to be discovered. This more general use of a variable is what Russell is invoking. A propositional function would then be a way of thinking of a proposition that was partially undetermined, with a variable holding the place that many other possible constituents might hold in different, related versions of the proposition. So, we could write 'Bx' and have that serve as a function for the propositions expressed by English sentences of the form 'x is bald.' The 'x' could be filled by lots of different people, though we would leave it undetermined in an analysis like Russell's, because our aim is to spell out the general form that such propositions might take.

Russell could then define how different denoting phrases would function in terms of how the truth of different propositions would be evaluated. Suppose we have a generic propositional function, 'Cx.' We could then substitute different denoting phrases into the spot held by 'x' and ask when they would be true. For the phrases 'everything,' 'nothing,' and 'something,' we get:

$C_{everything}$ means "Cx is always true."
$C_{nothing}$ means "'Cx is false' is always true."
$C_{something}$ means "It is false that 'Cx is false' is always true."

So it goes for the broadest sorts of denoting phrases Russell mentions. To analyze others, particularly definite descriptions, he gives a more fine-grained analysis of how those phrases function in propositions. So, let's turn to each of our three puzzles.

PUZZLE#1

'The' in this context implies uniqueness: there is exactly one such thing. How can we introduce this uniqueness as a logical matter, though? Take whatever properties play a role in something's uniqueness – being the author of *The Road* in (2), for instance. We'll say x has that property. Now suppose in some other context you come across a suggestion that y has that same property. Could there be a *second* thing with that property? Assuming something has that property uniquely, then no, but that's okay. It would just be the case that $x = y$. If there is just one author of that book, then any inclusion of that phrase in a sentence expresses a proposition involving that same person, even if there happens to be a different variable in use. If you found that there was a second author (or many more, somehow), then it would not be the case that $y = x$ for every value of y, but that's just to say that you would have found that the property was not uniquely held.

It is implied that there is exactly one thing that has the property of presently being King of France. We can introduce a propositional function for this, Kxy, which says roughly 'x is presently King of y.' (We could add a third variable space for the time at which someone is king, but 'present' is trickier to introduce than it seems, so we'll leave that for now.). Keeping our propositional function Bx for 'x is bald,' the proposition would be true just in case there was at least one thing that we could plug into that 'x' spot, for which the following would be the case:

(i) x is presently King of France.
(ii)   If any y is presently King of France, then $y = x$.
(iii) x is bald.[2]

Now we can evaluate the truth of this proposition. These three conditions are jointly necessary; if any one of them is false, the conditions are not met, and the proposition is false. As I write this, nothing makes (i) true, so the conditions are not met. There is no need to posit a non-bald person when we say this, because our analysis allows us to separate the baldness condition of the proposition from the existence condition.

PUZZLE#2

Gregg believes that McCarthy is McCarthy, but it's not the case that Gregg believes McCarthy is the author of *The Road*. How can these differ in their truth value when both are beliefs about the same reference (McCarthy)? The propositions have significantly different logical forms. 'The author of *The Road*' can be analyzed much like 'the present King of France' was: there is some x such that x is the author of *The Road*, and any y that is the author of *The Road* is identical to x. But (3) only requires McCarthy to be identical to McCarthy.[3] While those happen to work out for the same referent, Russell thought that there was nothing surprising about the fact that (3) and (4) would differ, assuming that beliefs are themselves functions of the propositions believed (which are different in this case).

PUZZLE#3

To deny the existence of something as (5) does, we should say "it is false that there is some x such that (i) x is prime, and (ii) nothing is both prime and greater than x."[4] We would then have to further elaborate these conditions to cash out the 'nothing' as Russell does in his original definition, but that's not difficult. Again, grasping the logical form shows us what is being said without committing ourselves to the existence of something.

RESPONSES

Russell would go on to argue that almost *all* noun phrases – including many apparent proper names – were subject to this sort of analysis. Russell's account of definite descriptions was also criticized by Peter Strawson, who argued that Russell had not distinguished between descriptions (and sentences, more generally) as linguistic *types* and particular *uses* of them on different occasions. For many phrases and sentences, it was only in the context of their use that a proper analysis of the function of their noun phrases could be made. Whereas Russell argued that the phrase 'the present King of France' in a proposition *entails* the king's existence, Strawson argued that it merely *presupposes* it, and thus utterances of (1) at different times may have different truth values. (See entry #29.)

A related line of criticism was pursued by Donnellan, who noted that definite descriptions were used by speakers in two different ways. In some cases, they would be interpreted strictly: whatever the content of a description implied determined what it would denote, and thus many such descriptions would fail to denote. Suppose you were at a philosophy conference and saw me speaking to someone in the lobby. You might speak of that person as "the philosopher that Michael was talking to." If, in fact, the person to whom I was speaking was not a philosopher, that description would fail to denote. But in ordinary conversation, with a little stage-setting, we often use descriptions in a less strict, more fallible way to focus fellow speakers' attention on a referent. Thus, if you say to someone "the philosopher that Michael was talking to" and that presumption succeeds in drawing your fellow speaker's attention to the person with whom I'm speaking, then the description may function satisfactorily, even if that person does not do philosophy. Donnellan called the first, stricter reading an "attributive" use of a definite description, while the latter he called a "referential" use. (See Donnellan (1966) and Predelli (2003) for more.) This suggested that some uses of phrases have a purely referential role – signifying some referent, plain and simple – that is only contingently associated with any description of that referent. This would influence the development of accounts of rigid designation discussed in entries #46–50.

NOTES

1. The puzzles here are well-known, but Edward Zalta's SEP page helped my thinking about how to frame this.
2. For those who have done some symbolic logic: $(\exists x)([Kxf \wedge (\forall y)(Kyf \rightarrow y = x)] \wedge Bx)$.
3. Let c = Cormac McCarthy, r = *The Road*, and compare $c = c$ with $(\exists x)([Axr \wedge (\forall y)(Ayr \rightarrow y = x)] \wedge x = c)$.
4. $\neg(\exists x)(Px \wedge \neg(\exists y)(Py \wedge Gyx))$

RECOMMENDED READINGS

MAJOR WORKS

Hylton, P. 2003. "The Theory of Descriptions." In *The Cambridge Companion to Bertrand Russell*, edited by N. Griffin, 202–235. Cambridge: Cambridge University Press.
Russell, B. 1905. "On Denoting." *Mind* 14: 479–493.

RESPONSES

Donnellan, K. 1966. "Reference and Definite Descriptions." *The Philosophical Review* 75 (3): 281–304.

Landini, G. 2002. "Russell's Theory of Definite Descriptions as a Paradigm for Philosophy." In *A Companion to Philosophical Logic*, edited by D. Jacquette, 194–223. Oxford: Blackwell.

Ludwig, K. 2012. "Logical Form." In *The Routledge Companion to Philosophy of Language*, edited by G. Russell and D.G. Fara, 29–41. New York: Routledge.

Predelli, S. 2003. "Russellian Description and Smith's Suicide." *Acta Analytica* 18 (1–2): 125–141.

Soames, S. 2014. *The Analytic Tradition in Philosophy (Vol. 1: The Founding Giants)*. Princeton: Princeton University Press.

Stevens, G. 2011. *The Theory of Descriptions*. New York: Palgrave Macmillan.

Strawson, P. 1950. "On Referring." *Mind* 59 (235): 320–344.

PEIRCE ON MAKING IDEAS CLEAR

Background: Among English-speaking philosophers in the Western world, there was a growing sense at the end of the 19th century that the predominant schools of philosophical thought in Europe faced intractable difficulties. One response to this was the emergence of analytic philosophy, which was profoundly influenced by the work of Russell and Frege. Contemporaneously, several American philosophers began developing a new school of thought stressing practical interests that came to be known as "pragmatism." We discuss a seminal pragmatist work here, and its themes of melding the semantic with the practical.

How could we spell out the meaning of a word or sentence? We do this in rough and ready ways all the time: I ask you what a word means, and you tell me a handful of suggestions to give me a sketchy understanding. In entries #5–6, we saw efforts to analyze more complex expressions in search of their logical form, which allowed us to speak of the senses of words and phrases and the truth values of declarative sentences. Those accounts have been very influential among Western philosophers, but there has been a parallel set of accounts that diverge significantly from Frege and Russell. In many of those accounts, there is a steady emphasis on how language plays a role not just in representing or picturing the world, but also in how we use language to cope

DOI: 10.4324/9781003183167-12

with the world. Our question in this entry is: how fundamental to the meaning of a word or sentence is the *use* that we put it to(?).

Much of modern Western philosophy has been influenced by the work of René Descartes (1641/2017), who offered an ambitious framework for synthesizing the methods of philosophy, natural science, and mathematics in our search for knowledge. It was central to his work that certain ideas were "clear" and "distinct," and due a special sort of authority because of this. But what does it mean to say that an idea is "clear" and "distinct"? Descartes claimed that a clear idea is "present and fully revealed to the mind attending" to it. A distinct idea would be a clear one that "is so separated and demarcated from all other ideas, that it contains in itself absolutely nothing which is not clear." As definitions, these may leave us a bit unsatisfied. When would the content of an idea be "fully revealed" to us? Descartes's answer suggests a special psychological state – an intellectual *feeling* of completion, like that "lightbulb" moment when an important point suddenly comes together. He appealed to what he called "the natural light of reason," which would give us a feeling of completeness and mastery of what was contained in the idea. That sort of feeling can be deceptive though, and it often happens to us regarding things that we later realize are false.

Descartes was a believer in "knowledge by acquaintance" – the view that our most fundamental knowledge is not gained by deduction or construction, but simply by being acquainted with certain phenomena. Consider a color: how do you know what green looks like? Your explanation is likely to come back to simply having seen green things. Descartes suggested the same is true for the content of more abstract concepts, which we could access through introspective reflection. Many philosophers had reservations about this for important concepts. For centuries after Descartes's death, there were rounds of philosophers refining and reintroducing this idea of clearness in our concepts, followed by rounds of criticism.

Charles Sanders Peirce entered this debate in the 1870s. His aim was to challenge the fundamental assumptions of Cartesian methods. Most of his professional life was spent doing work that would be better characterized as science, and he typically spoke of himself in those terms. His most widely read work, "How to Make Our Ideas Clear," (1878/1992) appeared in *Popular Science Monthly*. His immersion in scientific methods matters greatly here. He had developed a distaste for *a priori* intuitions and an appreciation for the rigorous scrutiny and self-correction that scientific practice requires. Where Descartes aspired to grand philosophical theory-building full of eternal truths revealed by introspection, Peirce embraced the provisional character of science, where hypotheses are put to the test, with the best kept on and the rest abandoned. There was a practical character to this kind of inquiry that resonated with him – pieces of equipment *work* in certain ways, chemical reagents can *make* new substances, physical materials can be *used* to fabricate structures, etc.

This all led Peirce away from Cartesian methods, but he retained the hope of an account that would articulate the ideal of clearness in our concepts. That would require a method for determining when a concept was clear, rather than appealing to introspection. To address this, Peirce offered what has been called the "Pragmatic Maxim":

> Consider what effects, which might conceivably have practical bearings, we conceive the object of our conception to have. Then, our conception of these effects is the whole of our conception of the object.
>
> (1878/1992, p. 132)

This maxim asks us to consider what effects there would be – what sort of *difference* it might make – in our taking up one concept rather than another. (Or, if we're concerned with language more directly, how differences in meaning between different words or sentences pay off practically.) So far, this does not sound unlike Descartes's view. After all, we were supposed to have clear and distinct ideas, so we're being asked to do some distinguishing, either way. The important turn comes in the clause that appeals to "practical bearings": what should distinguish our concepts is the differences they would make in how we might *use* them.

This implied that there would be some form of test by which we could decide when the concept applied. Ideally, these would have the rigor of logical proofs, or strictly controlled laboratory experiments. If we had no way of pinning a concept to our reason and experience, then we should treat it with some suspicion, as it might simply be empty noise when we use it. Peirce held a rather dismal view of much of the philosophical discourse of his time, feeling that it had declined into idle wordplay with ungrounded distinctions. The pragmatic maxim was an attempt to build that sort of grounding and testability back into philosophy and make it part of the gold standard for good concept usage. (Hookway (2004) addresses the finer details of Peirce's statement of the maxim over the course of his career.)

This was also an extension of his understanding of meaning, thought, and knowledge in general. Rather than being grounded in something abstract, or prior to our experience, Peirce saw them as bubbling upward from our practical engagement with the world. We develop and adopt concepts when we find some useful distinction to be made in how we cope with the world and work toward our goals. As Peirce put it, "The essence of belief is the establishment of a habit, and different beliefs are distinguished by the different modes of action to which they give rise" (129–130). The beliefs we have and the meanings of the words we speak are not simply static pictures or representations of our world; they are more like tools that we use to navigate and share in the work of pursuing our various interests.

All of this runs up against an objection, of which Peirce was aware. To say or believe 'Pittsburgh is west of Philadelphia' may guide my travel; to say or believe 'titanium melts at 1668°C at 1atm' will guide my work in a laboratory or factory; both will do so successfully. But to more traditionally minded philosophers, this success does not explain their meaning – rather, their success is waiting to be explained. The explanation, some say, is simple: those beliefs succeed because they are true, and they are true insofar as they represent facts. The practical guidance they offer is welcome, but to get at their truth, we must look at how they relate to something other than ourselves and our interests. So, Peirce must say something about truth on his view, and how these concerns can be addressed.

He did see truth and objectivity as central components of his philosophy, but he resisted the pull of representation here. To say that there were facts independent of whatever we might say about them, and that true sentences represent those facts, was appealingly intuitive, but it did not yet make matters fully clear. To make things so, we must return to the pragmatic maxim. How can we distinguish true beliefs and sentences from false ones by the differences that they make to us? What we can do is test them, as his maxim suggested. The true sentences and beliefs will pass our tests (we will get to Pittsburgh, we will melt that titanium, etc.), and the false ones won't. Those successes and failures may take considerable time and effort, but Peirce asserted that those who work on such problems were joined in the "cheerful hope" that these efforts would one day come to satisfactory resolutions. That is an ideal, but an ideal that extends the work and attitudes that we already take up in ways we can readily understand. He suggests that to say a sentence or belief is true is just to say that it is one that all who investigated it would one day converge on its acceptance. This is not to identify truth with anyone or any group's opinion; truth is not simply whatever we say. But it is to articulate the nature of truth in ways that essentially involve us and how we deploy our languages. (See Wiggins (2004) for more on this.)

RESPONSES

Peirce's philosophical works were not widely read in his lifetime, and he was only occasionally mentioned by other philosophers for decades after his death. His emphasis on use, testability, and the intersection of philosophy of language with science were immensely influential on other work, however. In particular, Quine and Sellars both studied with C.I. Lewis, who studied Peirce's work extensively, and many of their works continue themes from Peirce mentioned here. (See entries #9 and #14 for more.) We can think of Peirce's work here as the first great salvo in a series of disputes that animate many of the entries in this book: is language to be understood primarily in terms of representation (truth, reference, logical form, etc.) or in terms of use (practical interests, shared conventions, etc.)?

A revival of pragmatist themes and methods has led to a philosophical movement, sometimes called "neopragmatism," thanks to the work of philosophers such as Richard Rorty (1972). Rorty's take on pragmatism emphasizes parts of earlier works that deemphasize or reject expectations that language will "mirror" the world as a representation. Haack (2006) colorfully illustrates some of the tensions between Peirce's work and Rorty's interpretation by constructing a fictional dialogue between them built entirely from direct quotes. These were aspects of fellow pragmatist William James's work that caused friction between the two in their own lifetimes, and there has been a corresponding rise in interest in the more realist themes in Peirce's work. Misak (2004, 2016) and Lane (2018) have approached Peirce's account of truth historically, but with an eye toward reintroducing it to contemporary debates. Legg (2017) has done similar work, with attention to both truth and knowledge in Peirce, with direct responses to various neopragmatists.

RECOMMENDED READINGS

MAJOR WORKS

Descartes, R. 1641/2017. *Meditations on First Philosophy*. Edited by J. Cottingham, 2nd ed. Cambridge: Cambridge University Press.

Peirce, C.S. 1878/1992. "How to Make Our Ideas Clear." In *The Essential Peirce: Selected Philosophical Writings*, edited by N. House and C. Kloesel, vol. 1, 124–141. Bloomington, IN: Indiana University Press.

RESPONSES

Haack, S. 2006. "'We Pragmatists . . .': Peirce and Rorty in Conversation." In *Pragmatism, Old and New: Selected Writings*, edited by S. Haack and R. Lane, 675–696. Amherst, NY: Prometheus Books.

Hookway, C. 2004. "The Principle of Pragmatism: Peirce's Formulations and Examples." *Midwest Studies in Philosophy* 38: 119–136.

Lane, R. 2018. *Peirce on Realism and Idealism*. Cambridge: Cambridge University Press.

Legg, C. 2017. "Idealism Operationalized: How Peirce's Pragmatism Can Help Explicate and Motivate the Possibly Surprising Idea of Reality as Representational." In *Peirce on Perception and Reasoning: From Icons to Logic*, edited by K. Hull and R.K. Atkins, 40–53. New York: Routledge.

Misak, C. 2004. *Truth and the End of Inquiry: A Peircean Account of Truth*, 2nd ed. Oxford: Clarendon Press.

Misak, C. 2016. *Cambridge Pragmatism*. Oxford: Oxford University Press.

Rorty, R. 1972. "The World Well Lost." *The Journal of Philosophy* 69 (19): 649–665.

Wiggins, D. 2004. "Reflections on Inquiry and Truth Arising from Perice's Method for the Fixation of Belief." In *The Cambridge Companion to Peirce*, edited by C. Misak, 87–126. Cambridge: Cambridge University Press.

'PITTSBURGH IS WEST OF PHILADELPHIA' IS TRUE

Background: Building on the work of his classmate C.S. Peirce, William James transitioned from a psychologist influenced by the British empiricists to the public face of pragmatism in the first decade of the 20th century. Where Peirce's work was precise and revisionary, James's was bold and ambitious. One of his most noted – and notorious – extensions of pragmatist themes was his account of truth, which departed in radical ways from the traditional views of Western philosophers and would both draw fire and inspire thinking about truth.

In entries #5 and #6, we saw that Frege and Russell placed special emphasis on the role of truth in an account of meaning. Roughly speaking, they shared the view that to know the meaning of a sentence is to know the conditions under which it would be true. Other types of sentences, such as questions and commands, don't have such truth conditions, but we might explain their meanings indirectly via other sentences that do have them. For instance, questions elicit responses that typically take the form of sentences that have truth conditions. ("When is your birthday?" "My birthday is June 30." The response here would be true under certain conditions, false under others.) Variations on this view of meaning remain widely popular among philosophers of language in the West today.

DOI: 10.4324/9781003183167-13

Peirce's view, described in entry #7, throws this assumption back into question. While Peirce did emphasize testing and affirming what we say and believe and made those concerns central to his account of meaning, it was "practical effects" and the guidance of our actions that formed the core of his view. A sentence might be true, but never used to guide a course of action; very useful statements might turn out to be false. If you press them on the matter, physicists and engineers will tell you that Newton's theories are false and Einstein's are true (at least as far as we can see at this point). But that doesn't stop them from using Newtonian mechanics for all kinds of engineering projects. We don't build bridges over black holes or accelerate midsize cars to the speed of light, so the differences that using Newton's (false) mechanics generates are small enough to simply ignore. Peirce was well aware of these kinds of objections, and he addressed them in his work, but he also spoke only grudgingly about truth in general.

All of this brings us to a big, fancy, high-stakes, win-big-or-go-home kind of philosophical question: *what is truth*? Given its central role in some accounts and the aggressive ways that we shall see it downplayed in others, we should ask what truth is in the first place. Note that this is not a question about *which* things are true. There are many particular statements whose truth may interest us. Is virtue its own reward? Does dark matter exist? Were the 1996 Baltimore Orioles robbed in the American League Championship Series by an umpire's blown call?[1] We can dispute such matters, but that is not the question at hand. Truth *itself* is our concern. The classical answer in Western philosophy has been that truth is correspondence. This would be a special kind of relationship between what is said and what is the case. If grass is, in fact, green, then a sentence (or proposition) such as 'Grass is green' would correspond to the facts, whereas 'Grass is purple' or 'Grass is magenta' would not. On this sort of view, language functions much like a map or a picture of the world. Things are functioning properly (i.e., true things are being said) when the points in the picture correspond to the facts in the world.

Note that these illustrations don't tell us anything precise or definitive about the correspondence relation. We're relying on intuition here, whether we're correct or not. What kind of relation would correspondence have to be? It doesn't seem to be a spatial or physical one. We can say "Grass is green" from all kinds of spatial relations to grass, and I seem to be able to at least talk about things that are not physical at all. How else might we characterize the relation? Note also our capacity to make true statements even about subjects where there is apparently nothing to which our sentences can correspond. We can say "A unicorn is a white horse with a horn on its forehead," even if there are not, never have been, and never will be any unicorns to which that sentence corresponds. We can even make true statements like "The largest possible prime number would have no factors but one and itself," which is true even though it is necessarily the case that there is no largest possible prime number.

These worries, along with others, led some philosophers to push back against the classical notion of correspondence. We might call that classical account an *inflationary* view: it suggests that truth is something substantive and real, adding its special character to the world and waiting to be uncovered by philosophical methods. By contrast, many philosophers of language since 1900 have adopted what are now called *deflationary* views: truth is not something substantive or real, and the role it plays in our languages can be explained away with the right kinds of analysis. While deflationists about truth would readily agree that we speak of the truth of sentences, and that doing so allows us to say important things, they hold that there is no extra-special, metaphysically exciting thing that is truth.

One early proponent of a non-classical, deflationary account of truth was William James. Inspired by the work of Charles Sanders Peirce, James criticized what he called "copy" theories of truth and meaning. By "copy" here, he was suggesting the sort of "map" or "picture" view I described earlier, on which language serves as a static representation of the world. James shared Peirce's enthusiasm for practical engagement, and scientific inquiry that had a dynamic, unfolding character by which we *added* truths to our inventory, as James put it. How could we do that? If grass just *is* green, how could we add such a truth to our inventory? James's view was that this sort of worry was beholden to old ideas about truth that had not panned out; the key is to change our way of thinking about truth instead. His view emphasized the practical side of Peirce's account, suggesting that we call a sentence or belief "true" because it tends to produce better outcomes for more people and more goals than competing beliefs and sentences.[2] We say that the belief or sentence 'Pittsburgh is west of Philadelphia' is true because believing so does a better job of directing our travel, reading maps, anticipating changes in the weather (if it's snowing in Pittsburgh and the front is heading east, it's best to believe it'll reach Philadelphia soon), and countless other tasks and goals we might have. We might investigate many such sentences and beliefs and find that one consistently serves us better than the others. That one gets called "true," but there is no special metaphysical relation between that sentence and the facts, beyond its contribution to our successful coping with the world.

An early form of deflationism about truth (offered not long after James's work) was called a "redundancy" view, notably suggested by English philosopher Frank Ramsey. Consider:

(1)   It is true that Pittsburgh is west of Philadelphia.
(2)   Pittsburgh is west of Philadelphia.

A redundancy theorist like Ramsey would note that no new information is actually added in (1) that is not already conveyed by an assertion of (2). If I tell you that it is true that Pittsburgh is west of Philadelphia, then I'm really just telling you that Pittsburgh is west of Philadelphia. Nothing substantive is added by the 'is true' in either sentence. Again, this was not to say that using a word like 'true' was meaningless or suspicious. Rather, the use of a word like that would only serve some other function – reaffirming or endorsing a sentence, for instance. We can think of this view as similar in spirit to James's, although with a more precise, formal character.

RESPONSES

To say that there have been many deflationary accounts since 1900 is not to deny that inflationary accounts have continued to find wide support, as well. One very common concern about deflationary theories in general is that many philosophers of language believe that our best hope for a theory of meaning involves the use of truth conditions, as we recalled in the opening of this entry. On those accounts, the truth conditions *explain* what the sentences we use mean, and the sort of correspondence relation that inflationary accounts assume would provide a word-to-world connection that grounded meanings in a more substantive fashion. 'Grass is green' is true because that sentence is related to certain stuff in the world that really does have that sort of property. There is a strong intuition among some theorists that, for the meanings of words and sentences to be about something, rather than merely sounds and inscriptions we exchange with one another, there must be some word-to-world relation at the heart of it all, and truth is the preferred one.

To adopt a deflationist approach, proponents of truth-conditions will argue, is to take away a crucial foundational block and leave nothing that will support that explanatory need. We do say that the sentence 'Pittsburgh is west of Philadelphia' is true, and we do say that Pittsburgh is west of Philadelphia. But we say the latter sentence precisely because it is true, and we know what would make it true. It is not just a noise or scribble of symbols that pops out of us in some primitive way, without further explanation. Our assertion of it (and our refusal to assert other sentences) is not independent of its correspondence with the facts, and our comprehension of its meaning is not independent of that grasp.

Two other themes have shaped debates over truth in recent decades, which I will mention briefly here. First, there has been great debate about whether the bearers of truth values are sentences or propositions. That is, should we think of truth values as belonging primarily to the surface-level sentences of natural languages like English, or to the propositions that such sentences express? This makes a difference to how we conceive of truth, and whether an inflationary or deflationary account is correct. On many accounts, propositions are arrangements of objects and properties, or sets of possible worlds (full of objects and properties). If truth resides at this level of substantial things, that might imply that truth itself must be substantial (hence, some inflationary view must be correct). Second, Polish logician Alfred Tarski offered a formal definition of truth for certain types of formal languages. This included a general schema for theorems about truth:

(T) 'S' is true if and only if S.

Here, 'S' on the left mentions a sentence, while the same sentence on the left is used in standard ways. To incorporate an earlier example:

(T') 'Pittsburgh is west of Philadelphia' is true if and only if Pittsburgh is west of Philadelphia.

What's the payoff? The sentence after '. . . only if' is being used just as you would typically use it, without any special metaphysical or theoretical implications. You're just talking about the cities and where they are, without invoking any special truth relation between them. If Tarski's definition suffices, then deflationists have said there is reason to favor their accounts. (See Field (1986), Wright (1992), and Horwich (1998) for examples of this; Gupta (1993) and Patterson (2003) for replies. Tarski is discussed in entry #16.)

NOTES

1. They were.
2. Peirce was suspicious of James's use of his work on this point, fearing that it was detaching language, science, and philosophy from the world. The debate got so heated that Peirce eventually said he should not be called a "pragmatist" any longer, even though he is often credited with starting that school of thought.

RECOMMENDED READINGS

MAJOR WORKS

James, W. 1907/2000. "Pragmatism's Conception of Truth." In *Pragmatism and Other Writings*, 87–105. New York: Penguin Books.

Ramsey, F. 1927. "Facts and Propositions." *Proceedings of the Aristotelian Society* 7 (Supplementary): 153–170.

Russell, B. 1906–1907. "On the Nature of Truth." *Proceedings of the Aristotelian Society* 7: 28–49.

RESPONSES

Field, H. 1986. "The Deflationary Conception of Truth." In *Fact, Science and Morality*, edited by G. MacDonald and C. Wright, 55–117. Oxford: Basil Blackwell.

Gupta, A. 1993. "A Critique of Deflationism." *Philosophical Topics* 21: 57–81.

Horwich, P. 1998. *Truth*, 2nd ed. Oxford: Basil Blackwell.

Moore, G.E. 1953/2002. "True and False Beliefs." In *Some Main Problems in Philosophy*, 270–287. New York: Routledge.

Patterson, D. 2003. "What Is a Correspondence Theory of Truth?" *Synthèse* 137: 421–444.

Wright, C. 1992. *Truth and Objectivity*. Cambridge: Harvard University Press.

'ALL BACHELORS ARE UNMARRIED MALES'

Background: The work of Russell, Frege, and the early works of Wittgenstein suggested that the task of philosophers of language was to analyze meanings. By various logical methods, they should uncover the structures and semantic contents that made thought and language possible. This committed them to the existence of some fixed, eternal meanings that these methods might uncover. By mid-century, scrutiny about such meanings was building. Quine's attack on the analytic/synthetic distinction thus marks a significant challenge to the very possibility of an analytic account of meaning.

Here's a question for you. Perhaps you take it that there are meanings to the words and sentences you speak. Perhaps you also take it that declarative sentences have truth values – that they can be either true or false and will be one or the other.[1] Can declarative sentences be true (or false) *solely* in virtue of the meanings of their parts? Consider a few sentences.

(1)   In 2020, there were 446 bridges in Pittsburgh.
(2)   Light travels at 3×10^8m/s in a vacuum.
(3)   All coroners are officials who investigate suspicious deaths.

DOI: 10.4324/9781003183167-14

All three of these sentences are true, but there are differences between them that interest philosophers of language. Sentence (1) is an oft-quoted statistic in Pittsburgh and was recently determined by a geophysicist. Although it's a high number for a city of its size, there is nothing special about the fact that there are precisely 446 bridges there. We could imagine a higher number if there had been more money for public works, or a smaller number under other circumstances. Sentence (2) does not seem accidental in that way. It has the kind of necessity to it that we expect in a law of physics, and it is a necessity that we discovered. It came as a surprise at the time of its discovery, but results confirming it were clear and have been strongly corroborated in the years since. The facts proved persistent in this case.

I stress "facts" here to emphasize a difference you may grasp between (3) and the first two sentences. If you want to know how many bridges there are in Pittsburgh, you go out and you count them. If you want to know how fast light travels in a vacuum, you design and build equipment, and you measure what light does. But what would you measure or observe to confirm the truth of (3)? Would you take your lead from nature documentaries and follow coroners around, taking notes? Set up a camouflaged perch beside the photocopier in their offices to watch them, undetected?

One way that some philosophers have tried to capture the difference here is to say that sentences like (1) and (2) are true in virtue of the facts, while sentences like (3) are true in virtue of the meanings of their words. In the 18th century, Immanuel Kant proposed a distinction between *synthetic* and *analytic* truths. Sentences like (1) and (2) synthesized distinct concepts – '446,' 'bridges,' 'Pittsburgh' – to create a new representation. Sentences like (3) took concepts and unpacked them, spelling out what they already contained. Someone who was not an official but investigated suspicious deaths would be something else (a private detective); an official not investigating deaths is some other kind of official. To a believer in analytic truths, (3) is true simply because that's what 'coroner' *means*.

Philosophers of language made a great deal of this in the first half of the 20th century. This grew in part from efforts to provide a foundation for mathematics within the bounds of logic, but it soon extended to a project covering all of formal and natural languages. In short, the goal was to distinguish sentences that were analytically true from those that were synthetically true and have the analytically true sentences serve as foundations in a theory of meaning, with an explanatory power more like the axioms of a logical or mathematical theory. What could tell us what the analytic truths were, though? Examples may seem obvious, but we need some clear theoretical distinction.

W.V.O. Quine rejected the prevailing assumptions in this debate: there was no principled, useful, theoretically interesting distinction between analytic and synthetic truths. Nothing, he said, is true solely in virtue of the meanings of words, because the meanings of words and truth values of sentences are themselves subject to revision, and much of what is revised or preserved comes down to our choices and interests. Some of those changes would scarcely be imaginable, much less tolerable or desirable, but Quine was arguing that there is no principled distinction between analytic and synthetic truths that would support other explanations. His initial argument begins with a review of the prevailing approaches of his day, and a series of objections to each of them.

The first suggestion that Quine considered was logical truth. Take a sentence:

(4)   No unmarried man is married.

This is a logically necessary truth. The right account of logic will simply show us the necessity of that truth, and we don't have to go out and observe anything to get it. Quine had no objection to necessary truth like this in logic. Some sentences are "logical truths," which are necessarily true solely in virtue of their form alone, e.g., 'A = A.' But analytic truths were supposed to include sentences like (3), which are not logical truths. Those were the analytic truths that were supposed to be informative for other purposes. Analyticity was supposed to be a semantic notion about meaning, and it looks like logic is doing all the work in (4), while it can't do the work in (3).

The next two notions Quine considered may have already occurred to you: definition and synonymy. While we should not run the two notions together, they are closely related. Ideally (perhaps a little naïvely), a definition tells us a word or set of words that mean the same as the words we seek to define. Synonymous words or phrases would have the same meanings. Why not just say that analytic sentences are true by definition, or that they are true because their component terms are synonymous? "*By definition*, all coroners are officials who investigate suspicious deaths." Boom. Done. Or maybe not. When we write a definition, Quine argued, we're trying to capture an existing synonymy, and we look to usage as our guide. If that usage is to be *correct* and some synonymy is revealed by it, then something else must establish the synonymy. (Dictionaries don't *create* meanings; they *catalog* them.)

What if we tried the notion of "interchangeability" instead? Expressions would be interchangeable if we could always substitute them for one another in declarative sentences without changing the truth value of the sentence. So, if 'Freddie Mercury was born in Zanzibar' is true and 'Farrokh Bulsara' names the same person, then 'Farrokh Bulsara was born in Zanzibar' will also be true. If (3) is an analytic truth, then we should be able to substitute 'coroner' for 'official who investigates suspicious deaths,' and vice versa, into sentences without affecting their truth value. This would have to be possible for all contexts, minus a few exceptions. I won't belabor the exceptions here, because Quine's objection pertains to straightforward cases. He notes that different expressions might be interchangeable even if they don't mean the same thing. 'Creature with a heart' and 'creature with a kidney' can be substituted for one another this way. This does not show that they mean the same thing, however. When an organism needs a pump (its heart) it also needs a filter (its kidney) to remain viable; natural selection, not meaning, is responsible for keeping these two features connected. So simply being interchangeable is not enough to establish synonymy and cannot be the basis of analyticity.

Lastly, Quine considers what are called "semantical rules" in formal languages like those we use in logic. These had the virtue of being clear where the notion of analyticity was not. But they were also inventions of those who developed the formal languages, rather than discoveries of preexisting truths. Logicians could write a rule stating "All sentences in the set Γ are true in L" for some formal language called L, and simply place the sentences we took to be analytic in that set, but this stipulation wouldn't tell us any more about what made them true, or why we shouldn't pick some other set of sentences to assign this special privilege.

In the end, Quine says that there isn't a useful analytic/synthetic distinction to be had, and no sentence is true *solely* in terms of the meanings of its words. He thought it was a mistake to think of the meanings of words in isolation at all. The sentences of our language function instead as a great, interconnected whole – a "web of belief" as he called it. Meanings should be understood holistically, with each way of using them related to all the others, forming a framework that both guides our understanding of our experiences, and which adjusts in light of that experience. Each part of that great web might be revised if it conflicted with our experience, though we could not change them all at once. Conversely, any sentence we wanted to retain could be kept true, so long as we were willing revise other beliefs to accommodate that. Many revisions would be unwise, but none of them would be ruled out in principle. A sentence that was once taken to be analytically true might later be held false. Want an example? Try (3). Coroners did not originally investigate suspicious deaths; their role in 12th century England concerned property and tax collection. Their investigative role emerged centuries later as political institutions shifted around them. You might ask yourself: could we imagine the truth of apparently true sentences like these changing over time? What else would we have to give up, and to what else might we have to commit?

RESPONSES

Grice and Strawson (1956) argued that Quine had demanded too strict a definition for analyticity, and that not having a perfectly articulated distinction did not entail that there was no distinction at all. Over time, even Quine himself permitted a weaker sort of analytic distinction back into his own work. Putnam (1965/1975) pointed out to Grice and Strawson's objections that, while it was true that imperfect distinctions could do theoretical work, the nature of the analytic/synthetic distinction was of special explanatory importance. Intuitions and examples were not enough. Yet Putnam still insisted that Quine was wrong, and that there was a distinction to be had. He proposed that analytic truths in natural languages (as opposed to formal ones) would be exceptionless biconditionals ('A if and only if B') that were generally accepted and employed as a criterion for a single word. Later authors worried that "criterion" in this proposal is as fraught as "analytic" was. Fodor (1998) and Fodor and Lepore (1992) were critical of the holism that Quine's account entailed.

There has been some effort by cognitive scientists and philosophers inspired by the work of Noam Chomsky to resuscitate a version of analytic truth. In those areas, there has been greater acceptance of an innate set of mechanisms that permit humans to speak the natural languages we do. With grammatical rules "hardwired" into us, some associations like those expressed by analytic sentences might be part of the wiring. Note that this is still a weaker notion of analyticity than was widely held before Quine. These would be contours of our biological capacity for language, and not great truths about logic, mathematics, or the nature of truth itself. For other reviews of (and some attempts to revive) analyticity, see Putnam (1965/1975), Boghossian (2017), Chalmers (2011), Creath (2004) and Juhl and Loomis (2012).

NOTE

1. There are also more exotic views on truth to consider. Those are discussed in entries #16–20, but they would not affect much of what is at stake in this entry.

RECOMMENDED READINGS

MAJOR WORKS

Grice, H.P., and P. Strawson. 1956. "In Defense of a Dogma." *The Philosophical Review* 65 (2): 141–158.

Putnam, H. 1965/1975. "The Analytic and the Synthetic." In *Mind, Language, and Reality: Philosophical Papers*, vol. 2, 33–69. Cambridge: Cambridge University Press.

Quine, W. 1953/1980. "Two Dogmas of Empiricism." In *From a Logical Point of View*, 2nd ed., 20–46. Cambridge: Harvard University Press.

RESPONSES

Boghossian, P. 2017. "Analyticity." In *A Companion to the Philosophy of Language*, edited by B. Hale, C. Wright, and A. Miller, 2nd ed., 578–618. Oxford: Basil Blackwell.

Chalmers, D. 2011. "Revisability and Conceptual Change in 'Two Dogmas of Empiricism'." *Journal of Philosophy* 108 (8): 387–415.

Creath, R. 2004. "Quine on the Intelligibility and Relevance of Analyticity." In *The Cambridge Companion to Quine*, edited by R. Gibson, 47–64. Cambridge: Cambridge University Press.

Fodor, J. 1998. *Concepts: Where Cognitive Science Went Wrong*. Cambridge, MA: The MIT Press.

Fodor, J., and E. Lepore. 1992. *Holism: A Shopper's Guide*. New York: Wiley-Blackwell.

Juhl, C., and E. Loomis. 2012. "Analytic Truth." In *The Routledge Companion to Philosophy of Language*, edited by G. Russell and D. Fara, 231–241. New York: Routledge.

Putnam, H. 1965/1975. "The Analytic and the Synthetic." In *Mind, Language, and Reality: Philosophical Papers*, vol. 2, 33–69. Cambridge: Cambridge University Press.

10

'GAVAGAI!'

Background: Some accounts of language in this book treat meaning as a real but abstract sort of entity whose character can be revealed by the right sorts of logical analysis. However, there is an additional strain of thought running through Western philosophy that strives to naturalize our understanding of language, making it continuous with the methods and conclusions of scientific inquiry. Quine's "gavagai" thought experiment is a seminal work in this tradition.

When we use words like 'language' or 'meaning' in a philosophical way, they often take on a mysterious, abstract quality. The sense that there are fixed, determined meanings to which our muddled, everyday linguistic behavior must answer would seem to demand some sort of grounding, and Western philosophers since Plato have been accustomed to answering such difficult questions with exotic entities. That impulse to expand our ontology in response to explanatory demands has often been met with suspicion, especially among empiricists after David Hume and philosophers who assign greater priority to the methods and findings of science. That sort of post-Humean empiricism and openness to scientific thinking intersected among many English-speaking philosophers in the first half of the 20th century and shaped the thinking of analytic philosophers from the 1930s on.

DOI: 10.4324/9781003183167-15

The ideal for such philosophers would be a naturalistic account of language and meaning, on which there were no appeals to non-physical entities, and the methods that philosophy used were continuous with and sensitive to results in science. For the most ardent naturalists, much of the history of philosophy is portentous nonsense, and *good* philosophy consists in clearing up ambiguities and conceptual confusions to convert enduring questions into forms that scientists can take up. The business of philosophy would ultimately be putting philosophy out of business.

W.V.O. Quine was a naturalist in this vein and rejected any suggestion of meanings as abstract entities. But what would the alternative be? An important methodological move to make here is to get away from the expectation that a theory of meaning might be given from outside the standpoint of a user of the language. If there are no abstract entities with which our usage must align, then we have only one another to answer to. If so, then it is more important to think about *sameness* of meaning among speakers. If I'm competent in using a language, and you are as well, then we can communicate when our utterances, inscriptions, signs, etc., have the same meaning; confusion and disputes arise when those meanings are not the same. This much will be true however we account for meaning, so what we can then seek is a way of testing for the sameness of meaning that does not appeal to meanings as abstract entities.

Translation emerged as an important idea here. Whatever meanings might be, if we can successfully translate another person's utterances, inscriptions, signs, etc., into our own, then we have answered any important explanatory questions that might arise. (So says a naturalist, at least.) Translation between languages can be tricky of course, and there often won't be a single-word-for-every-single-word translation even between closely related languages. The German word '*Schadenfreude*' must be translated as 'pleasure derived from others' misfortune'; the Sanskrit word '*mudita*' must be translated as 'happiness from the well-being of others.' No single English word will do in such cases. Grammatical differences abound among languages, too, so there won't be word-for-word translations. But these are not failed translations, only cumbersome ones at the surface level. How do we test a proposed translation? Here, Quine appealed strictly to linguistic behavior. A successful translation would tell us what others would say, inscribe, sign, etc. – all forms of behavior – in a given set of circumstances.

Thinking like a behavioral psychologist, Quine put this in terms of stimulus conditions. When placed in front of a red color patch, a forthright English speaker would say, "It is red"; a forthright French speaker would say, "*C'est rouge.*" While the sounds, symbols, and signs may be different, users of those languages have dispositions to use them in the same stimulus conditions.

For a naturalist, this will all sound very appealing. But Quine was aware of another lingering concern. To illustrate this, he offers us a thought experiment. Imagine that you were a field linguist – someone traveling to remote parts of the world to meet groups of people who speak unrecorded languages, which you hope to study, learn, and share with other linguists. You would want to create a *translation manual* – a book of rules for substituting words and sentences in the new language with words and sentences from a language you already use. Quine imagines a case of *radical* translation, in which we have no knowledge of neighboring languages from which to start. How would we proceed? Quine suggests that we would repeat the sorts of moves we make as children. We would notice things in our environment, follow the behavior of others, make a guess about how their linguistic behavior tracks things in the environment, mimic that behavior, and adjust as we got feedback from them. Suppose we ingratiate ourselves with the new community and get to work. As we follow these speakers around, we notice that there is an abundance of rabbits in the local environment. Whenever a rabbit runs by, they shout, "Gavagai!"[1] After a while, you say "Gavagai!" in return; they repeat it. You appear to be well on the way to a translation for the English word 'rabbit.'

Are you, though? You have a finite set of observations and a hypothesis about them. There are many ways of interpreting that same set of observations, as any scientist will tell you about their data. Perhaps these people are saying something we would translate as 'Undetached rabbit parts!' or 'Rabbit stages!' or 'Dinner!' (if they eat rabbits). Quine noted that this was an issue both at the level of individual words and at the level of whole sentences. More observations would eliminate some of these possibilities; if they never eat the rabbits, and never say "Gavagai!" around mealtime, we can probably set 'dinner' aside. But there is no telling how many possible translations there could be, and no finite evidence set can establish the truth of a hypothesis with certainty. We may have much higher degrees of confidence in one hypothesis over its competitors, but we cannot conclusively determine that it is true from a finite evidence set. This is known to philosophers of science as "underdetermination," and it led Quine to claim that there is an indeterminacy of translation between any two languages that we could never wholly resolve. We do favor some translations over others, but our reasons for doing so are pragmatic: how simple or lucid the translations seem, whether the languages share a history and developed in parallel, etc. (Quine's definitive statement of these issues is in *Word and Object* (1960). For concise treatments, see Quine (1970) and Weir (2006).)

RESPONSES

Quine's appeal to behavioral dispositions was influential among analytic philosophers in the 1960s and 1970s. Every entry in this book requires some hard choices about which responses to discuss, but the volume of material written on this topic is dizzying. Two lines of criticism are discussed in other entries in this book. Saul Kripke's meaning skepticism arose in part from doubts about the sufficiency of dispositional accounts (see entry #15), while Chomsky's linguistic nativism was inspired by his view that deeper features of grammar could not be acquired in the ways that Quine's emphasis on observable behavior suggests (see entry #41). Both Kripke and Chomsky had studied with Quine to some degree, as did Donald Davidson, whose work hews more closely to Quine's. Davidson (1973) noted what some readers might have been thinking as the thought experiment played out above: the indeterminacy of translation between languages that Quine described would occur between speakers of the same language, as well. Where Quine spoke of radical translation, Davidson describes even those using the same language as engaged in a project of radical interpretation with one another. Each speaker must formulate a "theory" (which Davidson uses in a slightly idiosyncratic way) in which they assign beliefs and other attitudes to other speakers, given the empirical sources and constraints Quine suggested, even if they putatively speak one's own language. There will be many different possible assignments that we might consider, each compatible with our finite observations of others' behavior. This leaves us with the same sort of indeterminacy, even if pragmatic constraints lead us to settle on an interpretation fairly quickly. "The problem of interpretation is domestic as well as foreign" (1973, p. 125). For criticism of Davidson's approach here, see Krik (1985) and Khatchirian (2008) and Searle (1987), mentioned below.

Many responses to Quine's views on translation are critical of the argument being made from underdetermination. Jaggar (1973) noted that Quine was committed to a realist view of science and determinacy about which theories we were and should be adopting, despite their being similarly underdetermined. That might be resolved by giving up the scientific realism, though that might weaken the motivations for a naturalistic account. Gibson (1986) offers similar criticisms. Boorse (1975) argues that there are disjointed commitments in the background of Quine's work. His epistemology (informing the account of underdetermination) had moved on from his early days as a logical positivist, allowing greater holism among our beliefs. (See entry #9). But his semantics remained very positivist, failing to appreciate how accounting for meaning demanded more attention to inferential relations among sentences. (Here, compare with entry #14.) Bechtel (1980) suggests that the problems run deeper, and that Quine's claims of underdetermination and indeterminacy were inconsistent. If the theories by which we translate between the two languages are underdetermined, then we cannot say that they are empirically equivalent; but if we can say that they are empirically equivalent, then they are not underdetermined. Gemes (1991) similarly doubts that Quine has shown that there could be empirically equivalent translation manuals for entire languages, but attempts a reformulation of the indeterminacy thesis to salvage it. Allen (2010) also defends Quine to a degree on these points, arguing that indeterminacy remains an issue, even if we reject Quine's behaviorist approach.

A variety of other approaches merit mention, as well. Searle (1987) argued that Quine's deep commitment to linguistic behaviorism was an indispensable part of the argument for indeterminacy (cf. Allen 2010), and that such behaviorism was inconsistent with first-person authority about meaning. When I say, "The cat sat on the mat," I have a particular sort of authority over what I mean by 'cat' and 'mat,' and while my overt behavior should normally be expected to reflect that meaning, it cannot be said to constitute such meanings. (It will be useful for readers to compare Searle's claim here with work discussed in entries #46–50, which may bring first-person authority into question from a very different angle.) Conversely, Lance and Hawthorne (1990) argue that there is a type of indeterminacy of translation, but not the one that Quine suggests, nor for the reasons he presents. Whereas Quine treats a translation manual as a descriptive project – simply a mapping of the sentences of one language onto another – Lance and Hawthorne argue that it is a deeply normative one establishing rules to govern communication between linguistic communities – "more like writing a constitution than describing the properties of a metal" (1990, p. 29). A host of social, historical, and physical factors play into such choices. Thus, the choice of a translation manual is always "indexical" to that set of starting points, and the manual serves instead as an attempt to shape intersecting social practices going forward, rather than to describe them as they have always been.

NOTE

1.   I was taught to pronounce this "GAV" (like the first syllable of 'Gavin') "uh"-"guy."

RECOMMENDED READINGS

MAJOR WORKS

Davidson, D. 1973/1984. "Radical Interpretation." In *Inquiries into Truth and Inter-pretation*, 125–139. Oxford: Oxford University Press.

Jaggar, A. 1973. "On One of the Reasons for the Indeterminacy of Translation." *Philosophy and Phenomeological Research* 34 (2): 257–265.

Quine, W. 1960. *Word and Object*. Cambridge: The MIT Press.

Quine, W. 1970. "On the Reasons for Indeterminacy of Translation." *Journal of Philosophy* 67 (6): 178–183.

RESPONSES

Allen, S. 2010. "Can Theoretical Underdetermination Support the Indeterminacy of Translation? Revisiting Quine's 'Real Ground'." *Philosophy* 85 (1): 67–90.

Bechtel, P.W. 1980. "Indeterminacy and Underdetermination: Are Quine's Two Theses Consistent?" *Philosophical Studies* 38 (2): 309–320.

Boorse, C. 1975. "The Origins of the Indeterminacy Thesis." *Journal of Philosophy* 72 (13): 369–387.

Gemes, K. 1991. "The Indeterminacy Thesis Refomulated." *Journal of Philosophy* 88 (2): 91–108.

Gibson, R. 1986. "Quine's Dilemma." *Synthèse* 69 (1): 27–39.

Khatchirian, A. 2008. "What Is Wrong with the Indeterminacy of Language-Attribution?" *Philosophical Studies* 146 (2): 197–221.

Krik, R. 1985. "Davidson and the Indeterminacy of Translation." *Analysis* 45 (1): 20–24.

Lance, M.N., and J. Hawthorne. 1990. "From a Normative Point of View." *Pacific Philosophical Quarterly* 71 (1): 28–46.

Searle, J. 1987. "Indeterminacy, Empiricism, and the First Person." *Journal of Philosophy* 81 (3): 123–146.

Weir, A. 2006. "Indeterminacy of Translation." In *The Oxford Handbook to the Philosophy of Language*, edited by E. Lepore and B. Smith. Oxford: Oxford University Press.

PART III

WITTGENSTEIN ON RULE-FOLLOWING AND PRIVATE LANGUAGE

BACKGROUND III

Unlike the other sections of this book, this one is devoted almost entirely to the work of one person: Ludwig Wittgenstein. Like Quine, discussed in entries #9–10, Wittgenstein's work has both the hallmarks of Frege's and Russell's methods and a growing sense of the importance of practice and pragmatic concerns in natural language. In Wittgenstein's case, however, this set of themes appears over the course of the evolution from his earlier work to his later work, rather than as a mix throughout them. A key assumption among earlier analytic philosophers was that their approach would one day yield a *theory* of meaning; that is, a complex formal structure with well-defined foundational elements, rules, and methods for generating more complex arrangements of those elements, and a completeness to it that would allow us to interpret everything that could possibly be said. Wittgenstein's early work reflects this ambition. In fact, he was so sure he had laid the necessary groundwork for this that he quit philosophy after the completion of his first book!

Wittgenstein began to develop doubts about that earlier work and came to embrace a view of natural language with much greater emphasis on culture and shared social practices. This precluded a "private" language that we develop on our own in our thoughts from birth. Rather than a grand formal system, Wittgenstein came to think

DOI: 10.4324/9781003183167-17

of languages as loose collections of "language games" – small, specific practices over whose contours we gain an intuitive command through habituation and enculturation. To speak of a word or sentence having a "meaning" is misleading on such a view; better to think of them as having numerous uses to which we may put them. Wittgenstein's case for this took shape as a series of puzzles and problems surrounding how someone might follow a rule. Entries #11–13 and #15 look at this in detail. Entry #14 is an outlier here, but a close cousin in spirit. Wilfrid Sellars argues against the possibility of "foundational" beliefs that underlie all the rest of our knowledge. The possibility of any belief arises from the intersection of numerous social practices – many language games, Wittgenstein might have said – rather than any one of them having a special priority over all others.

11

WITTGENSTEIN ON FOLLOWING A RULE

Background: The early works of Wittgenstein were formative influences on the development of analytic philosophy of language. Those works owe a great deal to Frege and Russell and were embraced by the logical positivists. But by the 1930s, Wittgenstein's approach had shifted to focus on practical features of language use. Both this approach and the analytic philosophy he had inspired presume a competence with semantic rules – how to use words, what they imply, etc. Naïve conceptions of what rule-following involves present us with a surprising puzzle.

Let's play. What comes next?

(A)   1, 2, 3, 4, . . .

Yeah, that one's easy. How about this one?

(B)   1, 8, 27, 64, . . .

Maybe you think that's pretty easy, too. How about this? (Answer at the end of the entry.)

(C)   1, 27, 125, 343, . . .

DOI: 10.4324/9781003183167-18

I loved these kinds of problems in elementary school. Some people find them annoying, but it's not hard to see why teachers would use them as exercise. The form is simple, so most students pick it up quickly. We usually start such series with some function of the number 1, then the same function with the number 2, then 3, and so on. If you know your natural numbers, you have a starting point to tease out the function, and what that function gives you with the next natural number. They also require a little creativity and ingenuity once you get past the easiest ones. You don't simply repeat some pattern by rote in these exercises, as you do when you practice multiplication tables. You *carry on* into new cases (new to you, at least) and thus *follow* a pattern.

This sort of exercise caught the attention of some philosophers of language because it exhibits some of the important features of our capacity to follow a rule. By many estimates, it is fruitful to think about the meanings of words and sentences as a kind of rule. There are correct and incorrect ways to use them and sharing those ways of using them with fellow speakers of our language allows us to interact and communicate with them. If we did not share those rules for how the words are to be used, then that kind of shared linguistic coping with others would be impossible.

If grasping the meaning of a word or sentence involves grasping a rule, and for every rule there is some possibility of following it incorrectly – getting things wrong somehow – then a question presents itself: how does each of us know whether we're following a rule correctly? It's simple enough to check in routine cases, but as we said above, rules often guide us in dealing with circumstances that are new to us.

One answer that appealed to many people thinking about this question is that grasping a rule involves some special kind of internal state. In part, this is driven by the assumption that, if our grasp of a rule is guiding our behavior, it must be something internal to us that could cause us to behave in certain ways. Could we recognize this somehow, perhaps by recognizing a distinct feeling that accompanies our grasp? The experience of not grasping a rule might have this. When I'm put on the spot and don't know what to do next, my body tenses up, and I often feel a rush of anxiety. In moments like this, my internal monologue often stops completely for a moment. It's as though all the useful parts of my brain are hiding somewhere, trying to avoid getting chewed out.

What does it feel like when we grasp a rule and know how to follow it? It often does not *feel* distinctive at all. In many cases, an answer (or next move) will just "pop" into our thinking. If you ask me, "What is the third chord in the key of B major?" I will respond with "D# minor," and that will come without any deliberation or special event in my consciousness. For many things I can say with authority, the words often come out of my mouth before I can even formulate them "in my head." Coming up with those answers doesn't "feel" like anything. So perhaps the grasp we have of a rule is still an internal state, but something that does not have a particular quality we can feel at all. Perhaps it would be more like a mental or linguistic reflex – something that snaps into action without effort or deliberation. That would make it a bit murkier to us, but it would still be something internal to us.

Ludwig Wittgenstein was concerned with these questions, and came to a bold, unexpected conclusion late in his career. He claims that there is nothing within us that can tell us whether we're following a rule correctly or not – no thought, no interpretation of past results, no "linguistic reflex," nothing. This is not to say that we cannot follow rules correctly, but rather that we're confused when we look inside ourselves to determine that.

In *Philosophical Investigations*, he asks us to imagine teaching mathematics to a student. Suppose we're doing a very simple exercise like (A)-(C) above, where we count by twos. The student says or writes:

2, 4, 6, 8, 10, 12 . . .

Things seem to be going well here. But imagine that this is an especially rigorous school, and the exercise continues for a long time.

. . . 990, 992, 994, 996 . . .

All's well. The pedagogy's proceeding; student learning outcomes are being met.

. . . 998, 1000, 1004, 1008, 1012 . . .

Whoops.

Something has gone wrong here. Let's assume that this is not a case of a student fooling around, and that they are trying to give correct answers in an honest fashion. We might ask the student, "Why did you start doing things differently after 1,000?" We would expect certain kinds of answers: they got distracted; they forgot what the problem asked. But suppose we got a very different answer. Suppose the student said, "I did go on in the same way." Perhaps then we would review how numerals work, assuring that the student knew that the numerals '0' through '9' in the "ones" column still work the same way, and that you could still count by twos as you had before. "I know," the student might say, "And I was aware of those numbers, too. But this is how I had been going along before, and I kept going along the same way."

Here, we would be at a bit of an impasse. They may have felt that was the appropriate way to go on, but it wasn't correct. The student may have been honest about trying to do things as they understood them, but those weren't the ways to go on. If the point seems strained by the fact that this is a classroom exercise, think about more fundamental sorts of rules that we follow. Suppose our student started counting out the natural numbers in some unexpected way, or if their use of familiar words just stopped following the familiar contours of ordinary usage. This is so unfamiliar that it is difficult not to slip into thinking that someone who does this is playing a joke. But such breakdowns in following new-to-them rules do happen with children, and even as adults, we can find ourselves making mistakes when we thought we knew better.

Most importantly, for all of us and our misguided student, as well, the things that we can point to "inside" of us are not enough to resolve such breakdowns. If you ask me my favorite song or baseball team, my honest answer to that question has a special kind of authority to settle the question. When it comes to how a word is *to be used*, such a report cannot have the same authority. My *strong sense* or *feeling* that a word is to be used in a certain way may be there even when I'm making a mistake. When I have command of a rule, the way to proceed often feels comfortable, familiar – natural in an important sense. But again, all of that is often true when I make mistakes and fail to follow the rule, too.

Perhaps the answer lies in a deeper analysis. What if we were to take a rule that we're to follow, break our efforts down into smaller tasks, and spell out how they are combined in following more complex rules. For some rules, this might grant us some insight. In my example above where I knew that D# minor was the third chord in B major, I learned to make such judgments piecemeal: first I learned the 12 tones that Western music uses, then how to construct a major scale, and later how to take intervals in the scale to construct and name chords. I don't deliberate when I do that now, but maybe I'm just following rules quickly and unreflectively. Wittgenstein considered this approach (though not this example), but went to great lengths to emphasize that such analysis gave us only the illusion of philosophical insight. Each of these smaller tasks introduces further rules that must be followed – the order of the letters for the tones, the order of their names, how to count the steps to take between the notes, and more. You must admit, it's unsatisfying to ask, "How do we follow a rule?" and be told, "By following these twenty other rules." You could reasonably ask the same for each of those other rules, so we seem to have a regress.

Wittgenstein did not think that this cast our ability to follow rules into doubt. What it showed was that there must be some way in which we follow a rule that is not a further *interpretation* of the rule. An interpretation in this sense might be something like the analysis of my musical example, or it might be something like our earlier attempts to ground our rule-following in some special mental state, but it would be something that could be internal to us that we could affirm by reflection. No such thing would do, he was saying. Some of our rule-following might be the kind of deliberate construction that I described in the music example, but such possibilities rest on a kind of pre-reflective grounding common to members of a community. Following a rule requires being incorporated into what he called a *Lebensform*, or "form of life." Those who grasp the rule share something *practical*, deeply engrained into their everyday coping with the world, rather than something *intellectual* that analysis could unpack and formulate as a theory. This upended the consensus among English-speaking philosophers at the time, but more importantly, it suggested that our grasp on the world emerges from something that philosophy (and science too, Wittgenstein would have said) cannot further uncover for us. It suggested a hard limit on what philosophy could do.

RESPONSES

An extensive literature about Wittgenstein's account of rule-following developed over the second half of the 20th century. Some readings emphasized his views about the limits of what philosophy might do and interpreted much of his work as opposed to the very idea that philosophy can offer substantive theories or reveal eternal truths. Richard Rorty incorporated this interpretation into his own project, with controversial results. The emphasis on social practice in Wittgenstein's account has also been influential on the work of Robert Brandom and John McDowell, although with less opposition to theory-building than one finds in Rorty's work. (Their responses are discussed in entries #14–15.) There have also been efforts, contrary to Wittgenstein's views, to ground rule-following in psychological traits, such as dispositions. If successful, such strategies would defuse what is most radical in Wittgenstein's account and leave open the possibility of grounding future accounts of meaning in the natural sciences. Refuting such efforts is central to Saul Kripke's 1982 interpretation of Wittgenstein, discussed in entry #15.

RECOMMENDED READINGS

MAJOR WORKS

Wittgenstein, L. 1953/2009. *Philosophical Investigations*. Edited by P. Hacker and J. Schulte. Translated by G.E.M. Anscombe, P. Hacker, and J. Schulte, 4th ed. New York: Wiley-Blackwell.

Wright, C. 1980/2001. "Following a Rule." In *Rails to Infinity: Essays on Themes From Wittgenstein's Philosophical Investigations*, 9–32. Cambridge, MA: Harvard University Press.

RESPONSES

Hale, B. 2012. "Rule-Following, Objectivity and Meaning." In *A Companion to the Philosophy of Language*, edited by B. Hale, C. Wright, and A. Miller, 619–642. Oxford: Basil Blackwell.

Minar, E. 2012. "The Life of the Sign: Rule-Following, Practice, and Agreement." In *The Oxford Handbook of Wittgenstein*, 276–293. Oxford: Oxford University Press.

Pears, D. 1991. "Wittgenstein's Account of Rule Following." *Synthèse* 87 (2): 273–283.

Rorty, R. 1979. *Philosophy and the Mirror of Nature*. Princeton, NJ: Princeton University Press.

Stern, D. 1995. *Wittgenstein on Mind and Language*. Oxford: Oxford University Press.

Travis, C. 1989. *The Uses of Sense: Wittgenstein's Philosophy of Language*. Oxford: Oxford University Press.

THE PRIVATE LANGUAGE
ARGUMENT

Background: It was a dogma among early analytic philosophers of language that spoken language gives expression to some of the contents of our thoughts, and that this was its primary function. Overt speech or signing would thus be the public face of the private, internal worlds of our experience. This presumes a kind of linguistic competence internal to our thoughts and prior to social interactions in our explanations. Much like the problems of rule-following in entry #11, problems emerge.

As I write this, my right knee hurts a lot. It's probably from moving a couple of household appliances while doing repairs yesterday, though I didn't feel anything pop at the time. You probably know what this one is like, though. You wake up with it sore and a little hot, and it has that dull, constant ache. Not too many sharp, stabbing pains even when I bend it, so it doesn't feel the way a more serious sprain does. You know what that's like, right?

Most of us have pulled a ligament (or whatever it is I've done) this way before, and the sensations are familiar enough. How would we learn to make such distinctions and use those parts of a language, though? You, dear reader, have not been having my sensations all day, nor can I somehow tap directly into yours to report any comparisons. Suppose for the moment that each of my mental events is just some

DOI: 10.4324/9781003183167-19

process or event happening in my central nervous system. Even if our best neuroscientists made stunning breakthroughs, they could only tell us which sensations were brought about by which regions of the brain and the biochemical mechanisms by which it took place. That theoretical breakthrough might allow you to say which sort of sensation I'm having at a given moment, but it would not allow you to have my sensations as I'm having them. We just don't share our experiences in that sense, even though we appear to have experiences that are similar in important ways. Our access to our own consciousness has a distinctive sort of *privacy*, we might say.

How, then, could we talk about our sensations to others? Many Western philosophers have approached this with what we might call an "inside out" approach. They have suggested that we have special access to our own mental states from birth, that we recognize and manage those states with some facility, and learn to associate them with external signs, such as spoken words or the manual signs of ASL. If this were right, then I might spend my early life experiencing and recalling different types of sensations, and then noticing that other speakers make certain noises, write certain ways, or move their hands in some characteristic ways when things happen to them that cause me some sensation. It feels a certain way when I bang my toe, or burn my fingers, and I notice that when others do this, they make a certain sound, etc. With time and practice, I might then adopt those same sounds, inscriptions, and motions for the same apparent sensory events. On "inside out" views, we thus have a grasp of our mental lives prior to our social interactions with others and work our way "out" to give linguistic performances.

An "outside in" approach would reverse this order of explanation. It would suggest that speakers interacted with their environments and other speakers, developing ways of speaking or signing that they shared with others first. Speakers would then learn to distinguish their sensations and other internal states by turning their linguistic habits inwards upon themselves. Notice that, when I told you about my leg earlier, I had to make reference to external events or qualities in things that would be available in similar ways to all of us – *dull* and *sharp* pains, for instance. (Thankfully, I've never been stabbed. But I have nearly sliced fingers off more than once, so . . . we'll call it even.) This does not assume that we don't have consciousness, mental states, or anything "internal" until we acquire a language. Rather, it is to say that we don't have the resources to speak *to ourselves* about those states before we acquire a language, and we could not base the meanings of a language on things that were internal and accessible only to us. On this view, we could not have a *private* language.

Wittgenstein argued for this conclusion in *Philosophical Investigations*. He asked,

> 243. . . . But could we also imagine a language in which a person could write down or give vocal expression to his inner experiences – his feelings, moods, and the rest – for his private use? – . . . The individual words of this language are to refer to what can only be known to the person speaking; to his immediate private sensations. So another person cannot understand the language.

His answer to this question was clear: we could not have such a language. Not even the supposed speaker of this language, with access to the "private sensations" it supposedly discussed, could be in a position to speak such a language to themselves and understand its expressions. We should note that this is not a denial of some things that are already familiar or plausible. This does not rule out inner speech, or an internal monologue in which one "speaks" to oneself. While we only occasionally share the contents of our inner speech with others, the meanings of words in it are typically familiar from the languages we share with others. Nor would denying that there are private languages rule out the possibility that the meanings of some words or phrases would, *in fact*, only be known to one person. For instance, many different fields have technical jargon that is understood only by a very small number of experts. We could easily imagine some new term introduced by one of those experts – perhaps one they are keeping to themselves for now or have jotted down in a notebook that no one else has read yet. No one else, *in fact*, knows the meaning of this new word. But that in itself does not rule out others learning the meaning of that new word, and experts looking to expand a theory would typically define new terms with combinations of older ones. None of this would be private in the stronger sense that is relevant here.

Wittgenstein's choice to take up this question of a private language rooted in our sensations reflects the historical context in which he was working (and, I would say, one that is very common in everyday assumptions about thought and language). Many of his contemporary British, American, and German philosophers were deeply committed to an empiricist approach to language and knowledge. This committed them to accounts of meaning on which the most basic words signified sensations that might appear in our consciousness. Much was riding on the prospects for private languages among his peers.

Why should we reject private languages? Wittgenstein approached this question from a number of directions, but a common thread among them was the apparent impossibility of setting a rule for oneself that would give words in this private language their purported meanings. Something has to underwrite the substantial, meaningful quality of those words, though. Someone might use a word in their private language haphazardly, or without any order at all. This happens with natural languages all the time – someone "runs at the mouth" or "talks the talk" with pieces of a language that they really have no substantive grip on at all. It is not enough to simply make sounds or gestures to constitute using a language; you have to be doing something *correctly*.

So, to introduce a private name for a sensation, you would also need to establish a rule for yourself about how to use it, and which sensations it designated. This is where the real problem emerges. There must be something in a rule that we could check, or measure, or test against our own judgments. If I say that I'm seven feet fall, that could be checked with a tape measure, and I could be wrong. In that case, I might simply be in error, or I might not be following the rules for how to talk about height or to use numbers. In any case, there is the possibility of correcting me on this point. Now, imagine how our rule for a word in a private language must work. Suppose you were having a toothache. (Wittgenstein used this example so often that he and his students at Cambridge were known as "the toothache club" at the time.) You might propose that you could note the occurrence of that sensation and make a commitment (to yourself) to call all sensations like that "toothache," and not to call any other sensations by that name. To introduce that word, you would have to set some kind of standard for its usage, but you would only have yourself and your own sense that you were being faithful to the original standard. The measure of whether or not you were applying the rule correctly would be whether or not it *felt to you* like you were applying the rule correctly. This would not really be a genuine confirmation, Wittgenstein argued. That sort of feeling often accompanies successful judgments, but it also accompanies lots of mistakes. We often feel like we're getting something right, when in fact we're getting it wrong. The *feeling* of correctness does not constitute *being correct*. Yet this is all a speaker could appeal to in establishing a private language. If so, then we cannot have private rules; and if so, we cannot have a private language.

RESPONSES

The private language argument has also prompted discussion at the intersection of epistemology, theories of meaning, and philosophy of mind on the subject of self-knowledge. When it comes to knowledge about our internal states – sensations, moods, the content of our beliefs and other attitudes, to name a few – many philosophers hold the view that each of us has a privileged sort of access and certain types of incorrigible – perhaps even infallible – self-knowledge on some subjects (e.g., whether we're in pain, whether or not we believe something). Defenders of privileged access in this vein include Paul Boghossian and Jordi Fernández.

These accounts have clashed with compelling works by semantic externalists, such as Burge (1979), who have argued (in ways broadly sympathetic to Wittgenstein's view) that no one of us could have the resources and authority to say such things without the involvement of the external world and the community of speakers with whom we share the language. Some have gone further still. Schwitzgebel (2002) has challenged the assumption that introspection is a completely reliable source of knowledge, even for speakers of public languages under normal conditions. (Many studies in psychology address similar concerns about the reliability of self-reporting and the transparency of our own attitudes to ourselves, as well.)

Saul Kripke wrote a highly regarded (and highly divisive) book on rule-following and private language that is discussed in entry #15. A symposium with A.J. Ayer and Rush Rhees shortly after Wittgenstein's death also served as a touchstone for discussion that would later intersect with developments in linguistics and psychology. That debate is described in entry #13.

RECOMMENDED READINGS

MAJOR WORKS

Stern, D. 2011. "Private Language." In *The Oxford Handbook of Wittgenstein*, edited by M. McGinn and O. Kuusela, 333–350. Oxford: Oxford University Press.

Wittgenstein, L. 1953/2009. *Philosophical Investigations*. Edited by P. Hacker and J. Schulte. Translated by G.E.M. Anscombe, P. Hacker, and J. Schulte, 4th ed. New York: Wiley-Blackwell.

RESPONSES

Boghossian, P. 1989. "The Rule-Following Considerations." *Mind* 98 (392): 507–549.

Burge, T. 1979. "Individualism and the Mental." *Midwest Studies in Philosophy* 4: 73–122.

Fernández, J. 2013. *Transparent Minds: A Study of Self-Knowledge*. Oxford: Oxford University Press.

Hitchcock, C. 1995. "Wittgenstein on Private Language: Exorcising the Ghost from the Machine." *Philosophia* 24 (3–4): 127–147.

Mulhall, S. 2007. *Wittgenstein's Private Language: Grammar, Nonsense and Imagination in Philosophical Investigations*, 243–315. Oxford: Oxford University Press.

Panivani, C. 2008. "Rule-Following, Explanation-Transcendence, and Private Language." *Mind* 117 (466): 303–328.

Schwitzgebel, E. 2002. "How Well Do We Know Our Conscious Experience? The Case of Visual Imagery." *Journal of Consciousness Studies* 95 (5–6): 35–53.

Tang, H. 2014. "Wittgenstein and the Dualism of the Inner and the Outer." *Synthèse* 191 (14): 3173–3194.

Verheggen, C. 2007. "The Community Revisited." *Metaphilosophy* 38 (5): 612–631.

Wright, C. 1989. "Wittgenstein;'s Later Philosophy of Mind: Sensation, Privacy, and Intention." *Journal of Philosophy* 86: 622–634.

Wright, C. 1998. "Self-Knowledge" the Wittgensteinian Legacy." In *Knowing Our Own Minds*, edited by C. Wright, B. Smith, and C. Macdonald, 13–45. Oxford: Clarendon Press.

AYER ON ROBINSON CRUSOE

Background: After Wittgenstein's death in 1951, colleagues and students completed work on Philosophical Investigations. One early opponent of the private language argument was A. J. Ayer, who made a name for himself in the philosophy of language by importing and reinterpreting many of the central themes of logical positivism into Anglo-American philosophical circles. This committed him to precisely the sort of account that Wittgenstein had been so critical of in the Investigations. His arguments for the necessity and explanatory priority of private language are representative of much of analytic philosophy and anticipate themes from later linguistics and cognitive science.

Wittgenstein died in 1951, but the reputation of his work continued to grow. In 1954, the Royal Aristotelian Society held a symposium on the private language argument, at which Rush Rhees sat in for Wittgenstein, and Ayer offered an extended critique. Ayer's opinion of Wittgenstein's private language argument in this symposium was withering, to put it mildly. What could be more obvious, he wondered, than our capacity to speak to ourselves in ways that are inaccessible to others? Why should it not rest on an immediate grasp of our own sensations, and our introduction of rules to manage our apprehension of them?

DOI: 10.4324/9781003183167-20

A familiar literary trope appears in Ayer's critique: a person stranded on a desert island, in the vein of the protagonist of *The Adventures of Robinson Crusoe* by Daniel Defoe. Crusoe is an English slave trader who finds himself stranded on a desert island during a voyage to traffic enslaved laborers from Africa to the Caribbean. He spends decades on the island before managing to return to England. (The irony of urging readers to sympathize with a protagonist who might be swept away, never see his home and family again, while he was in the business of sweeping others away, never to see their homes and families again, does not appear to have registered with Defoe.)

The use of this character was intended to invoke the isolation that Crusoe experiences for much of the novel. Despite being without conversation partners, Crusoe narrates the events of his life during those periods. While this appeals to fiction, Ayer is emphasizing that there is nothing implausible about the events, given our own command of natural languages. We can carry on internal monologues, and we can imagine Crusoe extending his idiolect to include new names and general terms for things that he encounters. If we can imagine Crusoe doing this with objects *external* to him, Ayer suggested that there it was no great leap to imagine him doing so with sensations *internal* to his consciousness. At times, Ayer made an even stronger claim: not only was this sort of discernment of sensations and monologue in a private language possible for speakers, but that it is a necessary condition for any public language:

> But unless there is something that one is allowed to recognize, no test can ever be completed: there will be no I justification for the use of any sign at all.

> (68)

There is an intuitive appeal to this sort of argument, perhaps in that it validates a hope we have of grounding the meanings of what we say in something familiar and putting an end to these questions. Yet, Crusoe (or the Crusoe-like figure Ayer describes) appears to be someone who has *already* been trained to speak a language and is initially only extending those linguistic abilities to incorporate some new words – same game, just a few new pieces. Perhaps we should refine the thought experiment here. While the adult Crusoe has the advantage of being trained to speak a language, we could note how he extends his language in new situations and project those methods backward into his early childhood. In the present, Crusoe observes something, makes a note of its distinctive features, and introduces a word for it. Ayer argues that we must imagine Crusoe performing this kind of private process from the very beginning of his life in order to participate in a public language. Perhaps other people in his environment help by providing familiar words that he takes up, but the achievement would be largely private.

The suggestion here is that the public languages we speak with one another must have a sort of foundation in something private to us. I must have visual experiences, in which I pick out features to which I can then apply rules, to make judgments about what is being said. Only then can I convene with others to make judgments about whether people are following the public rules set out by our community. We must begin from inside our thoughts and work our way out to the public rules that a community shares, Ayer is suggesting, and that requires some degree of private language to make the public possible.

So goes Ayer's thought experiment. Does it succeed in reestablishing the *necessity* of private language? The scenario includes some generous assumptions that support Ayer's view. We should be cautious about projecting the abilities that we find in those who have been raised in a culture or trained in a set of practices back to the very beginnings of their lives. Thanks to some musical education (most of it informal) when I was younger, I can imagine new possibilities and write new pieces of music. It doesn't follow from that that you might have handed me an instrument at birth, left me in isolation, and reasonably expect songs and symphonies to have emerged. Actual cases of children who are deprived of linguistic contact in their early years certainly speak against this optimistic picture.[1] In the most severe cases, the absence of linguistic training and interaction at an early age seems to inhibit the development of linguistic competence altogether. Those accounts also tend to involve profound abuse and neglect of children, which may themselves cause further harms to their cognitive and linguistic development, so we should not rush to any conclusions here. But there won't be much empirical support for the assumption that we can project our abilities into early childhood in the ways the Crusoe thought experiment requires.

Ayer has also left the most critical part of this argument to a leap of our imagination. Crusoe can point to birds on his desert island, or to symbols printed on a train schedule, note some of their salient observable features, and introduce a new word for them that others could learn and use in the same way. (Crusoe is telling *us* his story, after all.) *Surely* that is no different from experiencing a sensation privately, setting up a rule for recognizing and remembering it (which no one else can check, and we can never directly explain to others), and then somehow sharing that word with others so that we might communicate, *right*? At the very least, this is a large assumption to make, and it is to assume precisely what Wittgenstein had thrown into question. Wittgenstein did not doubt that we had sensations, that we recognized them, or that we could use words to speak of them. Rather, he doubted that we could do all this by use of a special, direct access to our sensations in a way that was somehow guaranteed to be correct in every case, and instantly meaningful just by our choosing for it to be so.

RESPONSES

Could there be a better version of Ayer's idea here? Perhaps. A comparable idea has taken root among some cognitive scientists and psychologists, particularly those whose work overlaps with philosophical accounts of language. There, we can find accounts of a "language of thought" or "mentalese" that underlies our linguistic abilities. I stress that it is "comparable" because there is debate about whether such a thing (if it exists) should be thought of as a language at all. No one speaks it, at least not out loud. I cannot write a sentence of mentalese (if it exists) for you here, though it might be possible to represent some of its structures with the right sorts of psychological models.

The reasoning goes something like this. Human beings acquire linguistic competence at a young age, and they do so very quickly. As they acquire it, their command of the language exhibits great grammatical complexity and regularity, even in the early stages of acquisition. To have all of that structural complexity, there must be an underlying grammar hardwired into us from birth, just waiting for the right kinds of stimulation to activate it. Our best ways of understanding this involve thinking of our brains as a type of computer – not made of silicon and plastic, but performing functions on things that their parts represent. By some estimates, the best way to model this process would be to imagine each of us having a kind of hardwired private language – "mentalese" – that was active from our infancy, in which our brains could formulate hypotheses about which sounds, words, and phrases to use in which ways as we acquire the ability to speak natural languages like English. This would not be the voice of your "inner monologue," which is typically just a natural language that you also speak. Mentalese would be a layer somewhere *below* that, we might say. This is a line of thought that has been advanced most influentially by Jerry Fodor, and recently by Stephen Pinker. As Fodor put his general argument for some form of mentalese:

> Computational models of [thought and language] are the only ones we've got. Computational models presuppose representational systems. But the representational systems of preverbal and [non-human] organisms surely cannot be natural languages. So, either we abandon such preverbal and [non-human] psychology as we have so far pieced together, or we admit that some thinking, at least, isn't done in English.
>
> (Fodor, 1975, p. 56)

The inclusion of non-human organisms here is an insight that should not be swept aside. My cat, Bootsy Collins, seems to represent his world – staring expectantly at the cupboard where we keep cat food, jumping from bed to floor, chasing the elusive red dot when it appears. But Bootsy doesn't speak a natural language like English, and even the purrs, gurgles, and hissing sounds he does make don't have much that we could call a syntax or grammar to them. (At least nothing that compares with ours.). Should that lead us to say that he and creatures like him don't think at all? Fodor wants none of that.

The cost of such a move is not trivial, though. For one, we must ask whether such fundamental computational structures are really languages in the same sense that English is. This might be an open question even if those computational models were correct. A commitment to mentalese also suggests that most (maybe all) of our concepts and hence the grounding of the meanings of our words would be innate in us, packed into that hardwired grammar of mentalese. For simple concepts, that might not seem too great a stretch, but it can become so very quickly. Even Fodor pulled back a bit on this in his final years. After Pinker published a widely read book called *How the Mind Works* embracing a version of these ideas, Fodor flashed his dry wit and titled one of his last books *The Mind Doesn't Work That Way*. (Note that the theme of a hardwired "language of thought" is a theme that will crop up again in entries #41–45. Readers may find comparisons between those entries and this one fruitful.)

NOTE

1.   See especially the 1994 documentary *Genie: Secret of the Wild Child*.

RECOMMENDED READINGS

MAJOR WORKS

Ayer, A.J., and R. Rhees. 1954. "Symposium: Can There Be a Private Language?" *Proceedings of the Aristotelian Society, Supplementary Columes* 28: 63–94.

Fodor, J. 1975. *The Language of Thought*. Cambridge: Harvard University Press.

RESPONSES

Bar-On, D. 1992. "On the Possibility of a Solitary Language." *Nous* 26 (1): 27–46.

Cole, D. 1999. "I Don't Think So: Pinker on the Mentalese Monopoly." *Philosophical Psychology* 12 (3): 283–295.

Dunlop, C. 2004. "Mentalese Semantics and the Naturalized Mind." *Philosophical Psychology* 17 (1): 77–94.

Fodor, J. 1994. *The Elm and the Expert: Mentalese and Its Semantics*. Cambridge: The MIT Press.

Garfield, J. 1997. "Mentalese Not Spoken Here: Computation, Cognition and Causation." *Philosophical Psychology* 10 (4): 413–435.

Meyers, C., and S. Waller. 2009. "Psychological Investigations: The Private Language Argument and Inferences in Contemporary Cognitive Science." *Synthèse* 171 (1): 135–156.

Thompson, J.J. 1964. "Private Languages." *Amreican Philosophical Quarterly* 1: 20–31.

Verheggen, C. 1995. "Wittgenstein and 'Solitary' Languages." *Philosophical Investigations* 18 (4): 329–347.

Walton, D., and K. Strongman. 1998. "Neonate Crusoes, the Private Language Argument and Psychology." *Philosophical Psychology* 11 (4): 443–465.

'THAT IS GREEN'

Background: Early analytic philosophers of language had moved away from thinking of each word in a language as having a meaning unto itself, which was then cobbled together additively to give us complex phrases and sentences. As Russell's analysis of definite descriptions showed, it was sometimes best to think of a word like 'the' in virtue of its place in the logical structure of sentences and propositions. Some later philosophers argued that expressions and sentences were best understood in relation to a wide variety of other sentences. This suggests a holism about meaning: a word or sentence can be said to have a meaning only as part of the larger whole of its language.

Imagine you had a friend who was an especially boring conversation partner. We'll call her Chloe. Most of us know at least a few people who just drain the life out of a room, but Chloe is someone who is profoundly – even philosophically *interestingly* – boring. Imagine that Chloe says only one sentence. Let's imagine it's the English sentence 'That is green.' But imagine that Chloe also says this only when there are green things visible around her, and she doesn't say it otherwise. She recognizes green things very reliably. Walking by a grassy field in the spring? "That is green." A jade necklace in a jewelry store? "That is green." An old episode of *Sesame Street* where Oscar the Grouch is

DOI: 10.4324/9781003183167-21

talking to Kermit the Frog? "That is green. That is green." Let's assume Chloe doesn't have any further refinements of green in her color palate – no seafoam; no chartreuse; no Pantone 2258 XGC; nothing. 'Green' is a broad color term, so there may be some question about when things stop being green and start being teal or chartreuse. Those are questions for anyone who uses the word though, so we'll assume Chloe says "green" when most of us say "green," too. Some things we can observe are also green in some places, and other colors in other places. For now, let's assume that she says this when our attention is drawn to the green parts, rather than others.

Here's where we come to a philosophical question. Does Chloe know what 'That is green' means? She says that in the presence of green things, and not otherwise, but she can't say any more than that. When you ask a more typical English speaker, they can articulate the meaning somewhat further. "Green's a color. It's the color of well-watered grass in the spring, Boston Celtics road jerseys, and Kermit the Frog." They can tell you that green things aren't red things (again, speaking of parts that are one or the other), even if most of us need some practice discerning which shade is seafoam and which is viridian. Chloe isn't doing any of this further articulation and discernment, though. (And for the sake of the illustration, assume that she's not just doing it silently.)

In this scenario, Chloe's responses seem like instances of a very narrow reflex. Is that enough to grasp the meaning of a word or sentence? Infants sometimes exhibit this kind of early linguistic behavior, but many things react reliably to some condition just as Chloe does, and we would not think of them as using a language. Suppose I take a digital thermometer, add a few audio components, and rewrite the code on which it runs so that whenever it is 68 degrees around the end of the thermometer, the system produces sounds reminiscent of someone saying, "It's 68 degrees right now." We can draw conclusions from those sounds, but we could do so just as well if the system played a B-flat tone without any pretense to being a language-user. In the private language argument, Wittgenstein asked whether there could be a rule that only one person followed, and they only followed it once. (In short, no, he said.) We're inverting that question: would someone who followed only one such rule count as a language user at all, even if they followed it very reliably? How much of a language would someone have to speak to count as a speaker?

Answers to this question have ranged from "just the one bit is enough" to "a fairly large bit of it, actually." We can probably put Wittgenstein in the "fairly large bit" category here. Another philosopher who belongs in that category would be Wilfrid Sellars. He shared the view discussed in entry #15 that we should avoid thinking of meanings as special kinds of psychological or abstract entities. One thing that that sort of thinking was especially apt to obscure was how grasping the meaning of parts of the language entails making associations with other parts of it. We would expect someone who grasped the meaning of 'That is green' to be ready to say, "That has a color," or "That is not red," among other things. To be "ready" in the way that is relevant here is to have a command of the inferences that you would make between these sentences. Someone who knew which inferences to make and when would have the proper sort of command of all those parts of the language. We see minor local breakdowns in this sort of competence in fellow speakers all the time. We've all had the experience of someone who uses an expression or makes a claim, only to be struck dumb by the simplest follow-up question. "You keep using that word," we might say, "but I don't think it means what you think it means."

Someone who got all such inferences wrong would probably strike us as incoherent. Someone that really could not make *any* of these inferences probably would not strike us as a genuine language-user or concept-user at all. Brandom (2001) has illustrated this point with parrots who learn to mimic the sounds of human speech. We could teach parrots to make noises that sound like someone saying "That is green," but they would not be English *speakers* who were *saying* such a thing. (Even if the parrots were in rooms full of green things!) Preferences on my computer can be customized in various ways, and I could easily set them to say, "Good morning!" to me when I first logged in. But much like the parrot, they would be generating those sounds without any further capacity to draw inferences to them or from them. It would be . . . odd . . . to say to my phone, "Is that how you really feel? Be honest." My computer is not the kind of thing that can honestly reply to that. It has no command of the inferential role of these words and sentences.

Sellars presented this as a point about knowledge, and the sort of immediate, infallible access to knowledge of our own sensations that Wittgenstein doubted and Ayer defended. Suppose you had doubts about your knowledge of the external world. What could you still be certain about? One popular answer was that, even if we had doubts about the external world, we had an immediate grasp of the qualities of our sensations – the painfulness of our pains, the greenness of our green experiences, etc. These qualities could be known with certainty, because our powers of introspection are infallible, and simply directly perceive the qualities. Sellars noted that, if this were so, those intro-spective powers would have to produce a very special class of beliefs. They would have to be non-inferential (you just believe them when something green comes into your consciousness), and they would have to be self-justifying, not depending on any other belief to be had and had in a justified manner (rather than simply a guess, or a reflexive response, for instance).

This made for an incoherent cocktail of demands. The sort of well-justified belief that we can call knowledge has a wealth of infer-ential associations that we should be ready to make. To know that this is green on some occasion, not only should you reliably say (or think) "That is green" when green things show up, but you should say it with some authority. To say it with authority, you would need to be ready to *say* that you were reliable about such things, not just *be* reliable. That would imply acknowledging that you've had such experiences before, which would imply ways of distinguishing your experiences, as well as your being the kind of thing that can know, perceive, remember, and a host of other things. Sellars did not doubt that we could do all these things, but he did challenge the assumption that there was not some special way in which we could access our sensations that could underwrite all of our thinking and the meanings of things that we say. While this does not imply that one must speak a whole language to use a sentence like 'This is green,' he did insist that "it does imply that one can have the concept of green only by having a whole battery of concepts of which it is one element" (1956/1997, §20).

RESPONSES

Where to put animal intelligence in this account can be difficult. Sell-ars and Brandom set a high bar of linguistic competence if we're ascribing concepts to someone, but no other species speaks with the complexity and fluency that humans do. Should it follow from this that other animals don't grasp concepts or represent their world? Fodor made an objection along these lines in *The Language of Thought* (discussed in entry #13), though not to Sellars and Brandom in particular. It is certainly possible to read Wittgenstein as equally committed to a "high bar" and a distinctively human character to language, given the centrality of culture and shared social practices in his account.

A more pointed refrain in recent years has come from Fodor and Lepore, who reject the holistic picture of meaning given here – i.e., that a speaker must have a command of large portions (maybe all) of a language to grasp its meanings. They note that divergences and breakdowns are pervasive among communities of speakers; these may be errors, or they may be deeply held commitments to other ways of using words and sentences. So, your grasp of the language and my grasp of the language will never match up perfectly, and we must determine which of those differences are errors and which mark genuine divergences of meaning. Fodor and Lepore assert that there is no way to do this for a language like the one Sellars and Brandom suggest, unless we can appeal to analytic truths about meaning. (These are discussed in entry #10.) Most philosophers of language now doubt that there are genuine analytic truths about meaning.

Another common line of objection to the view of meaning that Sellars and Brandom provide is that it does not properly address how some parts of our language relate to the non-linguistic world. Hilary Putnam and Saul Kripke have both argued that expressions like proper names and natural kind terms have their reference fixed by some direct relation with the referent of that term. So 'Michael Padraic Wolf' refers to a particular person, me; 'water' refers to a certain physical kind, H_2O. Neither of those relations is determined by personal history or scientific theory; when you hear "Michael Padraic Wolf," you might make a variety of inferences, but none of those are the meaning of the name, nor could they somehow overrule that original fixing of the reference on me. (These views are discussed in entries #46–50.) Sellars and Brandom take the defining characteristics of words' and sentences' meanings to be word–word relations (saying "that is green" implies 'that is colored,' and that intra-linguistic connection is fundamental to the meaning of 'green'). Kripke and Putnam argue that the defining characteristics of some words are word–world relations ('Michael Padraic Wolf' refers to me, a non-linguistic thing, without any further help from the rest of the language).

RECOMMENDED READINGS

MAJOR WORKS

deVries, W., and T. Triplett. 2000. *Knowledge, Mind, and the Given: Reading Wilfird Sellars's "Empiricism and the Philosophy of Mind," Including the Complete Text of Sellars Essay*. Indianapolis: Hackett.

Fodor, J., and E. Lepore. 1991. "Why Meaning (Probably) Isn't Conceptual Role." *Mind and Language* (Wiley-Blackwell) 6 (4): 328–343.

Sellars, W. 1956/1997. *Empiricism and the Philosophy of Mind*. Cambridge, MA: Harvard University Press.

RESPONSES

Block, N. 1993. "Holism, Hyper-Analyticity and Hyper-Compositionality." *Philosophical Issues* 3: 37–72.

Brandom, R. 2001. *Articulating Reasons: An Introducxtion to Inferentialism*. Cambridge: Harvard University Press.

deVries, W.A. 2005. *Wilfrid Sellars*. Montreal: McGill-Queens University Press.

Fodor, J., and E. Lepore. 2010. "Brandom Beleagured." In *Reading Brandom: On Making It Explicit*, edited by B. Weiss and J. Wanderer, 181–193. New York: Routledge.

Maher, C. 2014. *The Pittsburgh School of Philosophy (Routledge Studies in Contemporary Philosophy)*. New York: Routledge.

Putnam, H. 1974. "Comments on W. Sellars." *Synthèse* 27: 445–455.

Sellars, W. 1974. "Meaning as Functional Classification." *Synthèse* 27: 417–437.

'KRIPKENSTEIN'

Background: The comments on private language and rule-following in Philosophical Investigations turned both issues into concerns for philosophers. Many readers interpreted Wittgenstein's arguments as implying a set of facts about meaning determined by culture or social practices. Others argued that the most fundamental sorts of rule-following are best understood as behavioral dispositions that we follow habitually. But Saul Kripke offered a very different reading of the Investigations that called meaning facts into question. Whether this was Wittgenstein's view is itself subject to debate, but the skeptical paradox Kripke offers has been central to subsequent debate.

In 1982, Kripke published *Wittgenstein on Rules and Private Language*, which generated fresh interest in this topic. His interpretation came to be known as "Kripkenstein" – a portmanteau of "Kripke" and "Wittgenstein," and more than a little suggestive of a creature lost from a horror movie. It may not be entirely true to Wittgenstein's original work, as Kripke acknowledged, but it raised important questions about meaning either way. Kripke's interpretation was especially bold in that it suggested a form of meaning skepticism – i.e., the view that there are no facts about meanings, or that we could never know such things if they did exist. In everyday usage, to say that someone is a skeptic often suggests only that they have doubts about a subject, or

DOI: 10.4324/9781003183167-22

that they would demand more evidence before settling on an answer. In philosophical circles, it tends to imply something even stronger. There, a skeptic is someone who actually asserts the non-existence of something, or the impossibility of some kind of status. Epistemological skeptics deny that we have any knowledge, or perhaps that we even could have any. Moral skeptics deny that there are moral facts or real moral properties of our actions.

Many analytic philosophers of language in Anglo-American circles had some sympathy with such a view about meanings. They were very wary of the idea of meanings as entities – that is, meanings as a special kind of abstract object, not present in the physical world, but accessible to our intellects by some mysterious process. (W.V.O. Quine called this the "myth of the museum," as though meanings were objects that you could visit and see in a display case.) But even those who doubt that meanings are real entities tend to think that there are objective facts about what words mean. Those facts turn out to be complex arrangements of social practices, psychological dispositions of speakers of a language, and historical patterns of usage. On views like these, there are standard conventional ways of using words, and we use them correctly and incorrectly. Meaning skepticism casts doubt even on that more modest view. There might not be *any* facts about what our words mean, even in principle.

The "Kripkenstein" interpretation takes its lead from the opening sentence of §201 of the *Investigations*: "This was our paradox: no course of action could be determined by a rule, because every course of action can be made out to accord with the rule." Wittgenstein mentions the reverse as well: without much difficulty, we can imagine a way in which anything we did or said conflicted with a rule, as well. When you have a rule, you take it that it will inform your actions and tell you how things are to be done or not to be done in a given situation. It's frustrating when a rule is stated so vaguely that it fails to give you that sort of guidance. But it's even more frustrating when you feel that you don't grasp a rule at all. This can happen when you start studying a new subject and some concept is first introduced to you. It has happened to me when I was thrust into new social circumstances and had to navigate customs and practices that were still alien to me. When all I can do is guess from a few hints or examples, I can imagine a way in which almost anything I do could be appropriate or inappropriate.

To find our way out of such quandaries, most of us typically try to pin down just what the rule at hand implies. When someone tells me that the standard of dress for an event is "business causal," I hunt for examples of this geared towards someone like me. When I learn a new concept in some subject, I look for cases of that concept in action, maybe with special attention to cases where it implies something I didn't expect. All of this seems to narrow the possible forms that a rule might take. But in what does that "grasp" consist? We cannot picture all the instances of such a rule, and writing a rule out more formally depends on further rules we would have to grasp. We need a definitive answer that speaks to what grasping a rule fundamentally involves.

One popular answer when Kripke was writing this (and one often glibly attributed to Wittgenstein) was that following rules consists in having certain *dispositions*, or habits to perform some action. When I add seven and five together, I don't work through an interpretation of the rules of arithmetic – I just say "twelve." I'm disposed to do this by years of training and repetition when I was a child. Even if I'm disposed very strongly to give an answer or use a word in a particular way, I have done so only finitely many times with finitely many examples. Those finite sets are compatible with infinitely many other rules that overlap with just those evidence sets. Where Wittgenstein imagined a student counting by twos until 1,000, Kripke imagines a student who purportedly learns the rule for addition, but once he comes to a computation of '68 + 57' writes '5' instead of '125.' That answer would be correct according to another rule – indeed, *infinitely many* other rules.

On a first reading, that probably strikes you as an idle point, perhaps even a silly one. Sure, there are infinitely many ways we could go on calculating or using a word according to various rules, but that's not *our* rule, and that's not what '+' or 'plus' *means*. Shouldn't we just say that Wittgenstein's and Kripke's students have trained themselves into some other rule – call it "quus" – and that it simply diverges from our well-established rule for 'plus?' In that case, how did we commit ourselves to *that* rule ('plus') in particular, rather than the one for 'quus?' We might say that we *intended* to pick out the familiar form of addition, or that we all share some special kind of mental state that is invoked in grasping such rules, which we can then use to reach an explicit consensus. Wittgenstein's original arguments cast considerable doubt on such moves, though, and Kripke takes those doubts to be decisive.

The problem here lies in the apparent absence of anything we could point to in order to ground an interpretation of a rule. Someone's intention or declaration that they are committed to 'plus' rather than 'quus' when the rule is introduced is only as good as their ability to select one of them in the first place. So long as they have only finitely many cases to point to, there cannot be a fact of the matter about which one they intended, Kripke suggests. And their dispositions to carry on in a certain way can only tell us that they agree in the finitely many cases we have seen so far. When someone's usage diverges from ours (like the errant students), we come right back to the question of which of us has the *correct* dispositions that match the supposedly well-established rule. We could consider many more speakers in a community, who perform many more uses of a word, but that will only give us a much larger data set while leaving us with the same fundamental problem. We don't seem to have something, even in principle, to which we can point to give us facts about meanings. As Kripke wrote, "It is not that calling a sensation 'pain' is easy, and Wittgenstein must invent a difficulty. . . . It appears that he has shown *all* language, *all* concept formation, to be impossible, indeed unintelligible" (62).

Kripke took this to be a serious skeptical problem and offered what he saw as a "skeptical solution." Theories of meaning in Wittgenstein's time typically stated their most central meaning claims in terms of the conditions under which a sentence would be true – e.g., "The sentence 'Grass is green' is true if and only if grass is green." But if meaning skepticism is correct, then there can be no facts of the matter about which conditions line up with which sentences to make them true. So instead, Kripke interprets Wittgenstein as arguing for the use of justification conditions. This would shift our attention from how the meanings of words depended on facts in the world to how meanings depended on our fellow speakers and what they would encourage, punish, or permit us to do. This is very much in keeping with Wittgenstein's frequent use of the word "games" in describing linguistic practices. If we're playing basketball and I suddenly start moving the ball by kicking it with my feet, my fellow players will punish me by taking the ball away. That's not how basketball is *to be played*, and fellow basketball players won't let me get away with that.

If we shift to the justification necessary for making a statement (or asking a question, giving a command, etc.) among fellow speakers in this way, then to say that a word or sentence meant something would be to specify the conditions and the manner in which someone would be permitted or required to use it. Following a rule in this way would never be a matter of consulting your dispositions or memories. Kripke notes that this will all be possible only when there is wide agreement within a community about these conditions, and ongoing vigilance about testing one another and articulating the criteria used in these justification conditions. But he does think that this can preserve most of what we ordinarily do in talking about meaning, even if there are no facts underlying it.

RESPONSES

The most prominent, almost immediate, response to Kripkenstein was from John McDowell, who claimed that Kripke's interpretation was simply not what Wittgenstein had said, and that Wittgenstein's actual view addressed the problem of meaning skepticism. In the very passage (§201) that Kripke quotes above, Wittgenstein later says:

> What this shows is that there is a way of grasping a rule which is *not* an *interpretation*, but which is exhibited in what we call "obeying the rule" and "going against it" in actual cases.

McDowell suggests that Wittgenstein's aim is to reveal a dilemma at the heart of our views about rules. On one horn of the dilemma, we have the paradox of §201 that Kripke focused on: that no course of action could be made to accord with a rule, because it is always possible to interpret an action as according with or violating the rule. On the other horn of the dilemma is the common "mythology" of rule-following that suggests we must find some extra-special, super-duper interpretation of a rule that is not susceptible to the sort of skepticism Kripke suggests. But as the latter part of §201 suggests, Wittgenstein's goal is to get us to see that the skeptical paradox and the hope for a skepticism-proof interpretation are two sides of the same coin. We should *reject them both* and seek a different understanding of rule-following, not embrace the skeptical solution Kripke offers. McDowell's influential reading places an emphasis on the role of shared customs that we follow "blindly" (as Wittgenstein put it), in which interpretation is neither necessary nor fitting. Subsequent responses have grappled with the implications for this, and whether we must appeal to some "primitive" form of normativity as McDowell does to underwrite shared customs, or whether there might be a naturalistic view that refined or replaced the dispositional views successfully.

RECOMMENDED READINGS

MAJOR WORKS

Kripke, S. 1982. *Wittgenstein on Rules and Private Language*. Cambridge, MA: Harvard University Press.

McDowell, J. 1984. "Wittgenstein on Following a Rule." *Synthèse* 58: 325–264.

Millikan, R.G. 1990. "Truth, Rules, Hoverflies, and the Kripke-Wittgenstein Paradox." *Philosophical Review* 99 (3): 323–353.

RESPONSES

Boghossian, P. 1989. "The Rule-Following Considerations." *Mind* 98 (392): 507–549.

Ginsbourg, H. 2011. "Primitive Normativity and Skepticism About Rules." *Journal of Philosophy* 108 (5): 227–254.

Green, D. 2018. "Semantic Knowledge, Semantic Guidance, and Kripke's Wittgenstein." *Pacific Philosophical Quarterly* 99 (2): 186–206.

Hattiangadi, A. 2007. *Oughts and Thoughts: Rule-Following and the Normativity of Content*. Oxford: Oxford University Press.

Horwich, P. 1990. "Wittgenstein and Kripke on the Nature of Meaning." *Mind and Language* 5 (2): 105–121.

Podlaskowski, A. 2012. "Simple Tasks, Abstractions, and Semantic Dispositionalism." *Dialectica* 66 (4): 453–470.

Tang, H. 2014. "'It is Not a Something, but Not a Nothing Either!' – McDowell on Wittgenstein." *Synthèse* 191 (3): 557–567.

Wilson, G. 1994. "Kripke on Wittgenstein and Normativity." *Midwest Studies in Philosophy* 19 (1): 366–390.

PART IV

SEMANTIC PARADOXES

INTRODUCTION

Much of the more formal work in the philosophy of language has been driven by a set of semantic paradoxes, which are the subject of this section. When people speak of something as a "paradox" in everyday language, they simply mean that a situation is unexpected or confusing. The more precise conception of paradox at work in this section involves a sentence or set of sentences that appears to be well-formed (or even true) and yet entails a contradiction. That may sound harmless (just remember not to say that sentence), but if there were genuine paradoxes, that would have disastrous consequences for our classical understanding of truth, rationality, and logic. The classical notion of "truth" presumes that no well-formed declarative sentence can lack a truth value or be both true and false. Classical logic in the Western tradition purports to give us rules of inference that would never lead us from true premises to false conclusions in deductive arguments. If there were genuine paradoxes that entailed contradictions, it would be possible to derive any conclusion we liked from any set of premises, as we see in entry #16. If any conclusion can be derived from anything, then logic tells us nothing and we lack a rational basis for any belief that we might hold. Entries #17–18 present additional paradoxes that deepen this threat.

DOI: 10.4324/9781003183167-24

What can we do in the face of such paradoxes? A good first tactic would be to show that the paradoxes were illusory – predicated on some mistake or misunderstanding – and thus readily dismissed. Each entry considers some refutations of this sort, but as you will read, the paradoxes have shown great staying power. More substantial changes to our understanding of truth and logic may be necessary. The most substantial of these possible revisions are considered in entry #20. There, we look at logical systems that would have three, four or potentially more possible truth values instead of just the familiar two (true and false) as a means to disarm the paradoxes. We also look at *paracomplete* logical systems that leave some paradoxical sentences without truth values at all, and *paraconsistent* systems that permit contradictions, but contain their more catastrophic implications.

WHEN WHAT IS ISN'T, AND WHAT ISN'T IS (THE LIAR PARADOX)

Background: In the entries so far, we have operated under some critical assumptions about truth-values. Every declarative sentence is either true or false and nothing else. Philosophers of language have often treated this as a fundamental part of their accounts, which constitutes a privileged sort of relation between the sentences of a language and the world. But there is a class of sentences and sets of sentences known as "the semantic paradoxes" that throw those standard assumptions into doubt.

> *One of themselves, even a prophet of their own, said, The Cretians are always liars . . .*
> *– Titus 1:12, King James Version*

Several entries so far have mentioned truth, and entry #8 was devoted to the subject. As we've seen, we can imagine assigning truth values to declarative sentences, but not to many other types – e.g., questions and commands. No problem there – those other types of sentences serve other roles. But even in the more in-depth discussion in that earlier entry, we were taking several things for granted. In particular, there are three we should make explicit:

Law of non-contradiction: There is no sentence 'A' such that both 'A' and 'not-A' are true.

DOI: 10.4324/9781003183167-25

Law of excluded middle: Every declarative sentence is either true or false, and not both.

Law of Bivalence: There are exactly two possible truth values for declarative sentences – true and false – and no more.

Each of these laws purports to be logically necessary. It's not just that there don't happen to be any contradictions, the law of non-contradiction (LNC) is saying, it is *necessarily* the case that there are none. Non-contradiction has been central to Western philosophy since Aristotle's work, and many logicians would say that logic and reasoning would be unintelligible possibilities without it. And you can think of the law of the excluded middle (LEM) as a way of ruling out any ambiguity or loose ends for truth. Every declarative sentence gets one of these two truth values, end of story.

When I teach logic, students often accept bivalence much more readily than they accept the LEM. There are some things that we will never be able to say are true or false, they say. They are right about that, but that's not really in conflict with the LEM. There is a difference between saying that every declarative sentence *has* a truth value, on the one hand, and saying that we *know* what the truth value of every declarative sentence is. The first of those is a non-ridiculous assumption about truth, while the second is surely not the case. Consider:

(1)   The number of grains of sand on every surface of the Earth 200,000 years before today was even.

That's a well-formed English sentence. No one will ever know what its value is, but that's not an issue with its *being* true. We can say what it would take to settle such a question (all the grains in a pile, space to split them into two piles, etc.), but *finding* that answer does not seem to be a prerequisite for there *being* an answer.

The assumption of the LNC, the LEM, and bivalence guided much of what we now call "classical" logic in the West for millennia. But that project has been haunted by examples like these:

(2)   This sentence is false.
(3)   I'm lying right now.
(4)   Sentence (5) is true.
(5)   Sentence (4) is false.

You may see the problems here. Let's say that (2) is true; if so, then it must be the case that (2) is false (that's what it says, after all). But it can't be both. Let's say that (2) is false; if so, then whatever it states must not be the case, so it must not be the case that (2) is false, and so the LEM tells us that (2) must be true. That doesn't work out any better. Sentence (3) does not mention truth or falsity explicitly, but truth values are implied by the use of "lying," so it has much the same effect. We can call these "Liar Sentences," a name inspired by the apparently self-refuting claim by the Cretan reported in Titus 1:12 (quoted at the start of this entry). Sentences (4) and (5) have what is called "cyclical reference." Neither one refers to itself, but they refer to one another in a sequence that loops back to whichever sentence you read first. (You could do this with larger sets of sentences, too.)

Are these sentences true? False? Anything else would violate bivalence or the LEM, but it's worse than that. These sentences are *paradoxical*. Despite being well-formed, valid reasoning from them would lead us to a contradiction. I'll show you a simplified version of such a derivation. To do that, let's introduce a principle:

(F)   For any sentence 'A,' if 'A' is false, then the sentence 'It is not the case that A' is true.

This will follow from the LEM and bivalence. Now, let's write a slightly different version of (2) to simplify some issues that the word "this" will cause:

(6)   Sentence (6) is false.

Suppose we assume (6) is false. Using (F), we can then derive:

(7)   It is not the case that sentence (6) is false.

Now, just conjoin them:

(8)Sentence (6) is false and it is not the case that sentence (6) is false.

Contradiction! If we assume that (6) is true instead of false, we get the same result with a slightly different series of steps. So, whether we say that (6) is true or false, we get a contradiction.

Why should that trouble us? The difficulty is that contradictions are what logicians would call *explosive*: once we allow a contradiction into a classical logic system, quite literally *any* sentence can be derived from it. In fact, most introductory logic textbooks (which teach you classical logic) make extensive use of this point. (This is often folded into "indirect proof" or the use of negation introduction/elimination rules, depending on which text you use.) This would make every proof trivial, and none of them compelling. Faced with the paradox, I'm often met with two familiar objections:

The sentences refer to themselves, or refer cyclically, so they're not well-formed!

These examples do involve self-reference or cyclical reference. Anyone who has ever written software or managed a spreadsheet knows the difficulties that can arise from circular references. (You need to determine the values to calculate with them, but the calculation is what determines the values, so the task cannot be completed.). That's in part because I have started with simple examples, and the simplest ones work self-referentially. As we'll see in entry #19, there are also examples that purport to be non-self-referring and non-cyclical paradoxes. But the objection itself is suspect. There is nothing troubling in these examples:

(2')   This sentence is true.
(2")   This sentence has seven words in it.
(3')   I'm telling you the truth!
(4')   Sentence (5') refers to another sentence.
(5')   Sentence (4') refers to another sentence.

You can see how these parallel the original examples, with (2") as a bonus. There doesn't seem to be anything wrong with sentences referring to themselves or referring cyclically in general. It would be special pleading to dismiss only those sentences that created the paradoxes when they are operating in ways that are perfectly acceptable otherwise.[1]

Maybe these are sentences to which we can't assign truth values, or they have some other kind of truth value.

That's not a bad intuition to have, though it would take some work to support. We do speak or write what appear to be declarative sentences without any pretense to their being true or false, like when we're telling a joke or making an expressive statement that should not be read literally – e.g. "The Pittsburgh Penguins are going to slaughter the Detroit Red Wings tonight!" yelled by a Penguins fan. But we're not doing that with (2)-(5). If we want to say that "liar" sentences don't have truth values, then we're denying the LEM. If we say that they have some other kind of truth value, then we're denying bivalence.

RESPONSES

The liar paradox is one of the oldest problems in Western philosophy, and the literature on it is very extensive. Some approaches to addressing it have already been hinted at in this entry, and further elaboration of them will come in entries #19–20. For the moment, I will focus on further readings that either attempt to address the paradox in a primarily classical vein or use "the liar" to make other important claims.

Tarski (1944) offered a formal definition of truth in a series of articles in the 1930s and 1940s. He made a methodological distinction between an "object language" and a "metalanguage." An object language would be one in which we spoke or performed other operations, such as a natural language like English or a formal language like those of mathematics. A metalanguage would be a language we used to talk about an object language. Suppose you're a native Japanese speaker and start learning to speak English. Your first classes would typically use Japanese as a metalanguage to introduce you to features of English, the object language. If you take a programming course, your metalanguage might be English, and your object language might be C++. So, a language could be an object language in some cases but serve as a metalanguage in others. The distinction lies in how we're using the language, not something intrinsic to it.

Tarski held that when we ascribe truth or falsity to a sentence, we have actually stepped into a different sort of language – a logical metalanguage. It has many familiar features of our native language, but it also has more sophisticated vocabulary that we put to various purposes. So given an object language sentence like:

(9)   Snow is white.

We can say in a logical metalanguage:

(10) 'Snow is white' is true.

How does this help? Tarski said that sentences like (2)-(6) are not well-formed sentences, despite their apparently sound grammar. They fail to distinguish between object-language sentences and meta-language predicates, so it's as though we're mingling two different languages in one ill-formed sentence. We should reject all of those paradoxical sentences. Many philosophers of language have been hesitant to follow Tarski's strategy here. For one, it takes some work to show why we could not create self-referential or cyclical-referential sentences in a metalanguage, too. Even if we succeed in showing that, few have been ready to throw out such a wide class of sentences without a better reason than saving classical logic's account of truth. (A more sympathetic reading of Tarski's view is given in Patterson (2007), and a review of Tarski's approach to "the liar" is offered in Ray (2006).)

NOTE

1. One outlier view on this topic is that of Pletiz (2018), which makes the case that there are no genuinely self-referential sentences in natural languages, at least not of a sort that lead to paradox.

RECOMMENDED READINGS

MAJOR WORKS

Aristotle. 1998. *Metaphysics.* Translated by H. Lawson-Tancred. London: Penguin Books.

Beall, J.C. 2004. "Introduction: At the Intersection of Truth and Falsity." In *The Law of Non-Contradiction: New Philosophical Essays*, edited by G. Priest, J.C. Beall, and B. Armour-Grab, 1–19. Oxford: Oxford University Press.

Sorensen, R. 2003. *A Brief History of Paradox.* Oxford: Oxford University Press.

Tarski, A. 1944. "The Semantic Conception of Truth: And the Foundations of Semantics." *Philosophy and Phenomenological Research* 4 (3): 341–376.

RESPONSES

Patterson, D. 2007. "Understanding the Liar." In *Revenge of the Liar: New Essays on the Paradox*, edited by J.C. Beall, 197–224. Oxford: Oxford University Press.

Pletiz, M. 2018. *Logic, Language and the Liar Paradox*. Paderborn: Brill, Mentis.

Ray, G. 2006. "Truth, the Liar, and Tarskian Truth Definition." In *A Companion to Philosophical Logic*, edited by D. Jacquette, 164–176. Oxford: Blackwell.

RUSSELL'S PARADOX

Background: In the early decades of the 20th century, many of the philosophers of language we have discussed in earlier entries were also working at the intersection between logic and mathematics, hoping to give a formal set of foundations for mathematical truth. Georg Cantor's development of set theory was an important precursor to this, and by 1900, many of the most important notions in foundations of mathematics were being articulated in set-theoretical terms. Russell's paradox threw all of this into doubt by presenting a type of set that meets all the requirement of the theory of its day yet entails a contradiction.

Consider a thought experiment here. Suppose you get a new job working in the IT department for a company. You find that the IT specialist before you left a real mess. Figuring out what needs to be done will take a while. So, you start making lists of things – what software you have, what has been backed up, etc. Soon, you realize that you need to make some lists just to keep track of your lists. You also realize that sometimes lists are included on your lists – e.g., you make a list of everything stored on a particular computer, and it includes lists of files. This is getting complicated, so you decide to make *a list of all the lists that don't contain themselves* for future double-checking. That's easy for most of your lists. Your morning

DOI: 10.4324/9781003183167-26

to-do list does not contain itself; your list of office numbers does not contain itself. But what about your list of all the lists that don't contain themselves – *the one you're now writing*? Does it belong on that list? (If so, it *does* contain itself.) Does it not belong on there? (Then it most certainly *does*.) At this point, you probably decide to go to lunch early.

Bertrand Russell (1903a, 1903b) had stumbled upon a paradox not unlike this thought experiment, focused on properties that would seem to place things into sets and exclude them at the same time. One type of truth that early analytic philosophers of language had great interest in was mathematical truth. A recurring theme in this work – a peril, perhaps – was that the logic and language of mathematics appears to permit the same sort of circularity that we saw in the liar paradox. There was a great deal riding on this, as it related to the fundamental concepts of set theory, and thereby to the groundwork for mathematics. It came to light through the work of Russell and others around the beginning of the 20th century that set theory was so conceptually and explanatorily rich that all mathematical objects, concepts, and arguments could be formalized in its terms. Logicians and mathematicians working before Russell could see the potential of set theory, but Russell saw a bit deeper, finding a contradiction that would upend the field and rewrite its most fundamental assumptions.

A set can be any collection of entities. Philosophers, logicians, and mathematicians usually only care about sets that are bound together by some defining property, like having a common feature – the right triangles, the prime numbers, etc. This allows us to speak in general of all the members of a set when that defining property has some implications, and it alleviates the burden of spelling out every member of the set in favor of allowing that defining property to guide us in new cases. So, rather than having to list every possible right triangle (as though that's possible!), we can say a triangle belongs to the set of right triangles when we notice its right angle. The entities in a set could also be other sets. For instance, when you look at the baseball standings, or the first-round groups in the World Cup, you're looking at a set of sets of teams. (And if the teams are just sets of players, then you're looking at a set of sets of sets of players.). A set could also be empty – e.g., the set of round squares. While the defining properties differ in these cases, logicians would treat them all as the same set – the empty set, or $\emptyset$, as it is written. Finally, a class would be a collection of sets that we can define in terms of a property that all the members of all their sets share.

Everything in the preceding paragraph states assumptions of what logicians would call *naïve set theory*. They are refined versions of concepts that people use every day, and they do resemble the conceptions that succeeded them. So "naïve" is not meant to suggest they are stupid, but rather that they are not yet mature. Crucial to refined versions of set theory were procedures for giving precise definitions of sets in the formal languages used in logic and mathematics at the time. Suppose we want to define a set of all the things that have property F. We could formally state this as:

$$S = \{x \mid F(x)\}$$

'S' is what we're calling our set here, and the curly brackets are used to denote sets. The "$x \mid$" inside the left bracket can be read roughly as "includes every x such that . . ." and what comes after the line denotes the defining property. Suppose we wanted to definite the set of even numbers – well, they're natural numbers ("whole" numbers, not decimals or fractions) that are evenly divisible by two. We can use $D(x,y)$ to denote a function we'd informally state as "x is evenly divisible by y," and N to denote the set of natural numbers. Thus, E, the set of even numbers is defined as such:

$$E = \{x \mid x \in N \land D(x,2)\}$$

This sort of definition will be important, because naïve set theory also assumes a very open, strong version of what is called the "comprehension axiom." It says that if a function $\phi(x)$ contains a free variable (like x here), then there will be some set of objects such that $\{x: \phi(x)\}$ is the set of objects that satisfy that function. Roughly, if we can give a property that defines a set, then there is such a set. It could be the empty set, but it will be there. However, Russell realized that he could define a set that not only lacked members, but the existence of which would entail a contradiction. Let $\phi(x)$ stand for "$x \in x$" and let's then define the following set, R:

$$R = \{x \mid \neg\phi(x)\}$$

This would make R the set whose members are those objects who are not members of themselves. We know that sets can contain sets, as we saw earlier. They could contain sets and other kinds of objects, assuming they share some defining property. It's strange to think of a set that contains itself, admittedly. The set of even numbers is not *itself* an even number; the set of all six-toed cats is not *itself* a six-toed cat. A simple way to illustrate the possibility is to think of the complement of a more ordinary set. Take the set of dogs, and then think of everything that is not a dog. Now, consider the set of all non-dog things: the set itself is not a dog, so that set includes itself.

Where is the paradox here? Ask yourself whether R contains itself. If it does, then it *is* a set that contains itself, and so it is not a member of itself. If it does not contain itself, then it is a set that does not contain itself, and so it is a member of itself. Either way, we reach the contradictory conclusion that R both is and is not a member of itself. This demonstrates the inconsistency of naïve set theory and the need for a dramatic revision of our understanding of sets, and by extension, the fundamental structure of mathematics.[1]

A variation on this paradox was once told to Russell. A barber is someone who shaves those who don't shave themselves. Does a barber shave himself? If so, then he must not be a barber, because barbers shave those who *don't* shave themselves. If not, then he falls into the category of those who don't shave themselves, rather than a barber. Thus, he is somehow both a barber and not a barber. This is cute, but not quite a paradox in Russell's estimation. We can deny that there are such barbers or assert that "barber" is ill-defined. Russell's paradox follows the postulates of naïve set theory; the barber case stipulates a definition that conceals a contradiction. And this presents us with a much more substantial problem. While the set of non-dogs or non-self-shaving barbers sound trivial, even silly, the formal methods by which we introduce them lie at the heart of mathematics. The credibility of mathematics lies not in particular results, but in the methods that we use to reach them. If Russell's paradox were real, then much of mathematics – and any other discipline that makes use of them – is in doubt.

RESPONSES

Russell himself responded to the paradox, offering what he called a "doctrine of types" to correct the deficiencies of naïve set theory. In

Russell's view (much of it later expressed in work co-authored by Alfred North Whitehead), all paradoxes arise from circularity. (Note that this assumption was also discussed in entries #16, 19–20.) We could evade this sort of circularity by sorting all possible sentences – including those of arithmetic and set theory – into a hierarchy of types. We could then spell out the conditions under which objects of a given type could be referred to, thereby prohibiting the sort of circularity within a type that gives rise to paradoxes. In "Appendix B: The Doctrine of Types," Russell lays out a hierarchy of types, beginning with individuals (or "classes of one"), then upward to classes of individuals, classes of classes of individuals, relations, propositions, and numbers. Each propositional function (which the sentences of a language express) would then have a "range of significance." That is, there would be some range of objects that would fall into each propositional function's scope, depending on the function itself. Some sentences will express propositions that range over individuals, others over larger classes, and so on.

Russell and Whitehead held that, with the proper formulation of this hierarchy of types, it would be impossible to create sets like those involved in the paradox: the collection itself would be of a higher order type, and so could not be within the lower order type of objects that it contained. There could be sentences expressing propositions that were themselves about sentences expressing propositions, of course – e.g., 'All English sentences contain at least one word.' Thus, they would have to be arranged in a hierarchy of their own, as well. Support for Russell's theory of types was somewhat muted after the release of his *Principles of Mathematics*, as well as later revisions of his position with Whitehead. The doctrine seemed designed to avoid the paradox, rather than reveal deeper insights, and even Russell acknowledged that further contradictions were derivable from it. (Recent discussions of those further contradictions and Russell's later responses are included in Deutsch (2014) and Linsky (2002).)

Part of the importance of Russell's paradox lies in its dimming the hopes for a foundation for mathematics in the vein that Frege had envisioned. Russell discovered the paradox while reviewing Frege's *Grundgesetze der Arithmetik* and exchanged letters with him concerning the paradox and its implications for Frege's program. For those interested in the history of this period, the correspondence is a striking look at two great logicians and philosophers coming to terms with a monumental setback, just as they felt they were on the verge of a great breakthrough. But the discovery of the paradox also induced many other mathematical logicians to address these matters in new ways. Several attempts to rework set theory would follow in the decade after Russell's publication of the paradox, culminating in the works of Zermelo and Fraenkel, which have become the standard in contemporary mathematics. (The important texts here are in German, and probably inaccessible to most of our readers, but are covered in any introductory text on mathematical logic.)

NOTE

1. Ernst Zermelo found the paradox before Russell did, but apparently did not think much of it. (Zermelo's later work shaped modern set theory and mathematics even more profoundly than Russell's, so don't feel too bad for him.)

RECOMMENDED READINGS

MAJOR WORKS

Russell, B. 1903a. "Appendix B: The Doctrine of Types." In *The Principles of Mathematics*, 523–528. Cambridge: Cambridge University Press.

Russell, B. 1903b. "Chapter X: The Contradiction." In *The Principles of Mathematics*, 101–107. Cambridge: Cambridge University Press.

RESPONSES

Beaney, M. 2003. "Russell and Frege." In *The Cambridge Companion to Russell*, edited by N. Griffin, 128–170. Cambridge: Cambridge University Press.

Deutsch, H. 2014. "Resolution of Some Paradoxes of Propositions." *Analysis* 74 (1): 26–34.

Linsky, B. 2002. "The Resolution of Russell's Paradox in Principia Mathematica." *Philosophical Perspectives* 16: 395–417.

Quine, W. 1966. "The Ways of Paradox." In *The Ways of Paradox and Other Essays*, 3–20. New York: Random House.

BERRY'S PARADOX

Background: In entry #16, we looked at liar paradoxes that related directly to the notion of truth. "The liar" and Russell's paradox apparently entails a contradiction, which would throw standard notions of truth in Western philosophy into doubt. Truth is an important semantic property in many accounts of language – indeed, the single most important one to many philosophers of language – but it is by no means the only one, nor the only one that might throw us into a form of paradox.

Russell and Whitehead mention another self-referential paradox in their *Principia Mathematica*, which they attribute to G.G. Berry, a junior librarian at Oxford at the time. (Don't presume that librarians just stack books!) It resembles "the liar" in that it can be used to derive a contradiction, but the structure of the paradox itself does not invoke truth. This suggests that paradoxes may not simply be the product of a wrinkle in our account of truth, waiting to be ironed out; they might also emerge from well-formed expressions on their own. In Berry's paradox, we shift from attention to sets and classes – which are fundamental to our accounts of mathematics – to denotation, specifically the denotation of a well-formed definition.

The paradox begins with the description or definition of a number, and the briefest, most compact terms in which it can be done.

DOI: 10.4324/9781003183167-27

To define a number in this sense would be to give a description of some property or set of properties that it held uniquely. "The largest prime number less than 100" would be such a definition. Counting back from 100, 99 is divisible by three, and 98 is divisible by two, so neither of them is prime. But 97 has no factors but one and itself, so it is prime, and it uniquely satisfies that definition. This definition also seems neat and concise. There are no extra concepts hanging around, doing work redundantly or not doing any work at all. If you took out any word, the definition would fall apart or change dramatically.

We could probably always give a longer definition of a number. How about 37?

'The largest prime number less than 40, which is three less than 40, which is one greater than a perfect square, which is one greater than the cube root of 46,656 . . .'

Given time, patience, and ingenuity, we could keep adding further conditions to the description. Perhaps we could keep doing so indefinitely. Continuing to add conditions doesn't add anything interesting to what is accomplished, though. Some of the conditions here don't even lead us to a unique number; many numbers are one greater than a perfect square, for instance. Once one of these conditions leads us to a unique number that the definition denotes, the others that follow repeat the work, at best. For various reasons, we might prefer whichever definition does so most briefly, simply, and elegantly.

Note that the question at hand is not about *merely* designating a number, which can be done even more concisely. Proofs often begin with the stipulation that we're seeking some number, n, which we then proceed to find. That 'n' designates a number with a single letter, but it does not define the number, telling us which one it is. What is at stake in the paradox is that the definition should do the work of leading us to the number that it designates, not just give us another way of designating it. We also shorten our designators for convenience with methods such as scientific notation, allowing ourselves to write 10^{37}, rather than a 1 with 37 zeroes after it, or "googolplex" rather than a 1 with 10^{100} zeroes after it. These are useful for many purposes but note that they allow us to specify an order of magnitude rather than providing a general recipe for pinpointing any number we like in a concise form. They serve a purpose, but not the one at stake in Berry's paradox.

So, what we have in mind is the most compact definition of a number that would uniquely identify it. Note that such a definition might be given without our knowing which number it designates: 'the smallest prime number greater than a googolplex' designates some very large number, but we have no hope of ever finding it.[1] The definition itself is well-formed, and probably as compact as any definition for such a number could be.

Now, consider the definition that gives rise to the Berry paradox:

'The smallest positive integer not definable in under 60 letters'

Where is the paradox? This definition seems well-formed and should designate some number. But the definition also has only 57 letters in it, so any number it does designate *can* be defined in under 60 letters. It appears that there should be some such number, as they become more difficult to define briefly as they get larger. But if some number *is* the smallest positive integer not definable in under 60 letters, then it *can* be defined in under 60 letters using Berry's definition, and thus it is *not* the smallest positive integer not definable in under 60 letters. Apparently, some number will both meet this definition and not meet this definition. Thus, we have a contradiction. (Some versions of this paradox put the definition in terms of the number of words or syllables in the definition, but we can generate the same paradoxical result in those ways.)

It might concern you that there are some loose ends here. Are we presuming the definition must be in English? Could we give shorter definitions in other languages, or other orthographies? We can answer questions like these any way you like, but they won't head off the paradox. Should we count spaces? Whichever answers we give, there will still be a Berry-style definition that meets the requirements for the paradox. What about the fact that there is a negation ("not definable") in the definition here? Maybe that negation smuggles in a much simpler contradiction into the definition, just below the surface, and we can resolve the paradox by pointing it out. Probably not. We could write an equivalent definition that did not include a negation – e.g., "the smallest positive integer requiring more than eighty letters in its definition." (The number of letters needed is slightly different here, but it gives us the same sort of paradox.)

Perhaps we should include familiar ways of writing numerals in decimal notation (so '983,745,984' would have nine "letters"). There would be a smallest positive integer that required more than 60 "letters" to be designated – it would be a "1" followed by 60 zeroes. No problem. But that's a numeral, not a definition, and simply changing the kind of expression we're using does not solve the apparent paradox. The heart of this paradox suggests that some well-formed expressions apparently both refer and don't refer to something, much like the sentence in the liar paradox was somehow both true and not true at the same time. If there are such well-formed expressions that lead us to a paradox, there is no comfort in the fact that other expressions don't.

RESPONSES

Some responses seek to defuse Berry's paradox without the need for substantial revisions to logic as a whole. These strategies focus on demonstrating that some part of the paradox rests on questionable assumptions about the semantics of the definition. French (1988) argues that the paradox arises only if we assume that the expressions in the definition have fixed, invariant meanings and that the same set of words cannot be used to describe different numbers under different conditions. Taking a cue from set-theoretical definitions of the natural numbers, French notes that we can define the empty set in fewer letters/words/etc. than stipulated in the paradox, and then define each subsequent number in sequence as, "The set that contains each and every number (and only those numbers) described in the preceding step." Thus, we could define every natural number within the confines set by the paradox. This solution involves the use of context-sensitive expressions ("preceding step"), but many philosophers have adopted more dynamic, context-sensitive accounts of meaning for a wide variety of purposes. The onus lies on proponents of Berry's paradox, French asserts, to show that there is some special reason to prohibit context-sensitivity here.

Grover (1983) also appealed to context-sensitivity as a solution to the paradox. She notes that some expressions serve as "inheritors" that connect one topic or piece of discourse with another. Paradigmatically, pronouns inherit their designation from other expressions in conversation, e.g., "*Flynn* is a musician. *He* plays guitar." Grover's view was that inheritors must connect with expressions that acquire their referents "independently," unlike inheritors; those that lack such independent expressions would be ungrounded, and this is how she characterizes the description at the heart of Berry's paradox. The paradox depends on finding the largest integer that can be described in a certain number of letters/words/etc., then using that as an antecedent and adding one to it. She suggests we must imagine all the possible definitions that meet the restrictions in ascending order of the size of the integer they designate. Any integer that purportedly met the definition would inherit antecedents from this chain. (It would be the integer right after the last, largest integer defined.) But this does not give the Berry definition an independent expression as its grounding, and so the definition itself is ungrounded. This is why it seems that, even if we were to find such an integer, it would simply be drawn back into the set of integers that could be defined within the restrictions – the paradoxical result. Thus, even though the definition appears well-formed, its reference cannot be determined, and so it does not refer. For those interested in Grover's solution, it is worth reading Simmons (2005), which takes its inspiration from Yablo's paradox in developing a version of Berry's paradox without self-reference. (Though this may still involve antecedents and inheritors in Grover's sense.)

Others argue that Berry's paradox is not only a genuine paradox, but an informative one. Chaitin (1995) notes the kinship between Berry's description and computable functions. Both would use finitely many steps or parts to determine some value, and so we might compare Berry's paradox with efforts to find the shortest program that would generate a particular output. Chaitin suggests the interesting question in computer science would then be whether we could show for a given program that no shorter program could produce the same output. (If we could do this with definitions like Berry's, we could then write out all the possible definitions of that length, find the one describing the largest integer, and add one to it.) Chaitin's aim here is to use Berry's paradox to motivate a way of thinking about the complexity and compactness of programs, but Roy (1999) interprets this in a more pessimistic fashion, showing that there is no effective method for finding the shortest (or most elegant) descriptions for any given output. There may very well *be* a shortest such description, but his proof suggests that there is no algorithm that could tell us what it is, or that we have found it. See also Kikuchi, *et al.* (2012) on Chaitin's argument. For readers with more extensive experience with symbolic logic, see Brady (1984), and Priest (2019) for deeper looks at the paradox's implications. Both Schlenker (2009) and Porpora (2021) make use of the paradox to draw conclusions in metaphysics.

NOTE

1. To give you a sense of the magnitude of that number, imagine writing a single numeral in a square millimeter of paper (about 5-point font), and stacking ten such sheets of very thin paper atop each other, giving you 10 numerals/mm^3 and 10^{10} numerals/m^3. The observable universe has a volume of about 10^{32} GLy^3, or 10^{80}m^3, so it could hold about 10^{90} of those numerals. You would need about 10 billion regions with the volume of our observable universe, full of paper, to write down the smallest prime greater than a googolplex this way.

RECOMMENDED READINGS

MAJOR WORKS

Chaitin, G.J. 1995. "The Berry Paradox." *Complexity* 1 (1): 26–30.

Grover, D. 1983. "Berry's Paradox." *Analysis* 43 (4): 170–176.

Simmons, K. 2005. "A Berry and a Russell Without Self-Reference." *Philosophical Studies* 126 (2): 253–261.

RESPONSES

Brady, R. 1984. "Reply to Priest on Berry's Paradox." *Philosophical Quarterly* 34 (135): 157–163.

French, J.D. 1988. "The False Assumption Underlying Berry's Paradox." *Journal of Symbolic Logic* 53 (4): 1220–1223.

Kikuchi, M., T. Kurahashi, and H. Sakai. 2012. "On Proofs of the Incompleteness Theorems Based on Berry's Paradox by Vopenka, Chaitin, and Boolos." *Matehamtical Logic Quarterly* 58: 307–316.

Porpora, D. 2021. "Supervenience Physicalism and the Berry Paradox." *Philosophia* 49 (4): 1681–1693.

Priest, G. 2019. "Berry's Paradox . . . Again." *Australasian Journal of Logic* 16 (2): 41–48.

Roy, D.K. 1999. "On Berry's Paradox and Nondiagonal Constructions." *Complexity* 4 (3): 35–38.

Schlenker, P. 2009. "Anselm's Argument and Berry's Paradox." *Nous* 43 (2): 214–223.

YABLO'S PARADOX

Background: Each of the paradoxes we've considered involves some degree of self-reference. They take forms like "This sentence is false," referring to themselves, or they go in cycles, with later sentences referring back to earlier ones. Some have deemed this suspicious, but most philosophers and logicians have dismissed this objection as simplistic. Diagnosing all paradoxes as products of self-reference would both explain them and suggest the possibility of a common solution to all of them. Yablo's paradox, if genuine, would suggest that paradoxes are not so easily tamed.

In entry #16, we looked at the liar paradox, in which a sentence or set of sentences that are well-formed and apparently harmless can lead to a contradiction. But the classic forms of the liar paradox depend on either self-reference, in which "the liar" sentence refers back to itself, or cyclical reference, in which a set of sentences refer to one another in a loop. We could think of all of these as *circular* references, with the single sentence being the smallest possible circle. Even if there are good reasons to allow these kinds of features in our language in general, it can feel like the liar paradox is playing on structural quirks, rather than revealing something important about truth to us. So, we should ask, is it possible to have a paradox that does not involve circular reference?

DOI: 10.4324/9781003183167-28

Stephen Yablo (1993) has argued that there are such paradoxes. They are still somewhat unusual, in that they require infinitely long series of sentences, and the sentences refer to other sentences in the series. But the sentences don't apparently involve circular reference. Let's look at the paradox. First, we imagine an infinitely long series of sentences, each of which we'll name S_k where k is the sentence's number in that series. $(S_1, S_2, S_3, . . .)$ Each one of these sentences will say that all of the sentences that come after it in the sequence are untrue. We could start writing the series out like this:

(S_1) For all $k>1$, S_k is untrue.
(S_2) For all $k>2$, S_k is untrue.
(S_3) For all $k>3$, S_k is untrue.
. . .

We can't finish writing the series, since it's infinitely long, but its structure should be clear. To show that it is a paradox, we need to derive a contradiction from the series.

We can do that by considering what happens when some member of the series, (S_n), is true. What (S_n) tells us is that for every $k>n$, sentence (S_k) is untrue. (So, if $n=8$, it tells us that (S_9), (S_{10}), (S_{11}) . . . and all the higher-numbered sentences in the series are all untrue.). Two things follow from this:

(a) S_{n+1} is untrue.
(b)   For all $k>n+1$, S_k is untrue.

Now we get to the contradiction. Condition (b) tells us that what (a) says is true, because (b) says that every sentence after S_{n+1} is untrue. But if (S_{n+1}) is true, then that would conflict with what (S_n) said, because it implied that every sentence after it was untrue. Go back to my illustration above for a moment and let's make $n=8$. If (S_8) is true, then (S_9), (S_{10}), (S_{11}) . . . and so on through the infinite series are all untrue. That includes (S_9), but since (S_{10}), (S_{11}) . . . are all going to be untrue, (S_9) would also be *true*, since it just says that all the sentences after it are untrue. Now, (S_9) somehow has to be both true and untrue, just like a "liar" sentence.

Can't we just make $n=1$? That's okay at first glance for (S_1), which just says that all the rest are untrue. (S_1) doesn't refer back to itself, so its being true is not a problem in itself. But once we get to (S_2), we realize that the truth of (S_1) entails the untruth of (S_3), (S_4), (S_5) . . . and on through the series, and that would entail the truth of (S_2), which was also supposed to be untrue in order to make (S_1) true. We get the same paradoxical sentence no matter what value we give for n.

We started this proof with an assumption that one of them had to be true, so why don't we try stipulating that *none* are true? Doing that won't help us, either. If every sentence after (S_1) is untrue, then (S_1) itself must be true, even though we're stipulating that it is not. In fact, if we stipulate that all of the sentences are untrue, then every sentence would be followed by an infinite series of untrue sentences, which would make every one of them true! And thus untrue, and thus true, and thus . . . you get the idea. We cannot coherently assign truth values to any of the sentences in the series. So, we have a "liar"-like paradox that suggests considerable trouble for the classical notion of truth. And none of these sentences refer to themselves, nor back to earlier sentences in the series, so there is no circular reference. (Readers may also want to check out Goldstein (1994), which presents a modified version of the paradox in set theoretical terms.)

RESPONSES

One thing I have assumed so far to keep things simple, as well as letting Yablo have his say, is that the paradox does not involve circular reference. That is apparently the case, but it has been disputed by some critics. The burden is on such critics to demonstrate the circularity, but Yablo's paradox would be far less significant if they succeeded, even if it remains a paradox.

Graham Priest (1997) argued that Yablo's paradox does involve circular reference. To make this case, he emphasizes the role of a "fixed point" in circular reference. For a sentence to refer back to itself, or for a series of them to loop back to some sentence, there must be a kind of "home base" for that return that distinguishes the circularity. In self-reference, the fixed point is just the sentence itself, and in the famous "liar" sentence 'This sentence is false,' the fixed point is fixed with the demonstrative 'this.' Priest's analysis of the paradox suggests that Yablo's use of natural numbers in formulating this sequence suggests that we must analyze it in the formal language we use for arithmetic, supplemented by a truth predicate. To derive the necessary contradiction, Priest shows that the predicate in each of the (S_n) sentences must be interpreted as saying (in more formal terms) "no number greater than x satisfies this predicate," which now includes 'this' to establish a fixed point. If that analysis is correct, then Yablo's case is still a paradox, but it implicitly includes the same sort of circular reference as "the liar." (See also Hardy (1995) on the dissimilarities between "the liar" and Yablo's paradox.)

Sorensen (1998) defends Yablo against Priest's objection, insisting that the arithmetical tools in Yablo's original formulation and Priest's analysis of it are not essential features of the paradox. Since Yablo's series has infinitely many sentences in it, but he and his readers are finite creatures, some finite means of delineating the series is a practical necessity, but not a logical one. "Our use of a self-referential specification is merely a useful heuristic" (1998, p. 145). Beall (2001) critiques Sorensen's defense, suggesting that he does not fully appreciate Priest's point about Yablo. Beall interprets Priest as saying that *any* description we can give of Yablo's paradox must invoke a form of circular reference. In particular, there is a question of how we select the referent for the expression 'Yablo's paradox.' We cannot write the whole of it out, as even Sorensen acknowledges, so we must instead give a description. (The version I wrote above would be a less formal version of that description than the actual one given by Yablo, including a few fragments from the early stages of the series for illustration.) And it is in the analysis of this description that Priest noted an implicit circularity. If that analysis or description provides our only route to identifying the paradox, then its occurrence is not incidental. Bringsjord and Heuveln (2003) are critical of Beall's response on this, arguing that it is possible to select a referent for the paradox without appealing to descriptions, undermining Beall's response. Bueno and Colyvan (2003) take a similar route, denying that descriptions are the only means to refer to the paradox, and then proceeding to argue that were we to use descriptions to select a referent, this would not entail circularity. Ketland (2004) criticizes Bueno and Colyvan's account.

Cook (2006) acknowledged Priest's point about needing fixed points for these sentences, but notes that the sort of arithmetical formalization Priest uses might be said to make any or even every possible sentence a fixed point of one sort or another. He makes a case that the sort of circular reference we find in the liar paradox is just one of many, and that Yablo's paradox does point toward the possibility of paradoxes in which the use of a fixed point does not explain the paradoxical nature of some cases. Thus, we should not conclude that paradoxes are simply a consequence of circular reference, as Priest and others have argued. See Cook (2014) for an extended discussion of Yablo's paradox and the possibility of non-circular paradox in general.

RECOMMENDED READINGS

MAJOR WORKS

Priest, G. 1997. "Yablo's Paradox." *Analysis* 57 (4): 236–242.

Sorensen, R. 1998. "Yablo's Paradox and Kindred Infinite Liars." *Mind* 107 (425): 137–155.

Yablo, S. 1993. "Paradox Without Self-Reference." *Analysis* 53 (4): 251–252.

RESPONSES

Beall, J.C. 2001. "Is Yablo's Paradox Non-Circular?" *Analysis* 61 (3): 176–187.

Bringsjord, S., and B. Heuveln. 2003. "The 'Mental Eye' Defence of an Infinitized Version of Yablo's Paradox." *Analysis* 63 (1): 61–70.

Bueno, O., and M. Colyvan. 2003. "Yablo's Paradox and Referring to Infinite Objects." *Australasian Journal of Philosophy* 81 (3): 402–412.

Cook, R. 2006. "There Are Non-Cicrcular Paradoxes (But Yablo's Isn't One of Them!)." *The Monist* 89 (1): 118–149.

Cook, R. 2014. *The Yablo Paradox: An Essay on Circularity*. Oxford: Oxford University Press.

Goldstein, L. 1994. "A Yabloeqsque Paradox in Set Theory." *Analysis* 54 (4): 223–227.

Hardy, J. 1995. "Is Yablo's Paradox Liar-Like?" *Analysis* 55 (3): 197–198.

Ketland, J. 2004. "Bueno and Colyvan on Yablo's Paradox." *Analysis* 64 (2): 165–172.

20

'TRUE, FALSE, AND WHATEVER ELSE YOU'VE GOT!'

Background: The study of logic, truth, and meaning in Western philosophy has operated on the assumption that there were two truth-values and no true contradictions. As we have seen in the last four entries, the paradoxes throw these assumptions into question. Here, we look at accounts that admit true contradictions to resolve the paradoxes.

We discussed a number of paradoxes in entries #16–19 that pose significant challenges to common intuitions about truth and other semantic notions. "The liar," Berry's paradox, and Yablo's paradox seem to entail that there are sets of well-formed sentences whose logical form entails a contradiction. Classical logic would suggest that such sentences must be either true or false, yet neither value seems quite right in these cases. There have been many attempts to address these issues that would save some version of classical logic, and many logicians remain committed to finding such solutions. But if you have read the last few entries, you may be ready to consider a more radical option: what if there were true contradictions?

Why should we fear contradictions in the first place? In the most general sense, to give an account of logic is simply to say what the well-formed sentences of it will be, and to give a logical consequence relation (how we should make inferences with those sentences). How

DOI: 10.4324/9781003183167-29

we assign or withhold truth values to sentences takes shape within our approach to those matters. But even if we add a third truth value, there is a serious issue concerning the logical consequence relation. In classical logic, contradictions are *explosive*. That is, with a little ingenuity and an introductory-course level of knowledge of the inference rules of classical logic, it is possible to derive any possible sentence from a contradiction. How so? Suppose we had a contradiction: 'Mingus plays bass and it is not the case that Mingus plays bass.' We can construct a derivation[1] like this:

(1)   Mingus plays bass and it is not the case that Mingus plays bass.
(2)   Mingus plays bass.
(3)   It is not the case that Mingus plays bass.
(4)   Either Mingus plays bass or there are round squares in Pittsburgh.
(5)   There are round squares in Pittsburgh.

Sentences (2) and (3) follow from (1); (1) just says that those sentences are jointly true. Sentence (4) will be true so long as at least one of the sentences on either side of 'or' is true, and we're assured by (2) that one is. (I just made up the other side; put in literally *anything* you like there.) Sentence (5) will follow from (3) and (4), since (4) is true and (3) eliminates one of the parts that could make it true, leaving us the other. So (5) must follow from (1)-(4). If that were so, then every sentence we could write would be trivially derivable (even absurd ones), so logic would not distinguish good arguments from bad ones and would offer us no guidance worth taking.

So, if any of the paradoxes we have considered so far entailed a contradiction, that would render every possible claim rationally irrelevant and every argument trivial. The stakes don't get bigger than that in philosophy. To get a sense of how we might fend off such a possibility even if we cannot find solutions to all the paradoxes, consider two kinds of intuitions people often have when confronted with the paradoxes. On the one hand, some people find it clear that the paradoxical sentences should be interpreted as *both* true and false. We can derive sentences with each of the two classical truth values without difficulty, so we should somehow assign *both* values to the same sentence. Others see this situation and find it so perplexing that assigning *either* truth value seems mistaken, and so we should assign *neither* one of them to the paradoxical sentence. This would imply that despite their well-formedness, some sentences simply don't have truth values, or they have some third value that we might call "undetermined."

This sort of non-value or third-value approach runs afoul of the Law of the Excluded Middle (LEM), which is a fundamental assumption of classical logic. Adopting it would require a significantly different approach, known as a *paracomplete* logic, in which the LEM fails, or is abandoned. This is a view that has gained traction with some mathematicians (and related logicians) who take mathematics to be a creation of the human mind. On such views, mathematical truths are not facts external to our theories, waiting to be discovered; they are true in virtue of the proofs that we construct for them. For some sentences about mathematics, no proof is yet available, and we may never find one. Take a simple example:

(6)   There are infinitely many twin primes.

Twin primes are pairs of prime numbers, one of which is two greater than the other, like 11 and 13, or 17 and 19. Mathematicians are almost certain that there are infinitely many such pairs, but no one has proven this. Perhaps we never will. If so, then we might want a paracomplete logic that allows us to say that (6) is neither true, nor false. This approach has been defended by Michael Dummett, who first adopted paracomplete accounts in mathematical logic but went on to apply them to other categories of sentences as well. As a solution to "the liar" and other paradoxes, three value approaches are quite simple: the paradoxical sentence simply has no truth value, or has the third, undetermined value. This would render it inert, without further logical consequences; the "explosiveness" is "defused." Thus, we might not assign a truth value to (1), and so it would not entail the truth of (2)-(5).

What about the second intuition, that a contradiction might actually have both truth values? Even then, would we really want to say that it *logically followed* from any given contradiction that round squares run wild in the streets of Pittsburgh at night? Probably not. So, some logicians would say that we need to refine and improve our understanding of logical consequence, making it more restrictive. In a *paraconsistent* logic, the Law of Non-Contradiction (LNC) can fail or be abandoned, but efforts are made to prevent the logical consequence relation from permitting explosion; explosiveness is thus "contained." To those most interested in paraconsistent logic, preventing explosiveness is even more important than the possibility of contradictions because of the faults that explosiveness reveals in classical logic.

With this in mind, developing a paraconsistent logic can be a very sober, technical matter. It would give us a logical system that was much more restrictive about the inferences it allowed, and we would have to decide how to prove important theorems using only those restrictive rules, and what we might have to give up in the process. True contradictions like (2) could remain hypothetical concerns, rather than live threats. The view that there *are* true contradictions – that some sentences can be *both* true and false – is known as *dialetheism* ('*di*' from the Greek word for 'two' and '*alethia*' for 'truth'). This has been a more controversial position to take; it seems to threaten rationality itself. How would anything count as a reason to accept anything if we left open the possibility that just the opposite is also the case? There is a story that Saul Kripke was once asked whether we should abandon the LNC in light of the paradoxes, and he said, "Yes! Then we can keep it, too!"

Given this long history of opposition in Western philosophy, why would dialetheists embrace the prospect of true contradictions? Graham Priest argues that this is an appealingly simple, elegant position when it complements a paraconsistent logic. For all the efforts made to resolve them, the paradoxes have not gone away. Many modifications have been made to address the paradoxes, only to see a new wave of "revenge" paradoxes emerge to confound us even further. If contradictions are inevitable, Priest suggests, why not accept them right from the start? Without the need to evade them, much of that arcane theoretical complexity is unnecessary, and a leaner, simpler, more intuitive approach to logic is possible.

The LNC won't go down without a fight, but it is challenging to offer a defense of the LNC once the law itself is thrown into question. The classical method of refuting a proposal would be to assume it and derive a contradiction, but that sort of argument would be circular if we were arguing about whether or not our logic (and our world) could allow contradictions. Whether a formal system of logic permits contradictions is a matter determined by the laws, definitions, and other assumptions that shape that system; what is at stake in the debate over dialetheism is *which such system* we should use (one that includes the LNC, or one that doesn't). Classical logicians may cry "foul" at this and insist that abandoning the LNC precludes the very possibility of rational discourse. Nothing would stop us from adopting some sentence, *A*, and accepting not-*A* at the same time, so no genuine disagreement would be possible. But the dialetheist argues that this begs the question against their view, too. Disagreement may be possible with more primitive notions than a formally defined negation operator, and the fear that *all* disputes would fizzle out in contradictions presumes the explosiveness that paraconsistent logic guards against.

RESPONSES

Graham Priest has been dialetheism's most vocal proponent, and his *In Contradiction* (2006) is both comprehensive and accessible to those with some coursework in logic. (See Parsons (1990) and Whittle (2004) for criticism of Priest's views on dialetheism.) Readers interested in the sort of paracomplete logic described above with some truth "gaps" (in which some sentences don't have truth values) should have a look at Kripke (1975). Much of that piece relates directly to the liar paradox, and responding to Tarski's work, so readers may also want to consult Skyrms (1970) and Ray (2006), recommended at the end of entry #16. Kripke's "gappy" approach built on the work of Kleene (1952, Chap. 12) and was further developed by Soames (1999). Soames introduced a system for "partially-defined" predicates, which don't assign truth-values at all to some objects.

Beall (2004) argues that dialetheism only strikes us as implausible (or "dizzying" as he puts it) when we import expectations about uncovering the nature of truth, as though it were an entity awaiting discovery. On "deflationary" views, talk of truth is simply an expressive tool within a language, and we have the option to adopt a dialetheic view if it serves our purposes (which Beall argues it does). Like Priest's account, this presumes that there is a simplicity and elegance to accepting contradictions to address the paradoxes. Littman and Simmons (2004) dispute this. They argue that no dialetheist view can cordon off its contradictions, and so they will inevitably infect critical theoretical assumptions at the expense of every theory's coherence.

One final view, more radical than all those discussed so far, is *trivialism*. Azzouni describes this as "the view that all the sentences of natural languages are both true and false" (2013, p. 3175). So, 'Mingus plays bass' is both true and false, as is 'Mingus does not play bass,' and so on for every truth-apt sentence. We can distinguish this from *metaphysical* trivialism, which would imply that every fact or state of affairs we could imagine both is and is not the case, which Azzouni dismisses as absurd. The trivialism of potential interest to a philosopher of language suggests that natural languages are inconsistent, and thus we can derive every possible sentence – and thus, the negation of every possible sentence. This does not require any appeal to paradoxes, or even to negation, and some proofs for it are very accessible, even to novices.

NOTE

1. This derivation is written in ordinary English to make it accessible even to those who have not taken a logic class. Bear in mind that whether the logical debate here applies directly to reasoning in natural languages or only to formal logical systems is itself part of this debate.

RECOMMENDED READING

MAJOR WORKS

Beall, J.C. 2004. "True and False – As If." In *The Law of Non-Contradiction. New Philosophical Essays*, edited by G. Priest, J.C. Beall, and B. Armour-Grab, 197–216. Oxford: Oxford University Press.

Kleene, S. 1952. *Introduction to Metamathematics*. Amsterdam: North Holland.

Kripke, S. 1975. "Outline of a Theory of Truth." *Journal of Philosophy* 72 (19): 690–716.

Priest, G. 2006. *In Contradiction: A Study of the Transconsistent*, 2nd ed. Oxford: Clarendon Press.

RESPONSES

Azzouni, J. 2013. "Inconsistency in Natural Languages." *Synthèse* 190: 3175–3184.

Littman, G., and K. Simmons. 2004. "A Critique of Dialetheism." In *The Law of Non-Contradiction: New Philosophical Essays*, edited by G. Priest, J.C. Beall, and B. Armour-Grab, 314–335. Oxford: Oxford University Press.

Parsons, T. 1990. "True Contradictions." *Candian Journal of Philosophy* 20 (3): 335–353.

Ray, G. 2006. "Truth, the Liar, and Tarskian Truth Definition." In *Philosophical Logic*, edited by D. Jacquette, 164–176. Oxford: Blackwell Pub.

Skyrms, B. 1970. "Return of the Liar: Three-Valued Logic and the Concept of Truth." *American Philosophical Quarterly* 7 (2): 153–161.

Soames, S. 1999. *Understanding Truth*. Oxford: Oxford University Press.

Whittle, B. 2004. "Dialetheism, Logical Consequence, and Hierarchy." *Analysis* 64 (4): 318–326.

PART V

CONTEXT-SENSITIVITY

INTRODUCTION

In section II, we considered the prospects of a *theory* of meaning: a formal system that spelled out the meanings of words and sentences in natural languages. The entries in section III cast some doubt on the prospects for such a theory, suggesting that meaning is not systematically grounded on some set of foundational elements, but rather emerges from collections of intersecting social practices. Not every philosopher accepts those arguments, but there is another significant challenge waiting in the wings. Most proposals for such a grand theory of meaning have presumed that the meanings of words and sentences were fixed and could thus be given precise theoretical characterizations.

However, many words and sentences that we use seem to have different meanings on different occasions of use. For instance, pronouns serve to designate different things contingent upon the occasion on which they are used. 'I' designates Michael Padraic Wolf when Michael Padraic Wolf uses it and designates other people when they use it. An adjective like 'tall' seems to imply very different standards when we're talking about children vs. professional basketball players vs. buildings. What we mean by it in one context and how we interpret and evaluate what others are saying with it can shift when we find ourselves in a different context (e.g., conversations about children vs. conversations

DOI: 10.4324/9781003183167-31

about buildings). The meanings of many words – and hence the sentences in which they occur – appear to be sensitive to the context in which they are used and change as the context changes. Note that the challenge here is not a matter of words having more than one fixed meaning; the same string of letters, sounds, etc., might have multiple meanings associated with it that we must sort through each time they are used, yet those meanings themselves are not changing. 'Bridge' can mean a structure over a body of water, or the command center of a ship, or the upper part of someone's nose, or a middle section of a song (and a few other things). However, when we use that first sense – a structure over a body of water – its meaning is not somehow shifting to designate a different type of object from one occasion of use to another.

It might still be possible to incorporate such context-sensitivity into a systematic theory of meaning. Entry #21 presents some of the prevailing attempts to do so; entries #22–23 respond to this with puzzles that suggest context-sensitivity might stretch much more widely across our language than it first seems. Entry #24 presents a puzzle related to pronouns that deepens the difficulties faced by accounts presented in entry #21. Entries #25–27 also present puzzles and problems related to pronouns, though these all concern the special practical implications that pronouns might have, rather than purely semantic ones.

21

'I CAN'T GET THERE FROM HERE'

Background: Most analytic philosophers began their accounts with a focus on general logical features and expressions whose meanings are invariant across different contexts. But natural languages are filled with expressions whose meanings do change in regular ways with the context in which they are used. In fact, for many classes of expressions, context-sensitivity is a defining feature. That sort of sensitivity required novel approaches, however, and these are the focus of this entry and the four that follow it.

Consider a sentence:

(1)   Maryland is south of Pennsylvania.

In previous entries, we discussed numerous approaches to accounting for the meaning of a sentence like this. Details will differ between those accounts, but the point to emphasize is that they all presume that there is a definitive, invariant answer to such questions. Once we articulated the meaning of a sentence like this, it would be as though we had solved a problem, and could bring that solution to every serious, literal use of it. I know what you mean when you say this, you know what I mean when I say it, and the answer is the same

DOI: 10.4324/9781003183167-32

in all cases. Now, suppose someone says the following, perhaps while pointing at something:

(2)   That is valuable.

This is trickier. What does 'that' mean? I suppose we could say that it depends on who's talking and where they're pointing, but such a response only highlights the concern. 'That' could designate many different – and wildly incompatible – things when different people say it. You might suggest that it's a kind of shorthand or abbreviation. If I say (2) while pointing to a Picasso painting in a museum, maybe we could just say 'that' stands in temporarily for the name of the painting. But I can use 'that' in just the sort of cases where I don't have a name or description available, too – e.g., "What the hell is *that*?" 'That' seems to defy attempts to give it a definitive meaning, once and for all. So, what could a word like 'that' mean?

There is an assumption that many people make that words and sentences that did not have fixed meanings would be useless. We communicate with one another via the languages we use, but if we don't share the meanings of the expressions in those languages, then we will simply be talking past one another. *Chaos! Anarchy! Ineffectual gibberish-mongering!* That certainly underestimates the degree of subtlety and facility we can deploy in conversation. But it also leaves out a more intriguing possibility: what about words and sentences whose meanings play roles in which their *purpose* is to change from one occurrence to the next? Some versions of that would be disastrous. If 'brown' started randomly designating other colors, or we started making radically different inferences from sentences including it, we'd be lost. The question here might be: how can the meanings of parts of a language change in ways that are orderly and understandable(?).

The first part of an answer to this is to note that there are possibilities besides being fixed and changing randomly. Some phenomena are what we would call "sensitive to conditions around them," and it may come in many forms. The mercury in a thermometer expands at higher temperatures; when I learn that someone has caused moral harm, my attitudes toward them change. The sort that concerns us most when we talk about meanings is sensitivity to conversational contexts, or simply *context-sensitivity*. Prime examples of context-sensitivity include expressions known as "indexicals," whose content has a sort of incomplete quality that is fixed by being interpreted in a context.

Pronouns such as 'he,' 'she,' and 'they' typically function in this way. In their most direct uses, we may use them demonstratively, in conjunction with a sort of demonstration of who or what we're referring to. Suppose we're standing in a parking lot, and I point to someone and say:

(3)   She has the keys.

Then, suppose I point to another object and say:

(4)   That is my car.

Whoever is selected by my demonstration in an utterance of (3) is the referent of 'she' in this sentence. Whatever is selected by my demonstration in (4) is the referent of 'that.' Without those demonstrative features of our conversational context, you would be left wondering how to interpret those expressions. In other cases, the selection of a referent is even more formally built into the utterance of a sentence:

(5)   I love John Coltrane's music.

Who is the 'I' that this sentence being said of? Whoever utters it on a given occasion.

In some cases, we do the same with other parts of a conversation to which later indexicals will link. (These would be called *anaphoric* uses of pronouns.)

(6)   Liz quit her job. She hated the hours.
(7)   If one man sins against another, God will judge him.[1]

In (6), both 'her' and 'she' have the incomplete quality I mentioned earlier; we fill those gaps in by recognizing that, in this context, our attention is turned to Liz. We take whoever that name refers to in the previous sentence and fill in those pronouns with that person as their reference. In another context, 'she' might refer to someone else, even if the entire sentence 'She hated the hours' occurs again. In (7), the reference is not really filled in at all. The 'him' is what logicians would call a "bound variable" and stands in for anyone that might fit the earlier description. We leave such referents unspecified on purpose, though we recognize how to fill them in as needed.

How should we spell out just what makes for a context, though? If we're to explain indexicals, we need a more systematic account of contexts, not just intuitions and simple cases. The most influential account among philosophers of language in recent decades is one offered by David Kaplan (1978, 1989). Kaplan distinguishes between *character*, *content*, and *context*. Character and content may be thought of as two distinct types of meaning, though they are closely related to one another. Sentences with indexicals in them will have the same character every time that they are used. These features will be determined by linguistic convention. In a sentence like (5), all the non-indexical parts of the sentence will have their familiar meanings, and competent speakers will know that 'I' is to be filled in with the speaker as a referent, much like a mathematical function may be filled with different numbers. We could give comparable accounts for each type of indexical. In a context, we can fill in those details, giving the sentence a determinate content. So, my utterance of (5) and yours will have the same character, but different contents as those details change. What makes for a context? Kaplan originally said each one would include an agent, time, location, and possible world. (Here, 'possible world' may be thought of as the totality of the facts that are true of the whole universe and its history.) Once we interpret such sentences in a context, we can evaluate their truth. Utterances of (5) from me would be false in contexts when I was young, true by the time I was an adult, and might not have been true at any point if the possible world I inhabit had worked out differently. Utterances from other speakers in other contexts would generate different contents, and thus vary in their truth, as well.

RESPONSES

One point of great interest has been the role of indexicals in beliefs. If someone has a belief that would be expressed by sentences such as (2)-(5) above, then they have an indexical belief. On Kaplan's view, these beliefs would express *singular propositions* – i.e., they would have an individual entity such as a person as a direct constituent, rather than a Fregean sense mediating between the belief and its referents. The content of my indexical belief "She has the keys" in context is about *that person* – whoever 'she' designates – and not something like a set of descriptions that uniquely specifies that person. This suggests a direct reference account of indexicals and demonstratives, consonant with recent accounts from Kripke and Putnam. (See entries #46–47.)

Many have noted that direct reference accounts run up against a puzzle that we may derive from Frege's work. Two beliefs or sentences that express the same proposition should have the same cognitive significance – i.e., we recognize them as no different. (See entry #40 for more.) Yet a sentence using only non-indexical expressions may express the same singular proposition as one with indexicals. For instance, suppose you believe "The meeting starts at 3:00," and then suddenly realize that it is 3:00 in your context, and come to believe, "The meeting starts *now*." Both sentences refer to the same time, and so they should express that same singular proposition. Yet Perry (1977) notes even if these would express the same singular proposition, we come to believe something with the second that we did not with the first. That implies that there is some cognitive difference between believing "The meeting starts at 3:00" and believing "The meeting starts now," yet this cannot be addressed solely by an interpretation that substitutes a specific time in for 'now,' as Kaplan's model originally suggested.

Perry's and Kaplan's views are that people can believe propositions *via* their characters in some fashion, giving us direct reference, but via a mediating abstract entity. They argue that this isn't a retreat to Frege because it's only appealing to facts about the context of utterance, not a sense, and these features don't become part of the proposition. To many proponents of direct reference, this seems like too thin a distinction, and marks a retreat. More stringent defenses of direct reference views are offered by Wettstein (1986) and Taschek (1987). Both argue that we should reject Frege's assumption that "any difference in the cognitive significance of two sentences must reflect an objective semantic difference" (Taschek 1987, p. 161), which drives the puzzles of indexical belief here.

Kaplan distinguished what he called "pure indexicals" from "true demonstratives." *Pure indexicals* were expressions whose content was determined entirely by objective features of the context of their utterance, while *true demonstratives* depended in some way on the intentions and performances by the speaker, such as pointing. Thus 'I' and 'today' would be pure indexicals, while 'that,' used demonstratively, requires a speaker to point out some referent, and it will be an open question which object is that referent. When I say "She has the keys" in a crowded room, different people might be designated by that pronoun, and we might need to determine from my intentions which one. Most occurrences of true demonstratives need no such unpacking, but this is not a logical or semantic point. That smooth interaction is the result of shared psychological traits among speakers.

Evans (1985) stressed this point in expressing qualified support for some of Kaplan's views. Agents that have indexical beliefs believe singular propositions that include the characters of indexicals among their constituent parts. But he also suggested that speakers using demonstratives and including them in their beliefs must have at least some conception of what they select in a demonstration, and hence there are some modest epistemic requirements implied by them (e.g., to select someone as my referent for (3), I must know that it is a person who is being pointed to). Evans saw this as pushing us closer to a Fregean appeal to sense for demonstratives (albeit a modified and corrected one), rather than a directly referential account in line with Mill, Kripke, and Kaplan. Bach (2010) comments on this debate, and Dickie (2015, particularly Chapter 4) does so with greater emphasis on details drawn directly from recent work in cognitive psychology on the perceptual and conceptual mechanisms by which we conduct such demonstrations. Baraski (2021) and Raftopoulos and Müller (2006) both make the case for direct referential views without conceptual or epistemic demands, contrary to Evans's account.

NOTE

1.   I Samuel, 2:25, *NKJV*.

RECOMMENDED READINGS

MAJOR WORKS

Evans, G. 1985. "Understanding Demonstratives." In *Collected Papers*, 291–325. Oxford: Oxford University Press.

Kaplan, D. 1978. "Dthat." In *Syntax and Semantics*, edited by P. Cole, vol. 9, 221–243. Oxford: Oxford University Press.

Kaplan, D. 1989. "Demonstratives." In *Themes from Kaplan*, edited by J. Almog, J. Perry, and H. Wettstein, 481–563. Oxford: Oxford University Press.

RESPONSES

Bach, K. 2010. "Getting a Thing into a Thought." In *New Essays on Singular Thought*, edited by R. Jeshion, 39–63. Oxford: Oxford University Press.

Baraski, M. 2021. "Are There Epistemic Conditions Necessary for Demonstrative Thought?" *Synthèse* 198: 6111–6138.

Dickie, I. 2015. *Fixing Reference*. Oxford: Oxford University Press.

Perry, J. 1977. "Frege on Demonstratives." *Philosophical Review* 86: 474–497.

Raftopoulos, A., and V. Müller. 2006. "Nonconceptual Demonstrative Reference." *Philosophy and Phenomenological Research* 72 (2): 251–285.

Taschek, W. 1987. "Content, Character, and Cognitive Significance." *Philosophical Studies* 52: 161–189.

Wettstein, H. 1986. "Has Semantics Rested on a Mistake?" *Journal of Philosophy* 83: 185–209.

'MICAH IS GETTING SO *BIG*!'

Background: Analytic philosophers of language now agree that natural languages include some classes of expressions whose meanings are context-sensitive. Indexicals are prime examples of this and of how such context-sensitive expressions could be incorporated into earlier accounts. These expressions are well-behaved and can be well-defined. In recent years, there has been a growing chorus of philosophers, linguistics, and psychologists who have argued that context-sensitivity extends much further into language, and in much more varied ways.

Friends of mine had a baby recently, and they named their child "Micah." As is customary, this had led to sharing countless pictures of Micah – Micah sleeping, Micah smiling, Micah smiling at their cats, their cats appearing confused by Micah – you name it. And as is customary, this has led to my saying things like:

(1)   Micah is getting so *big*!

Saying that sort of thing to new parents is almost a ritual, no matter the size of their child. But in this case, it is also true. Micah has grown quickly and steadily to a healthy size. I would say (1) seriously and literally, not just in that high-pitched baby talk voice that people use

DOI: 10.4324/9781003183167-33

when they see infants. Yet, at the same time, I also appreciate that 'big' can imply very different things. Micah is certainly big compared to, say, subatomic particles or other babies of the same age, but not compared to entire galaxies or human beings in general. That might seem beside the point. When I visit my friends and say (1), we're talking about babies, and it would be pedantic of someone to say, "Well, not in comparison with the Milky Way, or the current roster of the Milwaukee Bucks." Surely not, but who said *that*?

How can we account for this apparent tension? One type of answer given to this is that 'big' and perhaps a great many other words have a kind of context-sensitivity that we have not yet described. Micah is big *for a baby*, and features of the conversational context at my friends' house make that the appropriate class with which to compare Micah, setting a standard by which (1) may be true or false. In another context, another set of features might give rise to a different class – galaxies, basketball players, etc. – and a different set of truth-conditions. This sort of reading was offered by Travis (1996), who suggested that natural languages were rife with such contextual features. This context-sensitivity would invert a conception of language dominant since Frege. For generations of analytic philosophers of language, it was presumed that each sentence would have a single, specific set of truth-conditions that gave us its meaning. If the context-dependency suggested by Travis were correct, then many sentences (maybe *every* one) would have many different truth-conditions, and it would be up to those using the language to sort out which applied. Rather than truth-conditions accounting for sentences' meanings, the meanings would lead us to one of many different possible sets of truth-conditions any time we used them. The same sentence might express different propositions when uttered in different contexts. Call these *contextualist* views of meaning.

Here, some philosophers have cried foul. A language whose every detail was this dependent on details of particular contexts would put speakers in an impossible position. Almost every situation in which we find ourselves from day to day introduces novel combinations of conditions that speakers would have to navigate. Past experience would only be a limited guide, as we have little hope of saying in advance how many different parameters expressions might have, how many standards, reference classes, and other implications any one of them might have. I would say that the longer you think about how many different ways you might use the word 'big,' the less sure you will be that you listed them all. Yet, many philosophers of language will say that the primary purpose of natural language is communication. We speak, write, sign, etc. first and foremost to convey information to others. To do so, there must be a shared groundwork for communication, and thus any piece of the language in wide use must have a stable, context-independence to its meaning. Otherwise, the fact that we communicate with one another so successfully would be a miracle – not in the sense of divine intervention, but rather a result so improbably lucky as to defy explanation.

Cappelen and Lepore (2004) have offered an argument against contextualist accounts of meaning, in favor of what we may call *semantic minimalism*. On a minimalist view, there is very little context-sensitivity in natural languages, and those expressions that are context-sensitive are readily identified and characterized – e.g., indexicals and demonstratives. On a minimalist view, almost all meanings are invariant, and those few (the "basic list," as Cappelen and Lepore call them) that do vary do so in very regular ways. We do, of course, do much more subtle, apparently context-sensitive, things with words, but minimalists argue that the burden of accounting for those should be shifted to speech acts and studied as pragmatics. This would solve the problem of the "miracle of communication" that strong forms of contextualism seem to imply, but it might also leave us scratching our heads. What proposition does sentence (1) express? Does the occurrence of 'big' in it imply the galaxy-sized standard (in which case, my statement is false) or some much lower standard (on which it might be true)?

Cappelen and Lepore offer a striking view that they call "speech act pluralism." On such an account, "what an utterance says, states, claims, etc. differs from the proposition it semantically expresses" (2005, p. 190) and the content of any speech act – an actual statement of (1) for instance, which might use such a sentence to perform the act – may take a great many forms. "No one thing is said (or asserted, or claimed, or . . .) by any utterance: rather, indefinitely many propositions are said, asserted, claimed, stated, etc." (2005, p. 199). Speech acts may take such a wide variety of forms that Cappelen and Lepore despair of offering a systematic, theoretical account of it at all. Deciding what speakers are saying in a speech act instead involves attention to a wide variety of features – facts about the speaker, the conversational context, the world around us, and many more – but that attention won't lend itself to a single, uniform procedure for deciding the speech act's content. Perhaps my utterance of (1) conveys encouragement because Micah was born underweight and had a difficult time at first; perhaps it affirms my friends as parents, since things are going well; perhaps I'm making a point about the passage of time and how it seems to rush ahead when you start a family. All of these acts and many more are possible, but a minimalist will insist that none of them are part of the literal semantic meaning of (1) that would be given to us as truth-conditions. There is great variety in the ways in which we *use* language from one context to another, they concede, but the meanings of words and sentence with which we do this will be almost entirely invariant.

In different contexts, speakers and audiences may focus on one of these expressed propositions (my friends pick up on my note of affirmation, for instance), and when they share that focus, communication will be achieved. They readily admit that they can offer no theoretical account of how speakers do this, guaranteed to determine the proposition algorithmically in every case, but note that this accords with our experiences. Figuring out what people are trying to say to you in conversation *is* hard. But at the very least, in every one of these possible speech acts, competent speakers will have the benefit of understanding *part* of what is being said – the minimal, context-invariant proposition expressed by 'Micah is getting so big!'. (Similar minimalist views are offered in Borg (2004) and Hodgson (2018). Critiques of Cappelen and Lepore can be found in Recanati (2006) and Hawthorne (2006).)

RESPONSES

In his own contextualist account – one of the most radical in the contemporary literature – Francois Recanati (2002) characterizes the development of the philosophy of language in the last 150 years as split between a tradition invested in the notion of "ideal" language and formal semantics and "ordinary language"[1] philosophy, which privileged the actual use of most speakers. The ideal tradition originates with Frege and Russell, extends through Tarski and Carnap, to contemporary truth-conditional and possible-worlds theories of meaning. The "ordinary language" camp thought that this sort of logical analysis did not account for many important features of natural languages, and they forged a different path beginning with the later work of Wittgenstein and extending through Grice, Austin, and Strawson.

Those two paths have converged in recent decades; most philosophers of language take semantics (the study of linguistic meaning) and pragmatics (the study of its use in context) as complementary projects, rather than competitors. For minimalists, the primary bearers of meanings are sentences and propositions, and whatever uses we may put them to must be approached differently. For contextualists, the primary vehicles of meaning are speech acts, which are rife with great varieties of pragmatic features, and only in light of these in a real context does it make sense to think of a sentence having a determinate content at all. Thus, what animates the disputes outlined earlier in this entry is a general methodological and metatheoretical question: where should we draw the line *between* semantics and pragmatics? This became a standard way of framing the debate (with a tilt towards contextualism) in Sperber and Wilson (1995) and Carston (2002), and all the authors discussed here can be read as addressing this matter to some degree. Critiques of many of the standard arguments from those sources (among many others) for a more pragmatically enriched semantics (thus, more strongly contextualist) are offered in Stanley (2005). Stanley's primary concern is that contextualists posit a wide variety of context-sensitive features in ordinary sentences yet cannot point to constituent features that systematically explain their behavior. (By contrast, we posit logical operators like quantifiers and readily identify expressions like 'every' and 'all' by which they systematically appear in ordinary sentences.) Without such constituents, contextualism loses all hope of systemic explanation. MacFarlane (2007) expands the debate further, suggesting that both Stanley and minimalists like Cappelen and Lepore have hastily equated contextualism with indexicality; other varieties exist, and may be more promising to the contextualist.

More recently, there have been authors who have argued that there is no fact of the matter about where semantics ends and pragmatics begin, but only questions about how it is most theoretically fruitful to do so. Note that contextualists like Carston (2002) and Sperber and Wilson (1995) made their cases by invoking language's relation to thought and looking to psychology to see how speakers might share ways of determining context-sensitive features. But note also that,

when Cappelen and Lepore draw their line between minimal semantic contents and speech acts, the distinction is motivated in part by the
explanatory orderliness and success of semantic theorizing we can do
in that ideal language tradition vs. the unruly, ever-shifting conditions
under which we put them to a multitude of uses. To the minimalist,
those just seem like very different theoretical projects – complementary projects surely, but not to be mingled. Dever (2013) has explicitly
made the case that there is no fact of the matter about where to draw
the semantics–pragmatics distinction as part of his larger project of
offering an anti-realist view of semantics (i.e., there are no objective
facts about meanings to be found). Stotts (2020) makes a case for preserving the distinction, and even keeping it especially "sharp."

NOTE

1. "Ordinary language philosophy" is sometimes used to refer more narrowly to a group of British philosophers of the 1950s and 60s and their
   methods. Those philosophers fall within Recanati's category here as
   would many others.

RECOMMENDED READINGS

MAJOR WORKS

Borg, E. 2004. *Minimal Semantics*. Oxford: Oxford University Press.
Cappelen, H., and E. Lepore. 2005. *Insensitive Semantics: A Defense of Semantic
Minimalism and Speech Act Pluralism*. Oxford: Wiley-Blackwell.
Recanati, F. 2002. *Literal Meaning*. Cambridge: Cambridge University Press.
Sperber, D., and D. Wilson. 1995. *Relevance: Communication and Cognition*. Oxford:
Blackwell.
Travis, C. 1996. "Meaning's Role in Truth." *Mind* 105 (419): 451–466.

RESPONSES

Carston, R. 2002. *Thoughts and Utterances: The Pragmatics of Explicit Communication*.
Oxford: Blackwell.
Dever, J. 2013. "The Revenge of the Semantics-Prgamtics Distinction." *Philosoph-
ical Perspectives* 27 (1): 104–144.
Hawthorne, J. 2006. "Testing for Context-Dependence." *Philosophy and Phenome-
nological Research* 73 (2): 443–450.

Hodgson, T. 2018. "Meaning Underdetermines What Is Said, Therefore Utterances Express Many Propositions." *Dialectica* 72 (2): 165–189.

MacFarlane, J. 2007. "Nonindexical Contextualism." *Synthèse* 166: 231–250.

Recanati, F. 2006. "Crazy Minimalism." *Mind and Language* 21 (1): 21–30.

Stanley, J. 2005. "Semantics in Context." In *Contextualism in Philosophy: Knowledge, Meaning and Truth*, edited by G. Preyer and G. Peter, 221–253. Oxford: Oxford University Press.

Stotts, M.H. 2020. "Towards a Sharp Semantics/Pragmatics Distinction." *Synthèse* 197 (1): 185–208.

EPISTEMIC CONTEXTUALISM

Background: We've considered several ways in which the meanings shift with conversational context, especially those with a systematic context-sensitivity. Their shifts in meaning are not mere carelessness; they play roles that track and adjust matters that shift across contexts. Some philosophers argue that 'know' is context-sensitive and that this offers us special insight into problems in a theory of knowledge. The promise in such an approach is that it might dissolve problems in another philosophical field, requiring only theoretical tools already at our disposal.

If you have studied any Western philosophy, it is likely that you have been introduced to some form of epistemological skepticism – the view that we have little or no knowledge about anything at all, despite our everyday confidence that we do. Versions of these problems run through Western philosophy and most other traditions around the world. In fact, these are the sorts of problems that occur to many people on their own, which then *lead* them to an interest in philosophy.

Take an ordinary belief that you might have: that you're reading a book right now. You presumably have exceptionally high confidence in that and could offer exceptionally strong justification for your belief. Maybe you'd point out that you can see the pages; that you know what books are; that you know how to read, etc. But we can imagine circumstances in which you have experiences that look and feel just like such experiences of reading a book would, but which are not experiences of reading a book. Perhaps you're dreaming that you're reading a book, or you're lost in a vivid exercise of your imagination. Perhaps you have ingested the most boring psychedelic drugs ever created, which cause you to hallucinate a black-and-white, no-illustrations philosophy text. If anything like this were the case, then you would be deceived, and you wouldn't know that you were reading a book. When René Descartes offered a version of this in the 17th century, he imagined an "evil genius" tormenting him with false experiences, as we might imagine a mad scientist running evil experiments, or technologically advanced aliens placing our consciousness in a computer simulation.

In years of talking and writing about this subject, I have met almost no one who *actually believes* that they are a brain in a vat, or any other such thing, even when they spin these scenarios. But that's not the point. The point is that if we knew what we said we did, we should have some definitive way of showing that it is the case, and that we're not deceived. That proves far more difficult than people assume. We could sketch out the schema of the argument being made here. Let 'p' stand for any given belief you might have, and claim to know:

(1)   If I know that p, then I know that I'm not being deceived.
(2)   I don't know that I'm not being deceived.
(3)   Therefore, I don't know that p.

Both (1) and (2) are hard to deny, so (3) is hard to escape. Things look bad if we hope to have knowledge.

Here is where epistemic contextualists have stepped in with a novel argument. They suggest that 'know' (and perhaps some other epistemic terms) are context-sensitive, much like expressions that we considered in entries #21–22. 'Know' is not like a pronoun or other obviously context-sensitive expressions, but its meaning might shift in the way that an expression like 'tall' seems to shift. There is a standard at work (often implicitly) when we use that expression, and it shifts according to the topic of conversation. For adults, 'tall' might include anyone over six feet in its extension; for young children, that might be four feet; for buildings, it might be a few hundred feet. As we saw earlier, 'know' implies that someone has met standards for evidence or justification. Those standards might be higher or lower in different contexts, and so we might know that p in ordinary contexts, but not know that p in others (say, when we start discussing epistemology with skeptics). Thus, depending on what was said in an actual conversation to convince us of (2) in the argument above, we might even say that a shift in context had occurred, and that while we would have to admit (3) in this context, we might say just the opposite in others.

To see how this might work, Stewart Cohen (1999) imagines two people, John and Mary, who are flying from Los Angeles to New York. They believe that there is a layover in Chicago, and this is extremely important to them, because there is someone they expect to meet on urgent business in the Chicago airport before travelling on to New York. Suppose Smith, a fellow passenger, glances at his own itinerary and says, "Yes, I know – it does stop in Chicago." Smith's casual check of his itinerary is not enough assurance for John and Mary given all that they have at stake, and they seek better evidence. We could say that there are competing standards here – the casual, "low-stakes" standards of Smith, and the more demanding "high-stakes" standards of John and Mary. We could imagine even higher standards that might be in place, like perfect certainty. Which of these is the correct standard for knowledge? John and Mary's? Smith's? A demanding skeptic's? What does 'know' *mean* in this sense?

One answer would be that there is only one standard that never varies. It might be high-stakes or low-stakes, but it would give us invariant truth-conditions for sentences like 'Smith knows the plane stops in Chicago.' But Cohen gives a different answer: there is no one standard for knowledge, and no single correct answer. What 'know' means and what degree of justification requires varies with the context in which we ask the question. While these speakers may be using the same English words and perhaps uttering the same English sentences in some cases, they are expressing different propositions, which incorporate different standards for 'know.' This point about sentences and propositions can be difficult, but think of a sentence like 'I grew up in Maryland.' Given the context-sensitivity of the word 'I,' that sentence will express different propositions when I say it than when you do (perhaps it's even true when I say it, but not when you do).

So, it will go with 'know,' the contextualist is saying. The sentence 'Michael knows that p' may express different propositions in different contexts, not because 'Michael' refers to different people, but because 'knows' implies different standards, depending on what is at stake in the conversation.

Given his interests, Smith had adopted one (low-stakes) standard. The urgency of John and Mary's situation left less room for error and changed the conversational context, introducing greater demands and higher standards. As their interests shift, the nature of the context shifts, and the propositions expressed by the sentences they utter change, as well. Just as standards and truth-conditions for 'tall' shift when the conversation turns from people to buildings, so the standards and truth-conditions for 'know' shift as our interests do. It is not difficult to raise those standards with philosophical questions; for instance, as ambitions for a general theory of knowledge leave less room for error and amplify the importance of remote possibilities of deception and error. And this, the contextualist will say, is how the skeptic ensnares us. They shift the focus of our conversation, raising the standards much higher, but they smuggle in the assumption that the same standards must apply when we stop doing philosophy, even though the context has changed.

RESPONSES

Much of the literature on epistemic contextualism has been focused on epistemic issues with only passing attention to semantic ones. Readings and responses suggested here are thus selected for their focus on the linguistic aspects of this debate. Stewart Cohen (1999, 2000) and Keith DeRose (2002, 2005) have been the leading advocates for epistemic contextualism over the last 30 years. The semantic case for epistemic contextualism developed gradually, under the direction of numerous authors, alongside related developments of more general views on context-sensitivity. Ludlow (2005) offers a comprehensive and even-handed review of the relevant arguments for the context-sensitivity of 'know' and offers a tentative defense of its prospects against more pessimistic appraisals. The most pessimistic of those appraisals will come from semantic minimalists such as Cappelen, Lepore, and Borg, who hold that there is very little context-sensitivity at the semantic level, and that it only occurs in well-distinguished expressions like pronouns. (See entry #22 for more details.) A succinct case against epistemic contextualism from a semantic minimalist perspective is offered in Cappelen (2017).

Many critics of epistemic contextualism have raised objections to the purported context-sensitivity of 'know.' Stanley (2004) notes that, unlike other context-sensitive terms, 'know' is not gradable. That is, a contextualist view would suggest that knowledge comes in degrees of strength, and so we should be able to use modifying expressions on terms with such gradations – e.g., 'tall' can be modified to 'very tall' or 'really tall.' Stanley (2004) and Cohen (1999) both note that 'justified' can be modified this way ('well justified,' 'fully justified'), but Stanley doubts this can be done consistently for 'know.'

Several critics have noted that context-sensitive terms can also have their context-dependencies made explicit in certain ways, as when we say, "tall *for a building*." This sounds wrong, or at least strangely evasive, when done with 'know': "I know in an everyday sense, but I don't know with certainty." Bach (2005) points out that there is nothing illegitimate about this according to epistemic contextualism. We should be able to say:

I know relative to low standards that I'm reading a book, but I don't know relative to high standards that I'm reading a book.

Again, this seems to be at odds with how we normally speak when we use the word 'know,' at least when we're speaking literally and seriously. When confronted with skeptical challenges, speakers tend to gravitate toward one standard or the other, whether that entails confessing our ignorance or dismissing skepticism as academic chicanery. Yet for a term like 'tall,' it makes perfect sense to say, "Jack is tall *for a fourth-grader*, but not tall *for a building*." When we make explicit that we seem to have lower standards in some contexts that are then brought up by skeptical challenges, most speakers find it difficult to reconcile the two and return to lower standards once the challenges have been made. (This is the dismal trajectory of introductory epistemology classes.) Pritchard (2001) has called this the "problem of epistemic descent," and doubts that there is a satisfactory contextualist resolution of it (though it may be possible on non-contextualist grounds).

We might also read the standard epistemic contextualist response here as something like an error theory. Adopting an error theory toward some subject is to state that all the claims typically made about that subject are false because of some systematic misunderstanding. For instance, some ethicists defend error theories about moral theories because they believe there are no moral facts to report. Contextualists don't deny that there are true epistemic claims, but they do deny that philosophers and ordinary speakers correctly understand the context-sensitivity of 'know' when the skeptic starts toying with their intuitions. This would imply that the apparent tension between everyday knowledge ascriptions and responses to skeptical challenges is the result of a persistent, systematic error in our understanding of the meanings of our words. Schiffer (1996) would be the first of many to object that this was an implausible reading of our grasp of our own language. How much credence we can assign to epistemic contextualism depends heavily on how convincing we find Cohen and DeRose's characterizations of common usage in response to this.

RECOMMENDED READINGS

MAJOR WORKS

Cohen, S. 1999. "Contextualism, Skepticism, and the Structure of Reasons." *Nous Supplement (Philosophical Perspectives 13: Epistemology)* 33: 57–89.

Cohen, S. 2000. "Contextualism and Skepticism." *Nous Supplement (Philosophical Issues 10: Skepticism)* 34: 94–107.

DeRose, K. 2002. "Contextualism and Knowledge Attributions." *Philosophy and Phenomenological Research* 52 (4): 913–929.

DeRose, K. 2005. "The Ordinary Language Basis for Contextualism, and the New Invariantism." *The Philosophical Quarterly* 55 (219): 172–198.

RESPONSES

Bach, K. 2005. "The Emperor's New 'Knows'." In *Contextualism in Philosophy: Knowledge, Meaning and Truth*, edited by G. Preyer and G. Peter, 51–89. New York: Oxford University Press.

Cappelen, H. 2017. "Semantic Minimalism and Speech Act Pluralism Applied to 'Knows'." In *The Routledge Handbook of Epistemic Contextualism*, edited by J. Jenkins Ichikawa, 230–239. New York: Routledge.

Ludlow, P. 2005. "Contextualism and the New Linguistic Turn in Epistemology." In *Contextualism in Philosophy: Knowledge, Meaning and Truth*, edited by G. Preyer and G. Peter, 11–50. New York: Oxford University Press.

Pritchard, D. 2001. "Contextualism, Skepticism, and the Problem of Epistemic Descent." *Dialectica* 55: 327–349.

Schiffer, S. 1996. "Contextualist Solutions to Skepticism." *Proceedings of the Aristotelian Society* 96: 317–333.

Stanley, J. 2004. "On the Linguistic Basis for Contextualism." *Philosophical Studies* 119: 119–146.

'EVERY MAN WHO OWNS A DONKEY BEATS IT'

Background: In entry #17, we saw the seminal analysis of definite descriptions that Russell offered, resolving three longstanding puzzles and suggesting a distinctive account of propositions, just for good measure. We could think of that as beginning with an analysis of the logical form expressed by the English word 'the' in typical settings. The puzzle in this entry could be framed as starting with worries about how to analyze the English word 'a' (or 'an').

Our topic in this entry concerns further attempts to analyze the underlying logical forms of some garden-variety expressions. To motivate this puzzle, we need to understand two distinctions: indefinite descriptions and anaphora. To understand indefinite descriptions, it is best to start with a contrast. A *definite* description like 'the first person to run a four-minute mile' purports to denote exactly one thing; we call it a "proper" definite description if it does so. An *indefinite* description like 'a middle-distance runner' does not imply this sort of unique denotation; lots of people can be middle-distance runners, while only one person could be *the* first to run a four-minute mile. An indefinite description does not demand a unique referent in this way, even if we sometimes have one in mind when we use one. I might say, "There

DOI: 10.4324/9781003183167-35

is *a greatest prime number less than a million*" even if I don't yet know what that number is. Or I could announce to one of my classes, "I will select a student each day to complete a problem on the board," not knowing which student or which problem it will be until much later.

Anaphora is a type of relation that may exist between expressions in a sentence or a conversation. It occurs when one expression has its denotation determined by the denotation of the other expression, along with their syntactical roles. A prime example of this would be pronouns:

(1)   *Gregg* will attend the meeting if *he* can.

Here, 'he' denotes whoever is denoted by 'Gregg' earlier in the sentence. The pronoun stands in for the noun that was already introduced. It is typical for the anaphorically dependent expression (the 'he' in (1)) to come after the expression on which it depends, but it can precede it, too. ("*You*'re a mean one, *Mr. Grinch!*") Anaphora can occur across many sentences in a conversation, assuming all the speakers grasp what the pronouns are pointing towards. Sentences can also have overlapping anaphoric chains:

(2)   *Gregg* will drive <u>Hanna</u> to the airport if <u>she</u> calls *him*.

So now we come to the puzzle. It begins with an example from Peter Geach (1962):

(3)   Every farmer who owns a donkey beats it.

Note the indefinite description, 'a donkey,' and its anaphoric dependent, 'it.' Thanks to Geach's example, sentences with this sort of mix of indefinite description and anaphora have come to be known as "donkey sentences" or instances of "donkey anaphora." They seem to be linked in the same ways as the pronouns above, though here we have no names to anchor the anaphoric chains. We will find ourselves in the realm of quantifiers and variables, instead. But Russell showed us the way with that, right? We should seek some uniform way of analyzing indefinite descriptions like these, just as he did with definite descriptions. Russell suggested that indefinite descriptions should be read as implying existential quantification – i.e., implying that there is at least one thing that fits the description. Thus:

(4)   Michael bought a Warwick bass and it sounds great.

The appearance of the indefinite description, 'a Warwick bass,' implies the existence of such an instrument, and 'it' may be read as an anaphoric dependent that we can symbolize with the same variable, indicating that it is the same object mentioned earlier.

Indefinite descriptions will resist a simple, uniform treatment in this vein, however. Consider:

(5)   A dog has a spine.
(6)   A dog bit my leg.

Sentence (5) gives us a generalization about the class of all dogs: every one of them has a spine. A universal quantifier would be part of its logical form, and in this sort of case, indefinite descriptions are sometimes called *distributive* terms. (As in, they are distributing a property to everything in that class.) But in (6), just one dog is being denoted, and an existential quantifier would be part of its logical form instead. In these cases, indefinite descriptions are being used as *referential* terms.[1] So, back to (3). Is 'a donkey' a referential or a distributive term there? Paraphrasing a bit, which reading should we adopt(?):

(3')   Any farmer who owns a donkey beats at least one of the donkeys he owns.
(3'')   Any farmer who owns a donkey beats all of the donkeys he owns.

The 'it' suggests a single object. Suppose I said, "If we get a dog, you have to take care of it." But, in interpreting (3), that would lead us to the reading in (3'), and this seems like a very strange reading. We're generalizing about the donkey-owners and the donkeys they own, which makes it strange to think of a single donkey being picked out. It does not seem that a referential reading of the indefinite description fits. We seem to be generalizing over both the donkey-owners and the donkeys. But how can we read that sort of shift in the logical form of the sentence from the way it is composed at the level of its surface grammar? The heart of the issue is that we have an indefinite description inside the antecedent of a conditional (as part of the logical form of a generalization), and an anaphoric dependent inside another relative clause, but we lack a procedure for handling such distant parts of sentences that does not create problems of scope. This may sound abstruse and technical at first, but it strikes at the heart of the analytic approach to language that had been the orthodox view since Russell and Frege. Substantial revisions and extensions of the project would be necessary.

RESPONSES

Most of the responses to the problem of donkey sentences have fallen into one of two approaches. Most have either adopted a new category of "E-type pronouns" first introduced by Evans (1985) or adopted a form of dynamic semantics. Each of them marks a significant extension or departure from the models of denotation, quantification, and the interpretation of pronouns, so I will describe each at some length.

Evans notes that it is generally agreed that some pronouns with quantifier antecedents function like bound variables, but parts ways with Geach on how many do, and how we should treat others. Bound variables, strictly speaking, don't refer; the 'x' or 'y' in the scope of a quantifier is not secretly designating an object. Their purpose is to express logical forms that don't involve commitment to such designation, even if we happen to have someone in mind in the context of a conversation. (I might be thinking of LeBron James when I read a sentence like 'x is tall,' but that's not what that sentence *says*.). But Evans suggests that some pronoun–antecedent pairs do have referring pronouns that should not be interpreted as bound variables. Instead, in some cases, "a pronoun refers to whatever its singular antecedent refers to" (1985, p. 79). These are E-type pronouns. This is straightforward enough in sentences (1) and (2), but what of (3) and others where quantifier phrases appear?

Evans offers a principle (1985, pp. 89–92) by which the truth conditions of such sentences depend on an interpretation of their quantified phrases and whether there is a true substitution instance of the right form for existential quantifiers, or if every substitution instance comes out true in the case of universal quantifiers. So 'Some man loves his mother' is true just in case there is some substitution instance of the form '(β) loves () mother' where β is some singular term (like 'Gregg' or 'LeBron James') and the empty parentheses on the right are taken to co-refer with β. Universal quantifier phrases would operate in a similar fashion, except that we would imagine all the substitution instances of the form being true. In this way, the scope and quantifier ambiguities that plagued donkey sentences would be resolved. If those pronouns are not to be interpreted as bound variables, then scopes are not at issue, and they need not complicate our reading of the quantifier phrase.

Evans defends this account at length against Geach's arguments, but wrote little more on the subject due to his early death. Neale (1990) would later refine some elements of the E-type approach. The net effect of an E-type pronoun is thus much like a definite description, pointing back to the earlier referent in the sentence. We might paraphrase an E-type reading of (3) as "Every person who owns a donkey beats the donkey that he owns." Elbourne (2001) suggests that this should be understood as 'NP-deletion,' or the deletion of a noun phrase that an audience may infer from a speaker's earlier utterance – e.g., "I like Gregg's car, but not Hanna's" – in which 'car' is deleted from the latter phrase in the sentence. Abbott (2002) suggests that we might model anaphoric dependents on demonstratives instead – i.e., 'it' in (3) functions much like 'that' when we point to something. Berger (2002) critiques both Evans's and Neale's accounts, proposing revisions and a formal semantics for plural quantification to address the issues he raises. (He also critiques dynamic approaches to donkey anaphora, which are described below.) Morton (2015) has recently suggested a novel quantifier treatment – neither universal nor existential – to address donkey sentences that he defines in set-theoretical terms.

The second major group of responses to the problems of donkey anaphora come from a family of theories known as "dynamic semantics," inspired by the work of Heim (1982) and Kamp (1981), which departs from numerous assumptions in analytic philosophy. Dynamic accounts of semantics presuppose that truth-conditions belong primarily to entire discourses and to individual sentences only in a derivative sense. Different accounts will construe a discourse differently, but they will attempt to capture the information at work in a conversation as a structured whole, rather than as a collection of atomic parts. This de-emphasis on the truth-conditions of individual sentences allowed a dynamic understanding of their role and contribution to a discourse. Heim likens the information and structure of discourse to a filing cabinet whose files may be updated by adding, subtracting, or replacing informational contents. The "files" of a discourse will track sets of referents that are available in conversation for purposes of anaphoric reference. The details of dynamic semantics are challenging, and I'm only offering the briefest of glosses here. For a primer on dynamic semantics with special consideration of donkey sentences, see Yelcin (2012). Heim (1990) addresses E-type pronoun strategies extensively, focusing on the presupposition of uniqueness on which they depend, and finds efforts to develop a general strategy with them unconvincing. (See Elbourne (2001) for some criticism of Heim (1990).) Chierchia (1995) continues this critique of E-type strategies, but ultimately treats them as "coexisting mechanisms rather than mutually exclusive alternatives" (230), both of which are necessary parts of a general account of anaphora. Schlenker (2011) and Grosz *et al.* (2015) both describe empirical research that they contend supports a dynamic semantics approach over E-type strategies.

NOTE

1. For those who know some logic:

    (5★) $(\forall x)(Dx \rightarrow Sx)$

    (6★) $(\exists x)(Dx \wedge Bxm)$

RECOMMENDED READINGS

MAJOR WORKS

Evans, G. 1985. "Pronouns, Quantifiers, and Relative Clauses (I)." In *Collected Papers*, 76–152. Oxford: Clarendon Press.

Geach, P. 1962. *Refernce and Generality*. Ithaca: Cornell University Press.

Heim, I. 1982. *The Semantics of Definite and Indefinite Noun Phrases*. Amherst: University of Masschusetts.

Kamp, H. 1981. "A Theory of Discourse Representation." In *Formal Methods in the Study of Language*, edited by J. Groenendijk, T. Janssen, and M. Stokhof, 277–322. Amsterdam: Mathematical Centre.

RESPONSES

Abbott, B. 2002. "Donkey Demonstratives." *Natural Language Semantics* 10 (4): 285–298.

Berger, A. 2002. *Terms and Truth: Reference Direct and Anaphoric.* Cambridge: The MIT Press.

Chierchia, G. 1995. *Dynamics of Meaning: Anaphora, Presupposition, and the Theory of Grammar.* Chicago: University of Chicago Press.

Elbourne, P. 2001. "E-Type Anaphora as NP-Deletion." *Natural Language Semantics* 9 (3): 241–288.

Grosz, P., P. Patel-Grosz, E. Fedorenko, and E. Gibson. 2015. "Constraints on Donkey Pronouns." *Journal of Semantics* 32: 619–648.

Heim, I. 1990. "E-Type Pronouns and Donkey Anaphora." *Linguistics and Philosophy* 13 (2): 137–177.

Morton, A. 2015. "A Solution to the Donkey Sentence Problem." *Analysis* 75 (4): 554–557.

Neale, S. 1990. "Descriptive Pronouns and Donkey Anaphora." *Journal of Phliosophy* 87 (3): 113–150.

Schlenker, P. 2011. "Donkey Anaphora: The View from Sign Language (ASL and LSF)." *Linguistics and Philosophy* 34: 341–395.

Yelcin, S. 2012. "Dynamic Semantics." In *The Routledge Companion to Philosophy of Language*, edited by G. Russell and D. Graff Fara, 253–279. New York: Routledge.

25

'I'

Background: Entry #21 introduced classes of expressions whose "character" (to use Kaplan's term) was consistent, but whose designation varies with the context in which they are uttered and can only be fully interpreted once they are actually used. That approach remained consonant with the analytic philosophy of language that preceded it, as it suggested that the interpretation of those indexicals and the propositions their sentences expressed would be complete once we had assigned fixed semantic contents for those indexical ones. Arguments for de se content suggest there is more at stake.

In entry #21, we talked about words that could be called "indexicals." Those were words that derive at least part of their meaning from the context in which someone uses them. We know the meaning of pronouns like 'I' or 'you' or 'she' in part by knowing who is speaking, who they are speaking to, and who they are speaking about. Likewise, 'here' designates the place from which someone is speaking, and 'now' designates some span of time in which they are speaking. If a server in a restaurant says to me, "Your order is ready now" at 3:00 on December 1, 2022, then 'your' implies that the order belongs to Michael Padraic Wolf, and 'now' designates 3:00 on December 1, 2022. If that same server says that same sentence to someone else at another time, then it will be about another person's

DOI: 10.4324/9781003183167-36

order, ready at some other time. Even though 'your' and 'now' are the same English words in all those utterances, they mean slightly different things, because part of their meaning depends on the context in which they are uttered.

When we notice this, it is not unreasonable to wonder if these context-sensitive expressions are more trouble than they are worth. At first look, they seem to simply stand in for more precise sorts of expressions that tell us exactly what we're talking about. Assuming my full name – Michael Padraic Wolf – names me uniquely, then why not use that name instead of 'I' when Michael Padraic Wolf is the one who is speaking? We could do the same for all the other names and nouns, of course. This way, we would have fewer words to acquire in learning a language, but would be able to convey as much information, ask the same questions, etc. Admittedly, this sounds very strange to typical English speakers. Saying "Michael Padraic Wolf will be right back" before I left a room would sound . . . odd. People who talk about themselves in the third person this way often sound narcissistic or conceited, as though they are listening to someone else's play-by-play commentary on their successes. Still, feeling "weird" is not a very strong case for a philosophical point. Many things evoke that feeling at first, only to feel familiar later.

John Perry has made an argument that there are much stronger reasons for thinking that we must have indexicals like 'I' and 'now' in our language. If we did not have words like these in our language, we would lose the capacity to say and believe a wide variety of things. Other words – even if they referred to the same people and things – could not replace them. To see why this might be, imagine two scenarios, slightly adapted from Perry's original article. Suppose one day, I – Michael Padraic Wolf – am pushing a cart through a supermarket. I tend to weave between aisles when I shop, doubling back when I remember something I need. On this particular trip, I notice that there is a trail of sugar running through the middle of several of the aisles. I pick up my pace a bit, hoping to catch up with the person who's leaving sugar all over the floor. I look down at my cart, make a critical discovery, and I say or think to myself:

(1)   Oh! *I* am the one leaving sugar all over the place! It's *my* bag
        in *my* cart that's leaking!

Perry said that there is something more at work here than a report of a fact about whose bag of sugar is leaking. When I recognize that *I* am the person in question here, or that it is *my* bag that is leaking, there is an essential quality to my understanding the involves being the person saying and believing these things. In this case, that has a practical dimension: *I* am the one who needs to *do* something about my leaky bag; it is not just idle information about the world.

We can also see that similar things hold for indexicals that involve time, like 'now.' Suppose I look at my calendar and notice that there is an important meeting I need to attend from 2:00 to 3:00 today. A moment later, I look at a clock or my phone and see that the time is 2:03 p.m. I imagine I would say something like:

(2)   Oh no! That meeting is going on **now**!

Part of saying or thinking this – and properly grasping the meaning of it all – is recognizing that my utterance or thought is taking place at the time in question. Replacing that with a phrase specifying the time gives us a sentence that apparently reports the same fact:

(3)   Oh no! That meeting is going on at 2:03!

This leaves out the urgency of the original sentence, though – the *nowness* of what it says, we might say. Can we add that in this way?

(4)   Oh no! That meeting takes place from 2:00 until 3:00, and it is currently 2:03!

Sentence (4) does not seem as wrong as sentence (3), but of course this is because we added the word 'currently,' which is context-sensitive in much the same way that 'now' would be.

If Perry is right, then there is a way in which we center ourselves (or our position or time) when we say or believe these things. His work on this problem echoed themes from Castañeda (1968) and Lewis (1979), who had introduced the notion of *de se* content. This would be content that involves the self-ascription of properties: '*de se*' means, roughly, 'about oneself' and contrasts with '*de dicto*' ('about the word') and '*de re*' ('about the thing'). The ascription of properties to oneself, and recognizing oneself in that ascription, is an essential feature on these views. It is what was absent from my thoughts in our example above as I walked around, spilling sugar, and it is what is notably added when I say or think (1). It makes no difference to what is believed whether it is I or someone else who believes something like "There is no largest prime number." But (1)-(2) have types of *de se* content that do involve me in a way that cannot be replaced by an expression with no such content. This marked a significant challenge to the orthodox view of belief among analytic philosophers, which was that belief was a type of relation between an agent and a proposition. There are numerous schools of thought on how to account for propositions, but they tended to agree that propositions should be thought of as content independent of particular speakers and their thoughts and attitudes. *De se* content, if there is such a thing, would rule out that assumption, at least for some beliefs and propositions.

There are numerous different types of indexicals, but these two examples I have recounted from Perry are especially important to our reasons and explanations for action and our agency. It is one thing to speak in the abstract about the motives, intentions, and commitments that someone might have, but it is quite another to talk about what *I* must do, or why *I* chose to do it. Ideally, I could write out a list of all things I might do or have to do in a lifetime, but quite another to recognize that I'm living and acting at one of those times – that one of those is *now*! The urgency of getting to that meeting – of acting and having a reason to act – finds its place in the language through expressions like these.

RESPONSES

Given the profound effects that *de se* content would have for most accounts of belief and propositions, numerous objections have been raised since Perry and Lewis published their papers on this subject. Ruth Garrett Millikan (1990) argued that the purported examples motivating Perry were essential but were not indexicals. In her view, their contents do not shift with changes in context, even if self-reference figures prominently in the psychological functions they play. Banick (2019) follows suit in criticizing the inference from self-ascriptive thought to special types of semantic content. Instead, "*de se* thought rather places constraints on one's prior account of the way the self appears in experience, and not on the theory of propositions or propositional attitudes in semantics" (929). On Lewis's account, a possible world might be centered on something or some spatiotemporal region within it (such as the region a person occupies), and a class of such centered worlds would correspond to a property (1979, p. 532). Beliefs with *de se* content would have such properties as their objects, rather than propositions. Alward (2009) defends an analysis of beliefs as relations between agents and propositions and offers an account of explanations of behavior to refine a version of this view. Magidor (2015) contends both that Lewis's initial move to this view is unmotivated, and that several problems in the ascription of propositional attitudes are not solved even if we do make that move.

One of the most widely discussed set of criticisms of Perry and Lewis in the last decade comes in Cappelen and Dever (2013). They make a point of challenging the sufficiency of Perry's argument about the indispensability of *de se* and indexical content in explaining actions. Many of Perry's examples (including those above) turn on failures of explanation when co-referring terms are substituted for indexicals. (Thus, 'Michael Padraic Wolf is late!' differs from 'I am late!' as an object of belief, when believed by me.) But Cappelen and Dever note that co-referring expressions cannot be substituted for one another in explanation contexts in general. Adapting Perry's example, someone might believe that Freddie Mercury is spilling sugar in the store and try to alert him, while not believing that Farrokh Bulsara is spilling sugar in the store, even though 'Farrokh Bulsara' co-refers with 'Freddie Mercury' just as 'Michael Padraic Wolf' co-refers with 'I' when I utter it. Both Atkins (2016) and Bermúdez (2017) reply to these arguments in Perry's defense. Torre (2017) does the same, and also responds to Magidor's (2015) criticisms. Prosser (2015) revisits and revamps the role of *de se* and first-person indexicals in explanations of action, emphasizing what he calls *first-person redundancy*. An agent need not note their own position to locate themselves in space or time to use *de se* indexicals like 'here' and 'now,' and thus may take an "epistemological shortcut" in many of their judgments and beliefs. An account of first-person perspective is then built from this, and Prosser argues for its indispensability. Hanks (2013) takes an even more unorthodox path, defending *de se* content by reimagining propositions as types of actions that we perform when we make assertions or form beliefs. An indexical like 'I' leads us to perform actions that only we ourselves can perform, unlike other propositions that can be uttered or believed without such restrictions.

RECOMMENDED READINGS

MAJOR WORKS

Lewis, D. 1979. "Attitudes De Dicto and De Se." *Philosophical Review* 88 (4): 513–543.

Perry, J. 1979/2000. "The Problem of the Essential Indexical." In *The Problem of the Essential Indexical and Other Essays*, 33–52. Oxford: Oxford University Press.

RESPONSES

Alward, P. 2009. "The Inessential Quasi-Indexical." *Philosophical Studies* 145 (2): 235–255.

Atkins, P. 2016. "The Inessential Indexical: On the Philosophical Insigificance of Perspective and the First Person by Herman Cappelen and Josh Dever (Book Review)." *Analysis* 76 (1): 99–102.

Banick, K. 2019. "What Is It Like to Think About Oneself?" *Phenomenology and the Cognitive Sciences* 18 (5): 919–932.

Bermúdez, J.L. 2017. "Yes, Essential Indexicals Really Are Essential." *Analysis* 77 (4): 690–694.

Cappelen, H., and J. Dever. 2013. *The Inessential Indexical: On the Philosophical Insigificance of Perspective and the First Person.* Oxford: Oxford University Press.

Castañeda, H.N. 1968. "On the Logic of Attributions of Seld-Knowledge to Others." *Journal of Philosophy* 54: 439–456.

Hanks, P. 2013. "First-Person Propositions." *Philosophy and Phenomenological Research* 86 (1): 155–182.

Magidor, O. 2015. "The Myth of De Se." *Philosophical Perspectives* 29 (1): 249–283.

Millikan, R. 1990. "The Myth of the Essential Indexical." *Nous* 24: 723–734.

Prosser, S. 2015. "Why Are Indexicals Essential?" *Proceedings of the Aristotelian Society* 115: 211–233.

Torre, S. 2017. "In Defense of De Se Content." *Philosophy and Phenomenological Research* 97 (1): 172–189.

26

'YOU'

Background: The context-sensitivity of expressions such as indexicals and demonstratives became an enduring challenge for analytic philosophers of language. Kaplan's work treated them by adding functions that assigned context-appropriate designations to them, but Perry's work suggested that the content of first-person indexicals was not fully exhausted by such methods. A first-person perspective is necessary in using such expressions. A further departure from traditional assumptions would be implied if second-person perspectives (recognizing others as like oneself, not simply objects in the environment) were necessary.

In entry #25, we saw arguments for the claim that first-person indexicals such as 'I' had an essential role in natural language, and that this role had profound implications for the nature of belief and semantic content. It would be reasonable to ask whether there are similar lessons to draw from second-person expressions. Like first-person expressions, there is a type of perspective that they seem to invoke. To address someone in the second person implies a mutual recognition between fellow speakers, and not simply a report of a proposition. If we use a name or a third-person pronoun, we can do so without involving that third person in the conversation as a speaker. I can mention René Descartes and *his* contributions without talking *to him*,

DOI: 10.4324/9781003183167-37

or him talking *to me*, and whatever I may say in this mode, anyone else can typically say just as well. There is an agent-neutrality to what we say in the third person that mirrors names and other proper nouns. But second person hints at something more – a kind of content that necessarily involves other speakers.

There have been many authors who have stressed the fundamentally social nature of natural language, emphasizing that it emerges only among communities of speakers who regularly recognize and engage one another in conversation. As Donald Davidson put it, "The point of the concept of a language . . . is to enable us to give a coherent description of the behavior of speakers, and of what speakers and their interpreters know that allows them to communicate" (1992, pp. 256–257). Those interpretations in actual conversations are most typically expressed with the second person: I make a guess at what *you* are trying to say. Davidson's views on this appear to deviate from Wittgenstein's views on rule-following and the impossibility of private language, discussed in entries #11–15.

But even if we *typically* engage others in the second person in this and other ways, that doesn't yet show that it is *essential* that we do so. We can undertake a thought experiment here, much like those we considered in entry #25. Can we imagine a language with the expressive powers of our own, but without second-person expressions? Some uses of the second person are readily analyzed or paraphrased away. For instance:

(1)   You should drink eight glasses of water a day.

This makes use of 'you,' but only as a stylistic way of making a general ascription of a commitment. It could be replaced without apparent loss with:

(1')   Everyone should drink eight glasses of water a day.

Many uses of 'you' and related expressions have this sort of generic role. It might also be possible to paraphrase many second-person plural expressions this way. If I say "You're welcome to ask questions" to a roomful of people assembled for an event, that might be paraphrased as "Everyone in attendance is welcome to ask questions." These are just initial fragments of a strategy, but they already suggest a weaker position for second-person expressions.

What about more typical uses of the second person, where one person speaks directly to another using 'you?' Could these expressions be replaced with proper names, or third-person pronouns? It would sound very strange to meet someone for the first time and have them say to me, "It's a pleasure to meet Michael Padraic Wolf," instead of "It's a pleasure to meet you," but not incomprehensibly strange. To motivate this as a possible strategy, imagine an interaction. Suppose I work at a business where my manager sets the schedule every week. A schedule is regularly posted, but we also have a message board placed where all the employees can see it. One day, I come in and see a message:

(2)   Flynn called in sick, so Michael will cover the 12–8 shift.

Reading this, I think or say:

(3)   Oh, I'm covering the 12–8 shift.

Nothing here seems all that strange. I read (2) and infer what I say in (3) without difficulty. My manager could have found me and said, "*You* will cover the 12–8 shift," but my capacity for practical reason leads me to the same result in (2)-(3). Now, imagine a community of speakers that can use first- and third-person expressions in these ways (along with names and other nouns), but they also say things this way to one another in direct, face-to-face conversation. My manager says (2) to me, and I say or think (3). While this would feel strangely impersonal to our ears, it appears that this allows him to assign properties and commitments to me, and for me to interpret them, giving me the same payoff I would get from a second-person address. Speakers can report and ascribe properties, obligations, etc., to other specific speakers, and those speakers can recognize them. So, if we imagine a community of speakers with no second-person expressions, but all our other linguistic resources at their disposal, then what, if anything, would they lack?

What our thought experiment suggests is that any essential contribution that second-person expressions make won't be a matter of truth or designation. That was what we found with first-person indexicals, but the case for their essential role was located in our capacity for action and practical reasoning about actions. Darwall (2006) has argued that moral claims and moral discourse depend on a type of second-person perspective. It is a perspective we take up when we make claims to one another and acknowledge both those claims and the speaker making them. This may be made explicit with second-person pronouns, though it will often remain implicit among speakers who understand how they are interacting. Darwall notes that moral discourse involves numerous types of address (claims, commands, etc.) that state what he calls "second-person reasons," and that the second-person standpoint figures in the authority of the speaker making an address, the authority of their addressee to acknowledge that authority (or reject it), and the competence of the addressee to respond to those reasons and act accordingly. When a speaker addresses someone with a moral claim or command, a necessary condition of the speech act is that the speaker purports to have an authority to make it that the addressee can and should acknowledge. The speaker might not have that authority. In our thought experiment, I would surely reject the inconvenient demand of a midnight shift if I thought the message had been written by someone other than the manager. And offering such second-person reasons to another speaker presumes that there is an addressee who is competent to understand those reasons and acknowledge the addresser's entitlement to make them, and who is responsible for acting on them. These are conditions that can only be met by a language in which speakers can speak *to* someone and be spoken *to* in the second person. Darwall's work echoes themes in Anscombe (1957). (See Roessler (2014) for additional insight on Anscombe's work and its relation to Darwall's.) Garfield (2019) follows a related line of thought, suggesting that the second-person standpoint is even more deeply woven into our thought and identity, with attention to how this theme plays a role in Asian philosophical traditions. Garfield notes that, in both strains of contemporary analytic philosophy and classical Indian Buddhism, first-person access to our own states develops via interpretation of our interactions with second-persons figures: "we can only know ourselves as subjects to the extent that others address us, and that we address others, in the context of a mutual expectation of understanding" (2019, p. 49)

RESPONSES

Some critics have objected that appeals to a second-person stand-point are more suggestive than enlightening, especially if they are to play essential roles in such wide swaths of discourse. Heal (2014) and Lavin (2014) both attempt to articulate the distinctive features of the second-person standpoint. These are not necessarily defenses of Dar-wall's views, especially of the most granular details, but their responses will be useful to anyone with an interest in the topic. Heal's account emphasizes giving reasons to others to elicit their contributions to cooperative activity. Lavin suggests that the second person matters to us in light of the "problem of other wills;" that, in exercising prac-tical reason, we must ask, "What is it to encounter, recognize, and understand the practical significance of another will?" (280). Lavin sees efforts to incorporate the second person into ethics as an attempt to address this problem, but worries that much is left unsaid or unex-plained in Darwall's account. For more direct criticisms of Darwall on second-person reasons and the fundamental status of second-person indexicals, see Yaffe (2010), Börchers (2014), Rowland (2020), and Verdejo (2021).

Lance and Kukla (2013) acknowledge Darwall as an important contributor to the case for second-person reasons and their linguis-tic expression, but argue that he and earlier proponents have focused almost exclusively on contracting and agreement in second-person relationships. Those types of second-person reasons may entail that second-person expressions are essential parts of a natural language, as we have been considering, but they won't be rich or varied enough to account for the full range of moral and other normative relationships. Whereas other proponents of second-person interactions stressed speech acts that would result in contract-like obligations, they focus on a range of second-person "calls" (to use their term) that oper-ate differently and unpack their normative structures. Requests, for instance, are just as essentially second-personal as obligation-confer-ring calls, but for the person called to take a friendly request as obliga-tion-conferring is to misunderstand the call altogether. ("Hey, do you want to hang out this weekend?" "Well, if I *have to*, I guess."). Acts of defiance will also have a more rich, nuanced structure than a simple rejection of someone else's authority to make a second-person call. An act of protest may not explicitly deny that someone has the status and institutional authority to make such calls; transgressive responses typically acknowledge the norms and statuses that they transgress, but overtly defy them to a second party to make opposition to those norms explicit. These are just a few examples, and they serve to illustrate the sort of broadening of our second-personal palette. Thus, the challenge here is not that earlier accounts don't show that involvement of the second person is essential, but that they have not been radical or ambitious enough.

Amanda Roth (2010) makes a case that Darwall's work intersects fruitfully with an existing body of work in feminist epistemology, including authors such as Annette Baier (1981) and Lorraine Code (1987). An important theme running through this literature is that much of Western epistemology since Descartes emphasizes autonomy and self-reliance in the pursuit of knowledge to a degree that distorts our self-understanding. As Baier puts it, "The second person, the pronoun of mutual address and recognition, introduces us to the first and third, and to that relationship between first person ascriptions and others . . . ." (186). (On this point, it may be useful for readers to compare with Heal (2014), who contends that "'you' is 'we minus I.'") Knowledge is always pursued in cooperation with others to various degrees, and it is by calls to justify our beliefs to others that they rise to the level of knowledge, rather than mere habits.

RECOMMENDED READINGS

MAJOR WORKS

Darwall, S. 2006. *The Second Person Standpoint: Morality, Respect, and Accountability.* Cambridge: Harvard University Press.

Davidson, D. 1992. "The Second Person." *Midwest Studies in Philosophy* 17 (1): 255–267.

Lance, M., and Q. Kukla. 2013. "Leave the Gun; Take the Cannoli! The Pragmatic Topography of Second-Person Calls." *Ethics* 123 (3): 456–478.

RESPONSES

Anscombe, G.E.M. 1957. *Intention.* Oxford: Blackwell.

Baier, A. 1981. "Cartesian Persons." *Philosophia* 10 (3–4): 169–188.

Börchers, F. 2014. "Darwall on Action and the Idea of a Second-Personal Reason." *Philosophical Topics* 42 (1): 243–270.

Code, L. 1987. *What Can She Know?* Ithaca: Cornell University Press.

Garfield, J. 2019. "Second Persons and the Constitution of the First Person." *Humana Mente* 12 (36): 42–66.

Heal, J. 2014. "Second Person Thought." *Philosophical Explorations* 17 (3): 317–331.

Lavin, D. 2014. "Other Wills: The Second Person in Ethics." *Philosophical Explorations* 17 (3): 279–288.

Roessler, J. 2014. "Reason Explanation and the Second Person Perspective." *Philosophical Explorations* 17 (3): 346–357.

Roth, A. 2010. "Second-Personal Respect, the Experiential Aspect of Respect, and Feminist Philosophy." *Hypatia* 25 (2): 316–333.

Rowland, R. 2020. "Moral Error Theory Without Epistemic Eror Theory: Scepticism About Second-Personal Reasons." *Philosohical Quarterly* 70 (280): 547–569.

Verdejo, V. 2021. "The Second Person Perspective." *Erkenntnis* 86 (6): 1693–1711.

Yaffe, G. 2010. "Comment on Stephen Darwall's the Second Person Standpoint: Morality, Respect and Accountability." *Philosophy and Phenomenological Research* 81 (1): 246–252.

'WE'

Background: In entry #21, we saw how semanticists have attempted to interpret indexicals as context-sensitive expressions that could be associated with persons, times, etc., linked to the context of their utterance. In entries #25–26, we saw the introduction of first-person and second-person perspectives as essential elements for the use of some context-sensitive expressions. "Plural subjects" – groups of people joining in some statement – pose a further challenge. Groups don't share consciousness or beliefs in familiar ways, yet groups can announce commitments, attitudes, and other matters we typically assign only to individuals. Problems of collective intentionality thus present themselves when "we" say something.

Pronouns complicate the semantic models that many analytic philosophers have adopted. They demand interpretations each time they appear in a context of conversation; 'I' can be read as 'Michael P. Wolf' when I speak, sign or write something, but must be read as designating someone else when someone else speaks, writes, etc. As we saw in entry #25, this strategy may allow us to evaluate the truth of sentences containing first-person singular pronouns, but it loses something of pragmatic significance to our beliefs and actions in the process. As we saw in entry #26, there are parallel complications involving second-person pronouns.

DOI: 10.4324/9781003183167-38

All those earlier discussions centered on first- and second-person singular pronouns, we might note. They are 'I' examples, not 'we' examples. (For a review of the finer-grained semantic and grammatical details of first-person plurals, see Ritchie (2018).) Do we find the same features popping up again? As far as a substitution of context-insensitive expressions goes, this seems to be the case. Suppose you show me pictures of NBA legend Michael Jordan, actor Michael K. Williams, and former Orioles pitcher Mike Mussina. You ask me what I have in common with all of them, and I say:

(1)   We all have the name 'Michael.'

The 'we' here is what philosophers have called a "lazy" use of a pronoun. There are no important practical or logical entanglements between the four of us, so the sentence could be rewritten with all the names and not say anything informatively different. It's just easier to say (1) instead of a much longer sentence.

Perry's account also touched on the content of belief, which might add a wrinkle. Philosophers differ on how to account for belief, but most take it as a psychological state that could not be shared by two or more people simultaneously. You and I might have beliefs with the same content – e.g., we both believe that Pittsburgh is west of Philadelphia – but we're not "in each other's heads," experiencing the same particular state at the same time. Why is this a worry? Suppose a group of people have a friend with serious drug and alcohol problems. They might confront this friend by saying:

(2)   We believe you need some help.

A group might make a statement like this without an explicit survey of everyone's beliefs. Maybe one member of the group doubts that the measures that will be suggested (rehabilitation, counseling, etc.) are really needed, but feels obliged to at least urge the friend to slow down. This might be read as a "lazy" pronoun, distributing the belief to everyone in the group; but that sounds slightly dubious if we're going to suggest that it applies in every possible case.

There are even more challenging cases, though:

(3)   We support the current proposal.
(4)   We seek your help on this matter.

In (3)-(4), there are pragmatic features that aren't readily addressed by "lazy" collections of referents. Sentence (3) may be read as a commissive in Austin's sense; it commits whoever "we" are to do something. This type of statement is regularly made publicly by an institution or a group that states their position as a group, but it may not distribute to each of its members as an individual attitude. A policy statement like this ideally reflects consensus, but even in the best cases, that consensus is rarely universal. Sentence (4) solicits help from some party, but this does not entail a personal act of soliciting from each member of "we." The president of a university might make a statement such as (3), even if some faculty object, and probably regularly makes statements like (4) without most of the faculty, staff, and students being party to the request at all. None of this undermines what is said in (3)-(4), however.

Sentences (3)-(4) (and probably (2) as well) appear to invoke what might be called a *corporate body*, or an exercise of *collective agency*, in which a group of language users speak or act as a single, unified entity rather than a mere collection of individuals. Where there is collective agency – a group of people somehow acting, choosing, etc., as one – there is a question of their *collective* intentionality (or *joint* intentionality). And here, we found ourselves with a puzzle born out of conflicting assumptions. On the one hand, we typically assume that a particular intention to do something is a mental state that can belong to no more than one person, even if others have the same *type* of intention. Only I am having my particular thoughts, even if you're thinking the same types of things. On the other hand, perfectly ordinary uses of first-person plurals commit us to some sort of intention-like state that groups of people share. What sort of thing can have group intentions, and what form can they take if they are not the particular thoughts of particular people?

RESPONSES

One potent influence on contemporary accounts of collective intentionality is Wilfrid Sellars, whose work on this subject has seen renewed interest in recent years. Taking a cue from Kant, Sellars sought an account of intentions that have a universal, categorical form. My intention to write a book this year might be reasonable, but it is reasonable only in light my other desires, plans, etc. Even if others happen to have similar intentions in parallel with mine, my personal reasons for adopting that intention don't bear on others in the same fashion. Normative claims that purport to have universal force, such as moral claims, require a notion of shared intention – "we-intention," as he called it – that people can intend for a community to which they belong without special appeal to their own attitudes and preferences. Thus, in one of Sellars's examples, 'It shall$_{we}$ be the case that our welfare is maximized' is a we-intention (with the subscript to indicate this) that members of a community can will as a categorical, moral commitment and not simply a description of their own attitudes and intentions. Sellars's work can be especially dense and intimidating for first-time readers, however. A useful entry point on these topics is Koons (2018), who unpacks the idea of we-intentions as the core of Sellars's project in ethics and develops a reading that brings it into line with an expressivist account in contemporary metaethics. (See Dach (2021) for criticism of this reading of Sellars, and her novel reading that downplays the role of we-intentions.)

Sellars's approach would have the advantage of rendering some first-person plural statements as shared commitments without the need for more exotic psychological states somehow shared by multiple people. It is well-suited to big, normative claims like the earlier examples, but many philosophers have still sought to appeal to collective intentions in various other ways. We may broadly categorize responses to the puzzle of collective intentionality into two types. Reductive (or sometimes "deflationary" or "individualist") accounts say that all collective intentions can be reduced to collections of individual intentions, suitably coordinated and consistent in their contents. Non-reductive accounts simply deny that this can be done with all collective intentions, for various reasons. For the non-reductivists, there are at least some "irreducibly plural subjects," as Margaret Gilbert calls them. Notable proponents of reductive views include Tuomela and Miller (1988), Bratman (1999) and Ludwig (2016); notable proponents of non-reductivism include List and Pettit (2011), Rovane (1998, Chapter 4), and Gilbert (2013).

For reductivists, the reasons to adopt their view are a mixture of causal, ontological, and explanatory concerns. If collective intentions were something "above and beyond" the intentions of particular agents, what kind of entity would they be? If they don't have the kind of action-determining, psychologically real character of individual intentions, then they are only being called "intentions" in an analogous sense. If they do have those features, then we would be committing to a mysterious new class of entities or properties to do our explanatory work. While we can note complex arrangements of all sorts of entities exhibiting all sorts of complex behavior, intentional systems are supposed to be rationally goal-directed. McKenna (2006) notes this and expresses "extreme skepticism that any (alleged) irreducible collective agents in fact are sufficiently sophisticated to live up to the conditions for morally responsible agency" (29). Bratman (1999) describes shared intentions as "a public, interlocking web of the intentions of the individuals" (143) in which individuals in the group have intentions about what the group will do. There is a threat of circularity lurking here: if *I* intend that *we* do something, I appear to be smuggling in collective intentions that determine what *we* will do. Bratman attempts to address this by making the intentions conditional upon the intentions of others involved in the joint action. Sadler (2006) doubts this solution can save Bratman's account, but believes that a reductivist account in the same spirit may work, though it may deflate the "joint-ness" of the actions and intentions involved.

Non-reductivists make a priority of defusing the metaphysical worries surrounding group agents. List and Pettit (2011) argue that agents are simply systems that have representational states, motivational states, and the capacity to interact with their environment when their representations fail to match their motivations (i.e., when things are not as they want or intend them to be). Group agents can have all of these states (albeit in more distributed forms) by supervening on the states of their members. Thus, a group may jointly have knowledge and thus practical capacities jointly via the interactions of their members that no one of their members can have (and so on for intentions and other states). But no part of this "group agent" is anything mysterious – only biological organisms doing what they do. The very idea of a collective state such as intention may still seem mysterious, though. Gilbert proposes that we think of it as agents intending to "emulate as far as is possible a single body (perhaps better, person) that intends to perform that action" (2013, p. 86). Copp (2006) argues that most worries from the reductivists are misguided, as collective intentions don't require appeals to "phenomenal consciousness" – the sort of unmediated, felt, sensible qualities of our waking experiences. If they don't, then shared intentions don't have to be mysterious psychological events where we peer into one another's minds, and most of the worries about them simply vanish. He further argues that reductivism would imply that every collective-intention statement must be logically and semantically equivalent to some sum-of-individual-intentions statement, and this is untenable. We would end up either denying apparently true intention-declaring sentences for the sake of consistency or radically reinterpreting countless collective-designing terms. Roelofs (2017) considers an even more drastic path: we can imagine "moderately selfless agents" for whom first-person plurals serve the roles in rational agency and intention that first-person singulars do for us. This requires a bit of speculation about future technologies and great unity among agents on moral and epistemic matters, but Roelofs argues that none of this make such selfless agents impossible or individual agents necessary, contrary to prevailing views. For such agents, 'I' might not need to serve as a concept for them at all.

RECOMMENDED READINGS

MAJOR WORKS

Gilbert, M. 2013. *Joint Commitment: How We Make the Social World*. Oxford: Oxford University Press.

Koons, J. 2018. *The Ethics of Wilfrid Sellars*. New York: Routledge.

List, C., and P. Pettit. 2011. *Group Agency: The Possibility, Design, and Status of Corporate Agents*. Oxford: Oxford University Press.

Tuomela, R., and K. Miller. 1988. "We-Intentions." *Philosophical Studies* 53: 115–137.

RESPONSES

Bratman, M. 1999. "I Intend That We J." In *Faces of Intention: Selected Essays on Intention and Agency*, 142–161. Cambridge: Cmabridge University Press.

Copp, D. 2006. "On the Agency of Certain Collective Entities: An Argument from 'Normative Autonomy'." *Midwest Studies in Philosophy* 30: 194–221.

Dach, S. 2021. "Sellars, We-Intentions and Ought Statements." *Synthèse* 198 (5): 4415–4439.

Ludwig, K. 2016. *From Individual Agency to Plural Agency: Collective Action*. Oxford: Oxford University Press.

McKenna, M. 2006. "Collective Responsibility and an Agent Meaning Theory." *Midwest Studies in Phliosophy* 30: 16–34.

Ritchie, K. 2018. "Plural and Collective Noun Phrases." In *The Routledge Handbook of Collective Intentionality*, edited by M. Jankovic and K. Ludwig, 464–475. New York: Routledge.

Roelofs, L. 2017. "Rational Agency Without Self-Knowledge: Coule 'We' Replace 'I'?" *Dialectica* 71 (1): 3–33.

Rovane, C. 1998. *The Bounds of Agency: An Essay in Revisionary Metaphysics.* Princeton: Princeton University Press.

Sadler, B.J. 2006. "Shared Intentions and Shared Responsibility." *Midwest Studies in Philosophy* 30: 115–144.

PART VI

SPEECH ACTS AND PRAGMATICS

INTRODUCTION

Earlier entries (particularly #7 and #11–15) examined the degree to which meaning itself involved practical distinctions, but the matter at hand in this section is something different. Here, we look at accounts that set aside questions of meaning itself to ask what we can do with meaningful words and sentences. In sections II through V, we focused on accounts of meaning for words and expressions in natural languages. Whether we offered the grand theory of meaning that Frege and Russell hoped for or the loose configuration of overlapping "language games" that Wittgenstein described, such accounts would inform our understanding communication. Roughly speaking, communicating is conveying information from one language to another (or to a group of users, or from one group to another, etc.). By many estimates, this is the primary purpose of a natural language. Even if that is so, it is not the only use to which we can put words and sentences. Suppose I say, "I'll need reading glasses one day." In this case, I'm communicating information to some audience: I'm predicting something; thus, describing myself in the future tense. Now imagine you ask me a favor and I say, "I'll do that for you." In this case, I'm not really *predicting* my future actions; I'm *promising* you something. Even if I do anticipate some future actions, I'm saying something else here. These are not aspects of the meanings of the words and sentences at

DOI: 10.4324/9781003183167-40

hand. Instead, these are pragmatic features of our use of them. The range of other things we might do with words is considerable. We promise; we refuse; we invite; we honor; we mock; we command; the list goes on. Pragmatics is the sub-field within the philosophy of language in which these dimensions of our use are examined.

An important distinction within this field is that of a speech act. Presuming there are distinct types of purposes to which we can put words and sentences, there would be types of acts that we could characterize by their distinct pragmatic character. A promise commits someone to do something (or refrain from doing something), renders them blameworthy if they fail, and recognizes the moral importance and agency of those to whom something is promised. (This list might go on, too.) That list of pragmatic conditions will be different from those for invitations, refusals, etc. Some types of speech acts have explicit vocabulary associated with them: "I *promise* that . . . ." "We *invite* you to . . . ." However, many types of speech acts don't have such vocabulary associated with them and we must interpret what is implicit in context to identify them. Entries #28–30 all look at puzzles involving these kinds of implicit pragmatic features. Entries #31 and #35 both look at more pernicious pragmatic features, in which some language users' capacity to perform acts is undercut, or communities are systematically misled. Entries #32–34 consider the pragmatic features of slurs and profanity, and – to add at least a little more lightheartedness to the section – jokes.

28

' TRULY, YOU HAVE A DIZZYING INTELLECT.'

Background: Thus far, most of the accounts of language we have considered have stressed what we might call "literal meaning" and presumed that communication via language is primarily a matter of making statements (or asking questions, issuing commands, etc.) in which all the meaning there is to be found is found in the words that are uttered. In this entry, we consider cases in which what a speaker communicates is not stated explicitly and must be inferred by other means.

In many of the entries so far, we have considered the challenges of offering a theory of meaning. An unspoken presumption in much of that has been that we can spell out what the different parts of a language mean, and that this would account for what they communicate to one another in using the language. For most of the ways we speak, this presumption works quite well. But it is time to consider expanding our horizons. There are many ways in which speakers can communicate something to an audience without stating it literally. We convey something to others by saying something else and anticipating how they will interpret that. There's a hodgepodge of examples in the philosophical literature, but if you want a sense of what is at play, you could hardly do better than the 1987 film *The Princess Bride*. Consider a few samples:

DOI: 10.4324/9781003183167-41

(1) **Vizzini:**   [I]ocane comes from Australia, as everyone knows, and Australia is entirely peopled with criminals and criminals are used to having people not trust them, as you are not trusted by me so I can clearly not choose the wine in front of you.

   Westley: Truly, you have a dizzying intellect.
   [*You are very stupid.*]

(2) **Rugen:**   Come, Sir. We must get you to your ship.

   Westley: We are men of action. Lies do not become us.
   [*I know that you are not taking me to my ship.*]

(3) **Yellin:**   I have no gate key.

   Inigo: Fezzik, tear his arms off.

   Yellin: Oh, you mean this gate key.
   [*I will give the gate key to you.*]

In each of these examples, the last line says something that we can interpret literally, but in the context of those conversations, we can also readily interpret them conveying something in addition to or instead of that literal reading. (I've put that in brackets following the last lines.) In (1), Westley's comment is sarcasm: what would normally be said as a compliment is being said ironically, to mock Vizzini. Westley's reply in (2) is an artful way of saying that he knows that others have lied to him. And in (3), Yellin is abandoning his lie in the face of a threat, suggesting that he will give up the gate key. (Inigo's command in the second line may do this, too. It suggests that he does not believe what Yellin has said, even though it does not say so explicitly.) So here we have the makings of a puzzle. How is it possible to convey such things without ever saying them?

Grice (1968, 1969, 1975) offered an influential account of this phenomenon, calling such modes of communication "conversational implicatures." Note that in the examples above, the audience in each case is drawing an inference from what the speaker says. We call such inferences "implications" when they are matters of semantic or logical necessity. *Being red* implies *having a color* in this way. Grice uses "implicature" to distinguish inferences that are not matters of semantic or logical necessity, like those in cases (1)-(3) above. Some implicatures will be "conventional" – i.e., fixed across different contexts by social conventions. When you're shopping in a store and hear "The store will be closing in five minutes" over the loudspeaker, you recognize that statement's conventional implicature and conclude that you should leave very soon. Individual expressions can have conventional implicatures, too. 'But' implies logical conjunction, just like 'and,' but it also implicates a degree of surprise – e.g., "Margaret is a Yankees fan, but she's really a very nice person."

We could go on to distinguish ways in which whole sentences have such implicatures, and elaborate even further categories, but I will leave that level of detail for your later reading. In (1)-(3) and many other cases, the implicature is not fixed by convention. Outside of a conversation like (3), you would not infer that you should give someone the key, for instance. So, the speech act of saying the last line of each of these little conversations would be *illocutionary*; those speakers achieve some purpose (changing their audiences' beliefs) in addition to stating something. They are also *indirect*. Speakers *mean* (i.e., want their audience to believe or accept) one thing by saying something else with a different *meaning* (in the familiar semantic sense).

Conversational implicatures would include many interesting modes of speech, such as irony, metaphor, hyperbole, understatement, and many more. Wherever language turns colorful, you're likely to find conversational implicatures. All of that is good for our use of a language, but it also poses a substantial theoretical problem. If there are so many forms of conversational implicature, and their success depends on contextual features that are constantly emerging in novel combinations, how can those on the receiving end ever interpret them? Not only do we generally do this successfully, but we do it fluidly and effortlessly. Even if you have never seen *The Princess Bride*, you can likely read case (1) and discern that Westley is being sarcastic.

Grice's view was that this revealed how deeply *cooperative* communication is. We succeed because we typically start with similar background knowledge, interests, and habits, and we then contribute what is required by the mutually accepted purposes of our conversations. He referred to this as the "cooperative principle," which could be further articulated by maxims of quality, quantity, relation, and manner. ("Be truthful," "be as informative as required," "be relevant," and "be perspicuous," respectively.) Grice's crucial assumption is that speakers who follow these maxims will have their attention and expectations attuned to one another, narrowing the field of relevant possibilities and making some possible implicatures salient without the need to make them explicitly. One who hears a speaker making a conversational implicature can thus rely on the conventional, literal meanings of words used, the adherence of speakers to these maxims, background knowledge about the context in which the conversation takes place, and have confidence that all this information is available to both them and the speaker in interpreting conversational implicatures. (For a closer look at the details of this interpretation, see especially Grice (1975).) As a rule, Grice suggested that it was preferable to interpret cases like (1)-(3) as conversational implicatures, rather than expanding the sense of the words they contained. Interpretations of speakers in context make some additional demands on those who hear them, but this is preferable to expanding the conventional meanings of words and sentences to include every possible implicature, which would render them unlearnable.

RESPONSES

Grice's account has been profoundly influential in pragmatics, though it has been met with an increasing variety of challenges. While few dispute that pragmatic inferences like those implicated in (1)-(3) are regularly made, and many have welcomed the emphasis on the cooperative character of conversation and communication that drives Grice's work, doubts about this account have also taken root in recent years. Many critics have noted the problem of *overgeneration* – i.e., the maxims and background information, etc., in play in a context may generate many incorrect implicatures in addition to a correct one. When Westley says "Lies do not become us" in (3), he might be implicating that he knows that Rugen is lying. But he might also be implicating that he knows harm will come to him, that he's not afraid of this, that Rugen's lies are insulting in their transparency, etc.

Numerous modes of conversational implicature also achieve their ends by flouting the maxims underlying the cooperative principle, as even Grice noted. Westley's sarcastic comment in (1) has the appearance of a faithful assertion, but is made knowing that the proposition it expresses is false, thus violating the maxim of quality. Perhaps we should understand those maxims as defeasible, but that implies the need for some procedure to decide when exceptions are to be made. Offering an account that makes these tasks cognitively practicable has proven to be a challenge for proponents of Grice's methods. For recent attempts to revise accounts of conversational implicature in ways friendly to Grice, see Levinson (2000) and Horn (2004). Davis

(1998) offers an extensive critique of Gricean accounts of conversational implicature, which he argues are all doomed to failure. The core assumptions of such accounts generate many erroneous predictions and lack the rigor necessary to correct such flaws. In Davis's view, Grice's account underestimates the importance of both speakers' intentions and conventional implicatures in explaining conversational implicatures and the degree to which we rely on "conventional ways of conversationally implicating things" (1998, p. 132) that do the bulk of the work in conversational implicatures.

A much more radical departure from the standard Gricean model is relevance theory. (See Sperber and Wilson (1995), Carston (2002), Wilson and Sperber (2004, 2012).) While relevance theory shares Grice's assumption that communication is fundamentally devoted to expressing speakers' intentions to be recognized by others, and that much of the work in doing this takes the form of inferences that others make to glean a speaker's meaning, they have rejected his cooperative principle and its maxims in explaining this process. Instead, relevance theorists take the search for relevance to be a basic feature of all cognitive processes. (Note that this is a new, all-encompassing principle, not just Grice's maxim of relevance.) Any input into such processes – sensory, linguistic, activated memories – may have effects on someone's representation of the world. Such effects will come in degrees: the greater the changes they induce in those representations, and the less processing effort they require to do so, the greater their relevance. How does this play into communication? Humans will work to maximize relevance in their interactions with others, building on their abilities to discern, predict, and influence one another's mental states. We communicate with one another when these efforts to maximize relevance and influence one another's thinking take on overt forms. We comprehend one another by surveying all the stimuli from our interaction, the conventional meanings of words used, and processes to discern the assumptions at work in the context of conversation. While words in a language have much of their relevance encoded in them by convention, even the most straightforward statements will be comprehended by this sort of interpretive hypothesizing about speakers' intentions. What Grice treated as conversational implicatures are thus an extension of the same cognitive processes, giving rise to inferences about speakers' intentions, albeit with much more effort necessary for their processing. For some critical responses to relevance theorists on these topics, see Saul (2002) and Cappelen and Lepore (2007).

Two other points are worth mentioning briefly. Relevance theory has been influential in recent debates about the scope of context-sensitivity and would imply much more radical forms of it in our utterances. Semantic minimalists (like Cappelen and Lepore, mentioned above) have argued that this has implausible consequences. This debate is discussed in entry #22. Readers may also want to note that Grice's approach to semantic meaning shares some of the cooperative, intersubjective character discussed in this entry. Grice's model presumes the possibility of both ascribing mental states to those to whom one speaks, and the possibility of affecting those states in others. This has been influential in the study of animal communication, where other species' capacity for such ascription is disputed. Readers interested in this theme may want to read entry #42 after this.

RECOMMENDED READINGS

MAJOR WORKS

Grice, H.P. 1968/1989. "Utterer's Meaning, Sentence-Meaning, and Word-Meaning." In *Studies in the Way of Words*, 117–137. Cambridge: Harvard University Press.

Grice, H.P. 1969/1989. "Utterer's Meaning and Intention." In *Studies in the Way of Words*, 86–116. Cambridge: Harvard University Press.

Grice, H.P. 1975/1989. "Logic and Conversation." In *Studies in the Way of Words*, 22–40. Cambridge: Harvard University Press.

Sperber, D., and D. Wilson. 1995. *Relevance: Communication and Cognition*, 2nd ed. Cambridge: Harvard University Press.

RESPONSES

Cappelen, H., and E. Lepore. 2007. "Relevance Theory and Shared Content." In *Pragmatics*, edited by N. Burton-Roberts, 115–135. London: Palgrave Macmillan.

Carston, R. 2002. *Thoughts and Utterances: The Pragmatics of Explicit Communication*. Oxford: Blackwell.

Davis, W. 1998. *Implicature: Intention, Convention, and Principle in the Failure of Gricean Theory*. Cambridge: Cambridge University Press.

Horn, L. 2004. "Implicature." In *The Handbook of Pragmatics*, edited by L. Horn and G. Ward, 2–28. Oxford: Blackwell.

Levinson, S. 2000. *Presumptive Meanings: The Theory of Generalized Conversational Implicature*. Cambridge: The MIT Press.

Saul, J. 2002. "What Is Said and Psychological Reality: Grice's Project and Relevance Theorsts's Criticisms." *Linguistics and Philosophy* 25 (3): 347–372.

Wilson, D., and D. Sperber. 2004. "Relevance Theory." In *The Handbook of Pragmatics*, edited by L. Horn and G. Ward, 606–632. Oxford: Blackwell.

Wilson, D., and D. Sperber. 2012. *Meaning and Relevance*. Cambridge: Cambridge University Press.

29

'THE PRESENT KING OF FRANCE . . .' (YET AGAIN)

Background: Russell's account of definite description was enormously influential on British and American philosophers of language. It treated meanings as fixed semantic elements of names, descriptions, etc., whose logical forms could be analyzed with the right methods. Strawson was among a group of post-war British philosophers who rethought these assumptions to put greater emphasis on use and context, giving rise to the subfield of pragmatics. In this entry, we get his take on 'The present King of France' and what it reveals.

In entry #6, we considered Russell's seminal analysis of definite descriptions. Philosophers had struggled for some time to understand how to reconcile the assumption that meaning was grounded on designation with the fact that certain non-designating names, descriptions, and other expressions apparently remain meaningful. The definite description 'The present King of France' describes someone, but designates no one (thanks to the French Revolution), so how can it be meaningful if the meaning of an expression is ultimately what it designates? Russell believed that the sentence could still be meaningful (or "significant" as Russell put it), but its surface grammar does not immediately reveal how. He analyzed such descriptions as logically complex, expressing the conjunction of multiple propositions: for

DOI: 10.4324/9781003183167-42

some x, (i) x is presently King of France; (ii) if any y is presently King of France, then $x = y$; and (iii) x is bald. Each of these propositions can be true or false, but (i) won't be true for any x. Conjunctions are true only if all of their conjuncts are true, so 'The present King of France is bald' is false.

Strawson (1950) had considerable doubts about Russell's approach to this question, however. To see his point, imagine you have a budding interest in language and philosophical puzzles. Someone points you to 'The present King of France is bald' as a puzzle about language. You learn some logic and read Russell's "On Denoting," where he lays out his analysis. You now have a method for analyzing all definite descriptions, including empty ones like 'the present King of France,' and we'll assume you can deploy it proficiently. Now, suppose you leave your philosophy class and enter into an everyday conversation. Someone says to you, "The King of France lives in Paris. Right?" Let's think of the colloquial "Right?" as an invitation to truth-evaluation here. Knowing your history, you know that there is no longer a King of France, and knowing Russell's analysis, you know that you're supposed to deny this and insist that the sentence is false. Strawson suggests that most of us will be inclined to hesitate in saying that the sentence is false if we actually hear it in conversation. There is still something . . . uncomfortable . . . about assigning the sentence a truth value at all. If someone said this to me, I would probably say, "Well, there is no King of France anymore. Guillotines took care of that." In saying that, I'm sidestepping any evaluation of the sentence's actual truth. Why? I've read Russell! Why should this analysis suddenly fail us when we actually apply it to a natural language?

Strawson's diagnosis of this tension turns on distinctions about the *use* that speakers make of sentences and expressions. We must distinguish between: (1) sentences; (2) the *use* of a sentence; (3) an *utterance* of a sentence. We can draw the same threefold distinction for expressions. We might offer various types of analysis of the grammar and semantics of sentences, as Russell did. But we must then consider the different ways in which a sentence might be put to use. A sentence like 'The present King of France is bald' might be used in making an assertion to report facts, or it might be used in telling a fictional story, or as an example in a philosophy textbook, or put to many other possible purposes. An utterance of that sentence would be a particular occasion on which someone said, wrote, signed, etc. something. How a particular utterance operates is informed by those possible types of use and the syntactical and semantic features of the sentence. Two users of a language might thus create two distinct utterances that put a sentence to the same use: you and I might tell the same fictional story including this sentence, or Strawson, Russell and I might each offer utterances of it in our respective texts. But the same sentence might be put to different uses in different utterances or receive different truth evaluations in different contexts. An obvious way of seeing this is to imagine the truth values we would assign to our example if people were saying it at different times. It is hard to feel correct in assigning the example any value right now, but from the 10th century CE[1] until 1789, saying that it was true or false would be uncontroversial.

With this threefold distinction in hand, we can state Strawson's response. The *use* of a sentence or expression in an *utterance* presupposes certain conditions, but these conditions are not matters that are stated by an utterance of the sentence or expression itself.

> [W]henever a man uses any expression, the presumption is that he thinks he is using it correctly . . . The presumption is that he thinks both that there is some individual of that species, and that the context of use will sufficiently determine which one he has in mind.
>
> (1950, p. 332)

This introduces what philosophers and linguists have come to call *presupposition*. Strawson would later define matters by saying that one sentence presupposes another just in case the latter sentence must be true for the original sentence to have a truth value. Note that Strawson explicitly denies that this is part of the meaning of a sentence. As he says, "[t]o *use* 'the' in this way is not to *state* that those conditions are fulfilled" (332, emphasis added). The role that these conditions play is a matter of *pragmatics*, or the use to which sentences and expressions are put in conversation, rather than semantics. Strawson is concerned with definite descriptions in this article, but he and others have noted a wide variety of other forms of presupposition. There are too many to list here, but just for example, note how quantifier phrases and aspectual verbs involve presupposition:

All we love we leave behind.
Presupposition: *There are things we love.*

John Coltrane stopped playing with Miles Davis in 1960.
Presupposition: *John Coltrane played with Miles Davis.*

RESPONSES

One significant implication of Strawson's original account of presupposition is that it entails that many utterances of sentences will have no truth value. If we take that at face value, it would entail either a "gappy" or three-valued logic, which has itself been a contentious proposal. (See entry #20 for details.) Any account of presupposition also faces the challenge of determining which sentences are presupposed in a theoretically interesting sense, and which are merely associated in some weaker or idiosyncratic sense. One way to test for genuine presuppositions is to see what happens when a sentence is placed in various types of logical operators. For instance:

(1)   The present King of France broke the royal scepter.
(2)   There is a unique royal scepter.
(3)   The present King of France damaged something of great value.
(4)   It wasn't the present King of France that broke the royal scepter.
(5)   If the present King of France broke the royal scepter, then something was broken.

Given an utterance of (1), (2) follows as a presupposition. And (3) appears to follow as well, but is it a presupposition? We test this with (4)-(5). (We could list other presuppositions and further tests, but I won't here.) In (4), we embed (2) in the scope of a negation operator, and in (5), we do so with a conditional. In this case, (2) follows from both (4) and (5), but (3) does not. Maybe the royal scepter was a cheap plastic prop for ceremonies, and they can get another one easily, but that there was one such thing at work is still implied by (4)-(5). So, we can say that (2) is a presupposition of (1), but that (3) is not. Langendoen and Savin (1971) called this the *projection* of presuppositions, and tests like these for it have become a standard part of any account. However, there is an extensive literature on presupposition, and a great many examples in which presuppositions fail to project in some contexts or under some operators and not others. For detailed reviews of important parts of this literature, readers may consult Gazdar (1979, Chapters 5–6) and Beaver (2001, Chapters 1–3).

Strawson's account came to be known as a "semantic" or "semantical" approach in light of the centrality of truth-values in its definition of presupposition. But critics have argued that it is not necessary for the presuppositions associated with a sentence to be true, only for speakers to proceed *as if* they were true. Accounts that emphasized this point came to be known as "pragmatic" accounts of presupposition and followed the lead of Robert Stalnaker (1973). These accounts reject Strawson's definition of presupposition in terms of the intertwining of truth values between sentences in favor of an account that emphasizes the propositions "whose truth [a person] takes for granted, often unconsciously, in a conversation, an inquiry, or a deliberation" (1973, p. 447). Speakers presuppose some proposition when they are disposed to act *as if* they take the truth of that proposition for granted (whether it is true or not) and take it that their audience takes them to be doing so. Thus, presuppositions become attitudes – *accepting* something as true – of speakers, rather than belonging to the sentences themselves. Stalnaker revised this account over the years, as he and others have worked through the details of which "triggers" might activate presuppositions (such as 'the,' which is widely taken to trigger a presupposition of uniqueness), and how they might be added, deleted, or updated as conversation proceeds. See Karttunen (1974) and Schlenker (2008), Simons (2003) for pragmatic accounts that develop Stalnaker's central ideas. Atlas (1977) offers a pragmatic account that is particularly critical of semantic accounts, arguing that definite descriptions don't have logical forms that presuppose uniqueness.

The question of updating presuppositions as well as many other features of conversation were of great interest to theorists working in dynamic semantics. As the name would suggest, these accounts differ from earlier ones in the degree to which features of a context may change over the course of a conversation, or even a single sentence. While both semantic and pragmatic accounts of presupposition may introduce contextual features in the interpretation of expressions and sentences, the context by which this is done remains static throughout the interpretation. In dynamic accounts, the context itself may change as new information is added by language users' utterances, writings, signs, etc. The advent of this approach was Irene Heim's (1982) work, which disposed of quantifiers in the analysis of definite and indefinite noun phrases in favor of "files" of information that would be updated as conversation unfolds. Heim's original target was "donkey anaphora," which is discussed in entry #24, but she and others quickly adapted it to accommodate presuppositions. This link between anaphora and treating presuppositions dynamically was suggested by van der Sandt (1992). For further developments of these views, see Zeevat (1992), Chierchia (1995), and Beaver (2001). For some criticisms of dynamic accounts from a proponent of pragmatic approaches, see Schlenker (2007).

NOTE

1. Depending on when you think some version of the Frankish Kingdom turns into France. Consult your local medievalist.

RECOMMENDED READINGS

MAJOR WORKS

Langendoen, D., and H. Savin. 1971. "The Projection Problem for Presuppositions." In *Studies in Linguistic Semantics*, edited by C. Fillmore and D. Langendoen, 373–388. New York: Holt, Reinhart, and Winston.

Stalnaker, R. 1973. "Presuppositions." *The Journal of Philosophical Logic* 2: 447–457.

Strawson, P. 1950. "On Referring." *Mind* 59: 320–344.

RESPONSES

Atlas, J. 1977. "Negation, Ambiguity, and Presupposition." *Linguistics and Philosophy* 1: 321–336.

Beaver, D. 2001. *Presupposition and Asserion in Dynamic Semantics*. Stanford: CSLI Publications.

Chierchia, G. 1995. *Dynamics of Meaning: Anaphora, Presupposition, and the Theory of Grammar*. Chicago: University of Chicago Press.

Eijck, J.V. 1993. "The Dynamics of Description." *Journal of Semantics* 10: 239–267.

Gazdar, G. 1979. *Pragmatics: Implicature, Presupposition and Logic Form*. New York: Academic Press.

Heim, I. 1982. *The Semantics of Definite and Indefinite Noun Phrases*. Amherst: University of Masschusetts.

Karttunen, L. 1974. "Presuppositions and Linguistic Context." *Theoretical Linguistics* 1: 181–194.

Schlenker, P. 2007. "Anti-Dynamics: Presupposition Projection Without Dynamic Semantics." *Journal of Logic, Language, and Information* 16 (3): 325–356.

Schlenker, P. 2008. "Be Articulate: A Pragmatic Theory of Presupposition." *Theoretical Linguistics* 34: 157–212.

Simons, M. 2003. "Presupposition and Accommodation: Understanding the Stalnakerian Picture." *Philosophical Studies* 112 (3): 251–278.

van der Sandt, R. 1992. "Presupposition Projection as Anaphora Resolution." *Journal of Semantics* 9: 333–377.

Zeevat, H. 1992. "Presupposition and Accommodation in Update Semantics." *Journal of Semantics* 9: 379–412.

30

'WILL NO ONE RID ME OF THIS TURBULENT PRIEST?'

Background: Entry #28 covered Grice's notion of "conversational implica-
tures," or propositions that were communicated even though no sentence had
been used to assert them. Those examples involved inferring one proposition
from the assertion of another, thus involving only one speech-act type. This
only scratches the surface of the practical possibilities. This entry reflects an
ongoing project of expanding accounts of speech-act types beyond commu-
nicating information.

Will no one rid me of this turbulent priest?

This quote is often attributed to King Henry II of England (1133–
1189), speaking of Thomas Becket, the Archbishop of Canterbury. It is
almost certain that he never said precisely that sentence, but witnesses
did report him saying something similar in spirit. Henry and Becket
were engaged in an extended conflict over control of the Christian
church in England. Being the king, Henry was surrounded by people
who took whatever he said quite seriously, and four knights who
heard him took his words as a command, traveled to Canterbury, and
assassinated Becket. They took something that had the surface structure of one type of speech act (a question) as a different sort of speech
act (a command) that compelled them to act.

DOI: 10.4324/9781003183167-43

Such appearances of one thing that convey another are frequently invoked as examples of conversational implicature. But there may be something else at stake here, given that we have different types of acts rather than just an inference to an unexpressed proposition. We can vary both types of speech act involved and make matters less straightforward. If you've ever watched an old gangster film (or just a bad parody of one), the following will be a cliché:

(1)   Nice place you've got here. It'd be a shame if something bad happened.

The gangster saying this is making assertions, but in that context the gangster is also *threatening* the person to whom they're speaking. We might even take the assertions to be truthful and authentic. It might be a nice place, and the gangster may genuinely hope that nothing bad happens. "It's just business, not personal," as they say. There is no shortage of such examples, either:

(2)   Can you reach that jar on the top shelf?
(3)   The door is open.

In (2), we have a question that also sounds like a request. And (3) asserts that the door is open, but might also request that someone close it, assert that someone has neglected their duties, or invite someone to use it.

To lay some cards on the table and introduce a little terminology, imagine a brief conversation:

(4)   **Alex**:   Let's go out tonight.
       Claire: I have to study for an exam.

Claire's response in (4) can be interpreted as an assertion. But the more important speech act in this case is not made explicit by the literal meaning of the response. Claire is *rejecting* the invitation. Following Searle (1975), let's call the rejection the primary speech act, and the assertion that she needs to study the secondary speech act. The primary speech act is the one that Claire wants to complete by what she says, yet the secondary speech act is the one that is accomplished by the literal meanings of the words in her utterance. We could say much the same of (1)-(3) and the title of this entry, suitably adjusted to their various speech acts. Now we're coming to the heart of the current problem. How can someone saying, writing, etc., one of these sentences mean whatever is in their primary speech act by performing their secondary one? How can they convey something to their partners in conversation, and why would they do so in this fashion?

What we have in all these examples are what Searle called *indirect* speech acts: "cases in which one illocutionary act is performed indirectly by way of performing another" (1975, p. 60). They involve a type of redirection by those who undertake them, requiring a reevaluation by those who hear or see them. In (4), we can see Alex's initial speech act as a proposal, which one would expect to be met with a speech act of acceptance or refusal. But Claire's response offers other information that would be relevant to Alex's proffer only via a further chain of inference. Alex thus must infer that Claire means something in addition to what she explicitly says here and must discern her primary illocutionary intent. Given that they share background knowledge, such as how much time and effort academic work demands, that this work must be done before the exam, which is typically scheduled and cannot be rescheduled without better reasons than these, etc., Alex can probably discern that these would be grounds for a refusal, but not an acceptance. We could flip the resolution here by imagining another response from Claire:

(4') **Claire**: I've been wanting to try that barbecue restaurant over on Central Ave.

Here, given what both speakers know and the conditions of the different speech acts, Alex should infer that the proposal is being accepted, and that Claire is offering another (not just reporting her psychological states). Claire might reply in other ways – e.g.:

(4") **Claire**: Tautomers are interconverting structural isomers of chemical compounds.

In a case like this, the information asserted is not apparently relevant to either acts of acceptance or refusal. Alex's proposal lingers, unresolved, by Claire's response. At least her studying is going well (assuming it's a chemistry exam).

The key thing in Searle's view that allows responses like those from Claire in (4) and (4') to serve as indirect speech acts is the way in which they are relevant to the speech act and background conditions to which they respond. An indirect speech act could also take place without any speech act immediately prior to it. Imagine walking into a room and saying, "The door is open" amid people who are responsible for closing it, or starting a conversation with a tall stranger in a store with "Can you reach that jar on the top shelf?" In both of those cases, the background conditions for the command and request, respectively, are presumably common knowledge. Those who hear them, see the signs, etc., can infer the primary illocutionary act below the surface. Why do this at all? Searle suggests that politeness is most often the primary motivation. Claire's reply in (4) is not a flat rejection, and Alex need not take it personally; the tall person who hears (2) will feel that their help is freely given rather than demanded.

RESPONSES

It will be useful for readers to compare the notion of an indirect speech act with Grice's account of conversational implicature (see entry #28). Both involve an inferential path taken from the semantic meanings of words and sentences in a speech act to some further conclusion or effect to be drawn. The challenge of discerning what to draw from a speech act, given an enormous array of possibilities, looms as a problem for both conversational implicature and indirect speech acts. Searle suggests that much of that work would be done by an increasing degree of conventional stability around some grammatical forms used in indirect speech acts. Thus, "Could you___" has become a familiar form in English for issuing requests. The words have not lost their literal meaning and become mere idioms, but conventions for their use have allowed us to use them in a regular manner beyond those literal meanings (1975, pp. 75–78). We just hear them as requests straightaway, making their role more manageable. Sadock (1972) claimed that literal meaning in such speech acts became ambiguous and argued instead for treating the sentences in putatively indirect speech acts as idioms. Searle and others saw this as *ad hoc* and implausible, however.

Bach and Harnish (1979) tried to put intention back into a more prominent place in their account, contrary to Searle (and more closely aligned with Grice). Speakers provide a basis for hearers (or readers, etc.) to infer their intentions with the aid of "mutual contextual beliefs" (i.e., shared contextually salient information) and shared meanings from a language. They point to a conflict in Searle's account and others that solve the puzzle of indirect speech acts by qualified appeals to convention. As they note, Searle wants to both suggest that we hear 'Can you___' sentences (and similar others) directly as requests. Yet he also insists that those words retain their literal meanings (which do not form a literal request), implying that there are two illocutionary acts with the direct illocutionary act being something else. "The conventionality thesis cannot have it both ways" (179, p. 190, see pp. 187–191 for details). Rather than conventionality, they offer "illocutionary standardization," by which the utterance of a sentence in its context activates a mutual contextual belief about the standard way to interpret others' illocutionary intent. (So, a 'Can you___' sentence will have a standard illocutionary association with making requests.) This also makes for ready uptake of indirect speech acts. Morgan (1978) and Horn and Bayer (1984) take a deeper look at Searle's emphasis on convention, introducing a notion of "short-circuited implicature." On this account, the path to Searle's primary illocutionary act (as detailed above) is in principle calculable, but is frequently "short-circuited" by familiar conventions, obviating the need for most such efforts. This splits the difference between Searle's account and Bach and Harnish's, leaving room for conventions in indirect speech acts, but not ones that obscure the roles of literal meaning or distinct illocutionary acts in the account.

Bertolet (1994) considers a bold view on indirect speech acts: there are none. He argues that there are considerable grounds for skepticism about utterances having two illocutionary forces and speakers performing multiple illocutionary acts. While utterances in purported indirect speech acts are treated *as if* they are requests, etc., in addition to some other act, we can deny the inference to their *actually being* requests, etc. (See McGowan, *et al.* (2009) for a reply.) Asher and Lascarides (2001) offer a radical new view, as well, as they offer an interpretation of speech act types in terms of rhetorical relations. "Rhetorical" in this sense involves relations between utterances and previous utterances in discourse to which they are various sorts of replies. Explanations are a type of rhetorical relation, for instance: one provides an explanation not in a vacuum, but as a reply to a question. It is a matter of interpretation on their view whether a given utterance is an indirect speech act. The utterance may be interpreted as either of two incompatible semantic types (e.g., questions and requests), with the help of Gricean principles of rationality and cooperativity. (See Clapp (2009) for criticism.)

Finally, there has been increasing interest in recent years in the political implications of certain types of indirect speech acts. The surface form of political rhetoric regularly seems to mask other sorts of illocutionary acts, particularly calls to action against opposing groups where overt calls would be met with greater resistance. There has been an increase in the last decade in the use of "dog whistles" and other rhetorical strategies to stoke antagonism while giving political actors a veneer of deniability for their efforts. See Saul (2018) and Lopez (2014) for less theoretical, more political discussion.

RECOMMENDED READINGS

MAJOR WORKS

Searle, J. 1975. "Indirect Speech Acts." In *Syntax and Semantics, vol. 3: Speech Acts*, edited by P. Cole and J. Morgan, 59–82. New York: Academic Press.

RESPONSES

Asher, N., and A. Lascarides. 2001. "Indirect Speech Acts." *Synthèse* 128 (1–2): 183–228.

Bach, K., and R. Harnish. 1979. *Linguistic Communication and Speech Acts*. Cambridge: The MIT Press.

Bertolet, R. 1994. "Are There Indirect Speech Acts?" In *Foundations of Speech Act Theory: Philosophical and Linguistic Perspectives*, edited by S. Tsohatzidis, 335–349. London: Routledge.

Clapp, L. 2009. "The Rhetorical Relations Approach to Indirect Speech Acts." *Pragmatics and Cognition* 1: 43–76.

Horn, L., and S. Bayer. 1984. "Short-Circuited Implicature: A Negative Contribution." *Linguistics and Philosophy* 7: 397–414.

Lopez, I. 2014. *Dog Whistle Politics: How Coded Racial Appeals Have Reinvented Racism and Wrecked the Middle Class*. New York: Oxford University Press.

McGowan, M., S. Tam, and M. Hall. 2009. "On Indirect Speech Acts and Linguistic Communication: A Response to Bertolet." *Philosophy* 84 (4): 495–513.

Morgan, J. 1978. "Two Types of Convention in Speech Acts." In *Syntax and Semantics, vol. 9: Pragmatics*, edited by P. Cole, 261–280. New York: Academic Press.

Sadock, J. 1972. "Speech Act Idioms." *Chicago Linguistics Society* 8: 329–339.

Saul, J. 2018. "Dogwhistles, Political Manipulation, and the Philosophy of Language." In *New Work on Speech Acts*, edited by D. Fogal, D. Harris, and M. Moss, 360–383. Oxford: Oxford University Press.

SILENCING

Background: An account of speech act theory often begins with puzzles and thought experiments that accomplish some goal. Promisers make promises, priests declare couples married, etc. Accounts often stress the cooperative, action-coordinating qualities of speech acts. There can also be speech acts that inhibit the goals of others or prevent them from performing further speech acts. "Silencing" is one possible form of this and has been the subject of considerable recent attention.

(Readers should note that this entry includes mention of rape and sexual assault.)

The development of speech act theory opened up new terrain in the philosophy of language, both by highlighting the practical dimensions of speech and by broadening the range of forms that we might understand speech to take. This intersected with a long tradition in American law placing great value on the freedom of speech, which had also expanded the range of legally protected activities and subjects during the 20th century. Cinema was a beneficiary of these expanded protections, and more explicit depictions of taboo subjects became more common in commercially produced films. Pornography became much more widely available and openly produced as a result, despite

DOI: 10.4324/9781003183167-44

frequent attempts to label it obscene and thus unprotected. Opponents of pornography frequently cite its depiction of women as degrading, while its defenders cite their rights to free speech in producing and consuming it.

MacKinnon (1987) took a novel position on the matter, arguing that the production and consumption also infringed on the free speech rights of women. Pornography *silences* women, she argued: it systematically "strips and devastates women of credibility, from our accounts of sexual assault to our everyday reality of sexual subordination" (193). That is, it diminishes the capacity that women as a class have to engage in certain kinds of speech by robbing them of the authority to produce some speech acts. There are many limits we place on people's authority to perform speech acts, of course. Children cannot sign contracts, most people cannot perform weddings, etc. MacKinnon's claim was that pornography shifted the culture around us to adopt more permissive attitudes about heterosexual men's sexual demands while devaluing or discrediting women's refusals.

MacKinnon's work was intended for courts and legal scholars, so her account does not include further theoretical elaboration. Others have taken up the idea, though. Hornsby and Langton (1998) developed an influential framework for approaching this question. (I'll refer to this as "H&L.") They ask us to imagine a scenario as follows:

> A woman says "No" to a man, when she is trying to refuse sex; she uses the right locution for an act of refusal, but somehow her speech act goes wrong. The woman says "No" and the man does not recognize what she is trying to do with her words . . . She is rather like the actor in the story, who says "Fire!", intending genuinely to warn, using the right locution for warning, but who fails to warn.
>
> (1998, p. 27)

H&L suggest that there is nothing unrealistic about such a scenario, and there are large numbers of reports from women who have suffered rape and sexual assault that echo it. But if this is a point about language, what should we say has gone wrong? How is this "silencing?"

H&L take refusal to be an illocutionary act – i.e., a use of words that just by being said perform some action. The coach who says, "Drop and give me 20!" gives a command, and in saying those words, performs a specific type of illocutionary act. But illocutionary acts have "felicity conditions" as J.L. Austin called them − "things which are necessary for the smooth or 'happy' functioning of a performative" (1962, p. 14). These may be institutionalized (like "I do" uttered when prompted at a wedding) or woven subtly into the language itself. Among the important felicity conditions is what H&L call "reciprocity," or the capacity and readiness of other users of the language to take up the speech as an illocutionary act. Reciprocity may fail in many ways. Others may simply not speak one's language, or not grasp the fine details involved in more unusual speech acts. Where an audience was systematically encouraged to discount women's capacity to perform certain types of speech acts, this would poison the linguistic environment, undercut reciprocity, and strip away the possibility of performing those acts. This would be *illocutionary disablement*, as they call it. H&L suggest that most pornography exposes women to greater levels of sexual violence by priming heterosexual men's desires and expectations and disabling speech acts by which women might refuse.

Two concerns should be noted here. First, the predominant interpretation of this argument would suggest that pornography's association with illocutionary disablement is a causal one. It is an empirical question whether it has such effects. Second, if there is illocutionary disablement, it would be a further question whether legal prohibition was the best way of redressing this. I'm setting these questions aside, since our focus here is on theorizing about speech acts. With that said, others have agreed that silencing is possible, but differ on the details. Maitra (2009) offers an alternative to H&L that still takes pornography as silencing. She also takes refusal to be a communicative act, though one with non-linguistic goals (what we call a *perlocutionary* act). But she frames refusal in Gricean terms, suggesting that the act is communicative but not illocutionary. Silencing is "communicative disablement" by which an audience does not recognize a speaker's refusal, either because they don't recognize that the speaker does not want to have sex with them, or that this does not give them a reason to stop even if they do recognize the intention. Refusals in general would not be undermined on this account but *communicating* one's refusal might be; women simply would not be taken seriously when they said these things, even if they were things that would be taken seriously in other contexts. (Much like H&L, the failure to recognize someone else's intentions here is not meant to include simple confusion, but rather *systematic* effects on the audience's expectations caused by pornography.)

Bird (2002) insists that, even if we stipulate that pornography undercuts the uptake of women's refusals, this would not amount to illocutionary silencing on H&L's terms. The locutionary act of saying, signing, etc., "No!" still counts as an illocutionary act of refusal. The key point in his view is that refusal does not require uptake of the act by the person(s) to whom it is directed. If I refuse your invitation to attend a party, I successfully refuse regardless of what you make of my refusal. Bird is arguing that not all illocutionary acts are communicative acts, and thus not all require a reciprocal response. Thus, a woman who refuses sex succeeds in refusing and is not silenced, even if her refusal is ignored by her attacker. Mikkola (2011) agrees that not all illocutionary acts are communicative, but insists that refusals are communicative, and can be disabled by the failure of someone else's uptake. A refusal is made to someone else's illocutionary act (their asking for a favor, their soliciting sex), and it is part of someone's intention in refusing that the party who made the initial act recognize the refusal. McGowan *et al.* (2011) likewise insist on the communicative nature of refusal. They note that Bird's best examples depend on formal and institutional qualities that are not part of sexual advances, and this undermines his analogy.

RESPONSES

The field of epistemology has taken a more social turn since the beginning of this century, and work in this field intersects with speech act theory, as well. Greater emphasis has been placed on the ways that knowledge of individual agents depends on the work of others, as well as the means by which knowledge and justification may be transferred between agents. Offering testimony by speech acts such as assertion has thus become a theoretical concern. With this focus on testimony and the agents who testify have come issues of how agents may be marginalized for non-epistemic reasons, with considerable harm as a result. Miranda Fricker (1998) has called this "epistemic injustice," and points to practices by which the assignment of credibility to epistemic agents mirrors structures of social power, denying credibility to the powerless and assigning undue rational authority to the powerful. We may take these as another type of silencing wherever they may occur, in that they are systematic disruptions of the very possibility of performing certain speech acts for some classes of people. (McGlynn (2019) argues that testimonial injustice should not be understood as an extension of silencing, though she does not dispute that there is testimonial injustice.)

There has been interest in how these extensions of the idea of silencing apply to race. In Western philosophy and culture, speakers racialized as Black and other non-White groups have often been characterized as driven by anger, implying an intellectual deficiency by which testimony could be discounted. This type of silencing is more pronounced when the subject of testimony is race itself, or the injustice that surrounds it. Myisha Cherry (2021) makes a case for this view:

> Gaslighters do this in order to make the outraged doubt the existence of racism and to prove anger's unfittingness and inappropriateness, all with the hopes of quieting the rage . . . not merely to silence the noise but to prevent the communication of value of the oppressed, the reality of racial wrongdoing, and the need for justice.
>
> (59)

Cherry is using the term "gaslighter" where we have spoken of those who engage in silencing speech acts here, particularly those who strive to make members of marginalized groups doubt their own credibility.

Dotson (2011) speaks of "epistemic violence" in which there is "a refusal, intentional or unintentional, of an audience to communicatively reciprocate a linguistic exchange owing to pernicious ignorance" (238). This may take forms of "quieting" others' testimony (when an audience does not recognize a speaker as an authoritative epistemic agent), or "smothering" it (when a speaker is coerced into truncating their testimony). Tanesini (2016) offers a kindred account of these effects in light of the arrogance of certain speech acts, whose speakers "presume that their alleged or genuine superior intellectual authority entitles them to a range of privileges which they deny to others" (75). Where these types of acts systematically prevail, there are harms to the dignity and epistemic character of those denied such privileges, but also to the generation and dissemination of knowledge in general. Matheson and Chock (2020) acknowledge much of

Dotson's account of epistemic violence, but argue that testimonial smothering may be permissible on strategic grounds when one's testimony would fuel pernicious stereotypes amongst a biased audience. ("Don't air your dirty laundry in public," as the saying goes.)

Spewak (2017) concurs on the possibility of testimonial injustice, but takes issue with the intention-based models that many accounts of it adopt. In particular, he argues that H&L's account fails to explain cases in which there is silencing even though a speaker's intended speech act is recognized. In cases of testimonial injustice, the intention and action of speaking to a subject is often recognized, but the speaker's identity as a member of the marginalized group leads others not to take them seriously. Uptake occurs, but there is silencing anyway. He recommends instead a "dialectical" account of assertion (most relevant to testimony), on which such speech acts are characterized by their relation to other speech acts and the normative statuses of commitment and entitlement that speakers take on in light of speech acts.[1]

NOTE

1. Spewak characterizes this view in terms taken from Brandom. See entry #14.

RECOMMENDED READINGS

MAJOR WORKS

Austin, J. 1962. *How to Do Things with Words.* Oxford: Oxford University Press.
Fricker, M. 1998. "Rational Authority and Social Power: Towards a Truly Social Epistemology." *Proceedings of the Aristotelian Society New Series* 98: 159–177.
Langton, R., and J. Hornsby. 1998. "Free Speech and Illocution." *Legal Theory* 4 (1): 21–37.
MacKinnon, C. 1987. "Francis Biddle's Sister: Pornography, Civil Rights and Speech." In *Feminism Unmodified: Discourses on Life and Law*, 163–197. Cambridge: Harvard University Press.

RESPONSES

Bird, A. 2002. "Illocutionary Silencing." *Pacific Philosophical Quarterly* 83 (1): 1–15.
Cherry, M. 2021. *The Case for Rage: Why Anger Is Essential to Anti-Racist Struggle.* Oxford: Oxford University Press.

Dotson, K. 2011. "Tracking Epistemic Violence, Tracking Practices of Silencing." *Hypatia* 26 (2): 236–257.

Maitra, I. 2009. "Silencing Speech." *Canadian Journal of Philosophy* 39 (2): 309–338.

Matheson, J., and V. Chock. 2020. "Silencing, Epistemic Injustice, and Epistemic Paternalism." In *Epistemic Paternalism: Conceptions, Justifications and Implications*, edited by A. Bernal and G. Axtell, 219–231. New York: Rowman & Littlefield.

McGlynn, A. 2019. "Testimonial Injustice, Pornography, and Silencing." *Analytical Philosophy* 60 (4): 405–417.

McGowan, M., A. Adelman, S. Helmers, and J. Stolzenburg. 2011. "A Partial Defense of Illocutionary Silencing." *Hypatia* 26 (1): 132–149.

Mikkola, M. 2011. "Illocution, Silencing and the Act of Refusal." *Pacific Philosophical Quarterly* 92 (3): 415–437.

Spewak, D. 2017. "Understanding Assertion to Understand Silencing: Finding an Account of Assertion That Explains Silencing Arising from Testimonial Injustice." *Episteme* 14 (4): 423–440.

Tanesini, A. 2016. "'Calm Down, Dear': Intellectual Arrogance, Silencing and Ignorance." *Aristotelian Society Supplementary Volume* 90 (1): 71–92.

JOKES

Background: We have considered several types of speech acts that serve different sorts of goals. In addition to reporting facts straightforwardly, we may invite, command, request, etc. Many speech acts don't purport to state truths and their grammatical forms distinguish them. But there are speech acts that often deploy the sorts of sentences we do typically use to state facts, even though they don't purport to be true. We consider one such species in this entry: jokes.

How should we understand what is said in a joke? In one important sense, we should understand the words and sentences in a joke as we would in any other context. For instance:

A grasshopper walks into a bar.
The bartender says, "Hey, we have a drink named after you!"
The grasshopper says, "Why would you have a drink named Steve?"

I would suggest that the words and sentences in this joke are to be read literally. 'Bartender' and 'grasshopper' are not metaphors or euphemisms, for instance. Whatever the contours of our account of meaning might be, those sentences are about bartenders and grasshoppers. But they are not to be taken as true or taken *seriously* in familiar ways. To

DOI: 10.4324/9781003183167-45

interrupt the joke-teller to insist that grasshoppers cannot talk would be to miss the point. So, it is tempting to read jokes as a type of fiction. Indeed, the above conversation never took place. But not all jokes describe scenarios in this way, unless we want to say that every declarative sentence is a story (which fits our conception of stories poorly). And some jokes can be taken literally and seriously:

There are ten types of people in this world: those who understand binary and those who don't.

Not only does that sentence not purport to be fictional, but given suitable criteria for understanding, it's true!

So, conventional notions of truth and meaning don't reveal very much to us about jokes. We should then look to how they are used, and whether there is a particular type of speech act in which they play a role. One very common assumption is that jokes are made to induce a certain type of experience in their audience. Whereas an assertion is typically made to induce an attitude in an audience (to get them to believe what is asserted), a joke is told to induce amusement in its audience (to get them to feel a certain kind of pleasurable mood or sensation). Many different linguistic forms do this, and so we find enormous numbers of different forms of jokes. And given this emphasis on a distinctive sort of experience, it is a question on which the interests of philosophers of language and philosophers of aesthetics overlap. Just as we would want to say what (if anything) is distinctive about an experience of beauty, we would want the same for the experience of amusement that jokes provide.

What is characteristic of that species of amusement? Three types of theories (with plenty of variation within each) have predominated in Western philosophy:

Superiority: the amusement we feel from jokes is a sense of our own superiority, and thus our contempt for someone or something. The butt of a joke will typically be someone who is stupid, or morally corrupt in some feeble way, or an institution or practice that we can easily see is similarly inept. Some superiority theorists have worried that this type of amusement was itself symptomatic of moral corruption (enjoying what is contemptible) and should be discouraged. This view has been ascribed to Plato, Aristotle, and Thomas Hobbes. (See Hobbes (1651/1994, Book 1, §6).)

Relief/release: the amusement we feel from jokes is pleasure from the release of tension, which itself is caused by restraining our impulses or authentic attitudes. A joke says for us what we dare not say, and we feel a rush of energy at hearing it. Sigmund Freud (2003) is the most notable proponent of this account. There are also theorists who emphasize the role of surprise in humor, with a similar focus on sudden, involuntary release of tension that comes along with it. (Such views are sometimes lumped in with relief/release accounts, and sometimes treated as a further category.)

Incongruity: jokes amuse us because we perceive something in them that violates our expectations, defying our efforts to make familiar rational sense of them. Some authors suggest that this incongruous element dissipates when we look more closely, while others have said that it may present us with genuine contradictions that we cannot dismiss. To those adopting the latter version, humor may even be philosophically instructive. Immanuel Kant, Arthur Schopenhauer, and Søren Kierkegaard offered versions of this approach in the 19th century.

Having noted these theoretical approaches, it would also be fair to say that none of them are generally taken to offer necessary and sufficient conditions for jokes or the characteristic form of amusement that humor invokes. Many jokes seem to involve no apparent contempt, and make no comparison with others, which calls superiority into question. We laugh at matters that don't embarrass us, and jokes that bear the greatest social stigma (e.g., racist humor) are openly enjoyed by those with those attitudes (e.g., racist attitudes), calling relief into question. And not just any incongruity will be funny, or else entries #16–20 in this volume would be the funniest things you'd ever read. Kant, favoring an incongruity account, worried that humor's effects must be irrational and thus antithetical to the best, most authentic version of ourselves. Yet few would agree that humor is an indefensible feature of our language and experiences, nor one that cannot possibly enlighten us. (Schopenhauer and Kierkegaard differed from Kant on this point, but because they differed from Kant on the centrality of rationality to our authentic selves.) Dadlez (2011) offers a recent defense of this view of humor as a potential source of moral criticism. So, each of these families of accounts is suggestive, but also struggles to make sense of some jokes, and each would require considerable refinement and extension.

RESPONSES

As with many longstanding philosophical questions, one recent angle of interest in jokes and humor has been incorporating philosophical accounts of them into cognitive science and evolutionary biology. Even once we had a satisfactory philosophical account of these speech acts and experiences, we might still wonder *why* organisms such as ourselves should develop and deploy these capacities. Hurley *et al.* (2011) take a scientifically informed, empirical look at the cognitive and emotional dimensions of making and enjoying jokes. Their work suggests a deeply diverse account of humor, in which there is no unifying feature because there are so many widely divergent cognitive forms it takes. Those disjoint forms unite in contributing to cultural evolution and concomitant benefits, much like storytelling. Surprise, superiority, and incongruity all have a role to play, and "[e]ach has been wrong only in declaring itself an alternative to all the others" (287).

Another approach that emerged from such empirical inquiry during the 20th century was an emphasis on play, or the non-serious use of parts of the language (such as jokes) as a low-stakes setting to practice something new or unfamiliar. Children play with toys and games, by themselves and with others, and enhance their perceptual, motor, and social skills in many familiar ways. Jokes might serve analogous purposes, but with more complex arrays of conceptual possibilities. Morreall (2009) considers such strategies, and places them in context with the three big theories mentioned above.

In recent decades, many philosophers of humor have offered accounts that make social and ethical dimensions of jokes central to their functions. Cohen (2001) argued that all jokes are "conditional" – i.e., their success is sensitive to the audience to which they are delivered. Cohen's work is also notable for examining a neglected theme in much philosophy of humor: the potential for reflexivity, or groups and individuals telling jokes about themselves. Traditional Jewish humor is of particular interest to Cohen, in part for the value of shared responses to absurdity and grief. That sort of community-building is also key to Wolf (2002), in which the conditional nature of jokes that Cohen mentions is deployed in different modes (jokes about others, jokes about oneself, and jokes aimed at no one in particular) to develop and maintain solidarity. Cochrane (2017) considers similar questions about shared attitudes between speakers and audiences who share jokes. He argues that jokes can only influence our attitudes to the degree that we find them funny, and we only find things funny when they minimally disrupt our attitudes. (Revealing more serious disruptions that would significantly change our attitudes is possible, but we don't find such things funny any longer.)

Shifting to these social features of humor also leads us to questions of the moral dimensions of telling jokes. There are, of course, no shortage of racist, sexist, and other types of jokes that express or presuppose morally heinous attitudes. Ethicists and moral psychologists have long held that sharing jokes that denigrate other groups could have the effect of reinforcing or activating such views in others or numbing their sense of empathy towards those groups. (See Rodriguez (2014) for a representative account of such views.) But there is a further philosophical question at hand. Do moral flaws such as these make jokes less funny, or can they serve to make them more so? *Comic moralism* is the view that moral flaws in a joke can make their attempts at humor less amusing; *comic immoralism*, by contrast, would say that moral flaws in jokes sometimes increase their humor. (Bear in mind that this is about what makes these jokes *work*. Comic immoralists are not themselves endorsing the purported racism/sexism/etc. of the jokes.)

There have been few attempts to defend strong versions of comic moralism (that moral flaws *never* add to the humor of a joke), but moderate forms have their defenders. Smuts (2009) has argued that comic immoralists "lack a plausible mechanism whereby genuine ethical flaws could become relevant to amusement value" of their jokes (151). All the plausible examples offered by immoralists turn on outrageousness rather than genuine flaws, mentioning immoral things, but not actually making them central to the causal or explanatory core of the joke. Note, for instance, that many racist jokes have little to do with the actual race being denigrated, but rather depend on features like the supposed stupidity of the denigrated race. The same joke form could often be told by Germans about Poles, the English about the Irish, etc., and all such jokes flaunt their disrespect in outrageous ways. Woodcock (2015) responds to this in defense of moderate comic immoralism. He holds that Smuts's argument depends on discounting many plausible examples as not funny because finding them so depends on the attitudes of immoral agents (racists, sexists, etc.), whose judgments we may discount. But Woodcock argues that there is a relativity in the normative status of jokes – they are *for* an audience that already *shares* attitudes at work in the joke – even if that relativity is not the case for the moral attitudes themselves. So, racists find genuinely racist jokes funny, and those features are still immoral, despite their attitudes.

RECOMMENDED READINGS

MAJOR WORKS

Cohen, T. 2001. *Jokes: Philosophical Thoughts on Joking Matters*. Chicago: University of Chicago Press.

Freud, S. 2003. *The Joke and Its Relation to the Unconscious*. Edited by J. Crick. London: Penguin.

Hobbes, T. 1651/1994. *Leviathan*. Edited by E. Curley, Book 1, §6. Indianapolis: Hackett.

RESPONSES

Cochrane, T. 2017. "No Hugging, No Learning: The Limitations of Humour." *British Journal of Aesthetics* 57 (1): 51–66.

Dadlez, E. 2011. "Truly Funny: Humor, Irony, and Satire as Moral Criticism." *The Journal of Aesthetic Education* 45 (1): 1–17.

Hurley, M. Dennett, D., and R. Adams. 2011. *Inside Jokes: Using Humor to Reverse-Engineer the Mind*. Cambridge, MA: The MIT Press.

Morreall, J. 2009. *Comic Relief: A Comprehensive Philosophy of Humor*. Malden, MA: Wiley-Blackwell.

Rodriguez, T. 2014. "Numbing the Heart: Racist Jokes and the Aesthetic Affect." *Contemporary Aesthetics* 12 (Article 6).

Smuts, A. 2009. "Do Moral Flaws Enhance Amusement?" *American Philosophical Quarterly* 46 (2): 151–162.

Wolf, M. 2002. "A Grasshopper Walks into a Bar: Humor as a Tool of Normativity." *Journal for the Theory of Social Behavior* 32 (3): 331–344.

Woodcock, S. 2015. "Comic Immoralism and Relatively Funny Jokes." *Journal of Applied Philosophy* 32 (2): 203–216.

SLURS

Background: We have been looking at how different kinds of expressions might have qualities that stretch beyond literal meaning and semantic content. Much like some earlier examples, the question here is how we should treat the meanings of expressions where the meanings themselves are somehow repugnant. Do they have meanings that can play a part in the truth of sentences, or are their contributions simply expressive and pragmatic?

If you've seen the film *The Godfather*, you may recall a particular piece of dialogue. In this scene, Tom Hagen – a lawyer and advisor to Vito Corleone – visits Jack Woltz, a Hollywood movie producer. Sensing that he's about to be pressured into changing his film, Woltz erupts at Hagen with a barrage of outrageous language:

Woltz: . . . [L]et me lay it on the line for you and your boss, whoever he is! Johnny Fontane will never get that movie! I don't care how many dago guinea wop greaseball goombahs come out of the woodwork!
Hagen: I'm German-Irish.
Woltz: Well, let me tell you something, my kraut-mick friend . . .

In this exchange, Woltz's is trying to insult Hagen in a tactical fashion: if he seems vicious enough, Hagen and his boss may be intimidated

DOI: 10.4324/9781003183167-46

and hopefully back off. Hagen's unflustered response here suggests that won't be the case. It's also an odd response in the midst of all these insults, in that Hagen is *correcting* Woltz. Imagine someone insulting you by saying, "You're as dumb as a rock!" and correcting them with, "My intelligence is, in fact, greater than that of any rock." (Yes, surely, but that wasn't the point of the insult.)

What distinguishes this exchange is that Woltz is using slurs. These are expressions whose very nature is to be derogatory toward a group of people, usually with some connection to stereotypes about that group. In this way, they have the sort of hostile, insulting character of pejoratives like 'jerk' or 'asshole,' but anyone can be an asshole, and using this expression does not derogate a further class of people that we already identify in neutral ways – e.g., the slurs in the above exchange are used for Italian, German, and Irish people, all of which are classes we can identify without derogation. (Some pejoratives may do this, too – e.g., 'pencil-pusher' is a mild pejorative just for the class of bureaucrats. But all slurs have this quality.) Slurs will always be somewhat offensive, but their offensiveness may vary. The N-word stands out as highly offensive; 'mick' barely raises an eyebrow anymore, even among Irish Americans.

This makes explicit part of what is at stake in the exchange above. It makes some sense for Hagen to correct Woltz, because the initial slurs simply don't apply to Hagen. Woltz is eager to provide others in that case! If someone were to hurl slurs at me that were related to a group to which I did not belong, my reaction would be confusion, and probably some contempt for the speaker. I would think, "Wow. You're really racist. And you're not very good at it." Thus, it seems that there is something to get right or wrong (true or false, perhaps) in using a slur. This has some undesirable consequences, though. Like the character of Tom Hagen, my ancestry is mostly German and Irish, but in the time and place I live, that presents no systemic or inter-personal challenges to me. (I have privilege when it comes to race, as we say.) But suppose those circumstances were different, and groups to which I belonged were subject to various kinds of discrimination. In that case, if someone were to say, "Michael is a kraut-mick," you might hesitate to affirm this, as I hope you would any serious use of a slur. "Oh yeah, he *is* one of them!" seems to affirm the content of the slur with a shrug. Even if we're thinking solely about the semantics of these terms, many philosophers have been loath to accept that they co-referred with more neutral expressions for those classes of people. That presents serious challenges for many approaches to giving an account of their meaning.

RESPONSES

If we think of the problem at hand being where to locate the derogatory quality of slurs, we could think of responses to the problem as falling into three strategies: (1) putting it in the meanings of the words themselves; (2) in the pragmatics of utterances of the slurs, and; (3) a mixture of both.

Theories that place all the derogatory quality of slurs in their meaning could proceed in several different ways. One option is a purely expressivist account. That would imply that slurs had no content that would be part of the truth or falsity of a sentence in which they occurred, but they might still serve a role in expressing speakers' attitudes toward the derogated group. (Compare this with the sort of exclamations people make in support of their team or contempt of the opposition at a big game.) Someone who used the word 'mick' would be expressing a negative set of attitudes toward Irish people, for instance, but not necessarily using the word to classify or assert anything true or false. (See Richard (2018) for a version of this.) That purely expressive approach faces an uphill battle, though, as slurs seem to play a part in sentences that can be true or false. Hagen has to *correct* Woltz in our example, and it can be true or false to say, "Tom Hagen is not a goombah." A different approach here has been offered by Hom and May (2013). They suggest that the meaning of a slur includes some set of negatively evaluable moral traits (perhaps associated with stereotypes of that group) that members of the group have simply in virtue of being members. So 'mick' might mean 'Irish, and morally contemptible because of it,' and so on for other slurs. We might thus grasp their meaning without adopting such attitudes, and our rejection of a derogatory statement like 'Tom Hagen is a mick' is semantically well-founded, because there are no individuals who are Irish and morally contemptible because of it (despite what some bigots may say). On this view, slurs would be meaningful, but they would have null extensions (no members), just like 'unicorn' or 'Romulan.' For criticisms of this view, see Camp (2018).

Pragmatic accounts take the derogatory qualities of slurs to lie not in their meanings, but in how they are used to say or accomplish things beyond their literal meanings. Speech acts involving slurs can serve many such purposes. They may serve to intimidate or silence their targets, draw others into complicity with a speaker's bigotry, or many other ends. Camp (2018) suggests that each use of a slur accomplishes two distinct speech acts: first, a literal classification of the target that is suitable for truth-evaluation, and (2) a derogatory act, which may be likened to insulting the target or expressing a negative attitude. Nunberg (2018) takes a similarly pragmatic approach, denying that there is a distinctively semantic type of content that marks slurs, and opting to characterize their effects in terms of conversational implicatures instead. (See entry #28 for details on conversational implicature.). Tirrell (2012) examines concrete cases in which they were used to foment organized violence by one group against others, though her account weaves pragmatic ends into its account of semantics. There are many variations of this approach, but for now I will concentrate on pragmatic theories that emphasize the purposes that slurs serve in racist or otherwise discriminatory social practices. Those who adopt such views can assert that the literal meaning of slurs is no different from neutral terms for a target group; 'mick' would literally mean nothing different from 'Irish,' etc. Thus, it would make sense for Hagen to correct Woltz, as he is not a member of the groups that are being slurred. Woltz's last line make sense by the same token. So where does the offensiveness lie? Anderson and Lepore (2013) suggest that linguistic communities have norms about which such words are offensive. Violating those norms by using the offensive terms derogates the target group by disregarding their preferred modes of recognition and self-description.

These pragmatic approaches typically have one advantage over others we have discussed in that they readily account for what we might call *reappropriation* or *reclamation* of a slur. (See Hess (2020) for more on this.). Irish Americans may casually throw the term 'mick' about with one another without causing offense. How? Their violations of that general norm have an ironic character, akin to an inside joke. This is far more difficult to explain if we pack the derogatory character into the slur itself. But such a view would also need to give us some sense of why slurs would be worthy of prohibition in the first place. One group using a slur for another target group may very well disrespect and domineer the target group against their wishes, but those wishes would apparently reflect their view that the slurs are offensive in the first place. We would typically expect prohibitive norms to follow from some prior sense of offensiveness, or else the norms that some words are slurs and others are neutral would seem to be arbitrary.

Finally, some accounts combine different types of content to explain slurs. On these views, slurs have both a truth-conditional component and a second component that does the derogatory work in some other fashion. (Note that this is reminiscent of Camp (2018), mentioned above, but her analysis is at the level of speech acts.). The component doing the derogatory work could take a number of forms, some of which we have already described. One possibility would be that the use of a slur conveys two different sorts of descriptive content: first, the neutral description; and second, some additional description that has negative implications or value to it, such as a stereotype. 'Mick' might thus have both a first truth-conditional component of 'Irish' and a second truth-conditional component of 'drunken, violent, lazy' (or whatever belongs to negative stereotypes of Irish people). Bach (2018) offers one such view, which he calls "loaded descriptivism." Making this second component truth-conditional strikes some as implausible, as it would suggest that the application of a slur is simply a matter of agreement with the facts. What should we say if Hagen *is* drunken, violent, and lazy? That he really *is* a mick? (In that case, why would such a slur be "loaded" at all?) So, others adopting this two-component view have suggested that the second component is some expressive quality, such as the expression of negative attitudes towards the target group. Croom (2013) and Jeshion (2013) offer such views.[1] (See Bach (2018, pp. 67–70) for criticisms.)

NOTE

1. Jeshion (2013) introduces a *third* component to slurs, which she calls the "identifying" component. The user of a slur takes some feature of the target (e.g., race) to be their defining feature. This is slightly different from the other sources mentioned in this paragraph, but still more similar than to others.

RECOMMENDED READINGS

MAJOR WORKS

Anderson, L., and E. Lepore. 2013. "What Did You Call Me? Slurs as Prohibited Words." *Analytic Philosophy* 54 (3): 350–363.

Croom, A.M. 2013. "How to Do Things with Slurs: Studies in the Way of Derogatory Words." *Language and Communication* 33 (3): 177–204.

Tirrell, L. 2012. "Genocidal Language Games." In *Speech and Harm: Controversies Over Free Speech*, edited by I. Maitra and M.M. Kate, 174–221. Oxford: Oxford University Press.

RESPONSES

Bach, K. 2018. "Loaded Words: On the Semantics and Pragmatics of Slurs." In *Bad Words: Philosophical Perspectives on Slurs*, edited by D. Sosa, 60–76. Oxford: Oxford University Press.

Camp, E. 2018. "A Dual Act Analysis of Slurs." In *Bad Words: Philosophical Perspectives on Slurs*, edited by D. Sosa, 29–59. Oxford: Oxford University Press.

Hess, L. 2020. "Practices of Slur Use." *Grazer Philosophische Studien* 97: 86–105.

Hom, C., and R. May. 2013. "Moral and Semantic Innocence." *Analytical Philosophy* 54 (3): 293–313.

Jeshion, R. 2013. "Expressivism and the Offensiveness of Slurs." *Philosophical Perspectives* 27 (1): 231–259.

Nunberg, G. 2018. "The Social Life of Slurs." In *New Work on Speech Acts*, 237–295. Oxford: Oxford University Press.

Richard, M. 2018. "How Do Slurs Mean?" In *Bad Words: Philosophical Perspectives on Slurs*, edited by D. Sosa, 155–167. Oxford: Oxford University Press.

34

IF YOU HAVE BEEN SCANNING THE TITLES, LOOKING FOR THE ENTRY WITH ALL THE DIRTY WORDS, IT'S THIS ONE

Background: Every language seems to have a subset of "dirty" words, whose use violates norms of propriety and brings disapproval. Their "dirty" character is a difficult matter to explain in the usual semantic terms. They designate things that are designated by non-"dirty" words, but they can be used in all types of speech acts, as we expect of words with more ordinary meanings. Profanity proves to be a persistent feature without an obvious home in most theories of meaning.

In 2009, students at Danvers High School in Massachusetts received notice of a new school policy: use of the word 'meep' was now forbidden. Let's grant for the moment that this is a word at all, rather than simply a noise borrowed from *Road Runner* cartoons and the staff of Muppet Labs. If so, it is not a word that has been used by English speakers elsewhere, and so there is no taboo that the Danvers student were inheriting or exploiting. But no high school principal has *ever* overreacted to chicanery with needlessly draconian policies, so *something* must be in play here.

DOI: 10.4324/9781003183167-47

Guy Raz (2009) of National Public Radio interviewed Mike Spiewak, a Danvers student and frequent 'meep'-user:

RAZ: So, what are a few examples of how you would use the word meep?
SPIEWAK: Well, you can just say meep being a one-word sentence. You can say how the meep are you? Shut the meep up.
RAZ: Now, that sounds like a substitute for another word, a not-so-friendly word that some of our listeners might be familiar with.

In the Danvers case, Spiewak notes that usage of the term included this quasi-profane form but was also highly unstable and mostly just flippant fun. Clearly, some of that fun was to play with the possibility of both creating and violating a taboo that their elders did not control. Let's take this as a thought experiment. Could a small linguistic community like the Danvers students make a word like 'meep' dirty in the same way that words like 'fuck' are to English speakers? Could 'Meep off!' or, 'Go meep yourself, you pig-meeping mothermeeper!!,' as silly as they sound, have the same bite that other dirty words already do?

To address this we should ask, what makes dirty words "dirty?" It does not appear to be simply that they designate objects or subjects that are taboo. For every word like 'fuck,' 'shit,' or 'piss,' we have anodyne words like 'copulate,' 'excrement,' and 'urine.' Words like 'damn' and 'hell' sound dirty to socially conservative Christians, but also occur frequently in the sacred texts and apologetics of Christianity. You could hear both of them in any given Sunday's sermons. This does suggest that, to some degree or in some cases, what makes an expression dirty is how it is used rather than something intrinsic to the word itself. An outburst like, "Damn it! What the hell are you doing?" may include some dirty words, but "You will be damned to Hell for your sins" somehow doesn't. In the sorts of uses that are taboo, there is also an additional expressive quality to the words that permissible words will lack. They have an amplifying effect on the emotional and attitudinal features of what we're saying. There is a visceral thrill to shouting, "FUCK YEAH!!!" when your team wins, and there is added venom in saying, "Fuck Donald Trump and all his fucking lies!!" that doesn't come through in saying, "I strongly condemn Donald Trump and all his outrageous falsehoods!"

A straightforward response here would be to say that linguistic communities establish conventions for usage, and most will have a set of terms that have a supplemental taboo quality to them. 'Fuck' and 'copulate' can designate the same sort of actions – perhaps even have the same meaning, depending on the account one offers – but 'fuck' has a forbidden status that 'copulate' does not. An empirical point in favor of this assumption is the wide variety of different taboo statuses that such words have at different times and in different contexts and corners of the English-speaking world. No one will object too strongly if I drop a 'motherfucker' into conversation while drinking with friends at a rowdy bar, but the president and deans of my college will want a word with me if I do so during a speech at our commencement ceremony. Similar comparisons could be made between different English-speaking regions and the degrees of taboo they place on different words. All of this is suggestive of *mere* conventions, added to some underlying meaning, which can vary from one place and time to another without any inconsistency.

As explanations go, this has the virtue of being clearly true, but the vice of being superficial. Surely, there are linguistic conventions about what appropriate and inappropriate usage of an expression would be; *every* word will have such conventions. What we want is a better sense of what the "dirty" conventions would imply and why we have them. Distinguishing words as dirty in the present sense has something like a moral quality to it, rather than a simple matter of correctness or standardization. A field biologist who uses the term 'whistle pig' (common in some parts of Appalachia) instead of 'groundhog' or '*Marmota monax*' may be corrected for the sake of convention, but there won't be a sense that she has wronged the editors and readers. However, if I start my commencement speech with 'I want to thank you motherfuckers for . . ..' I will almost certainly have offended others, even if I'm speaking in jest. The implication here is that, when dirty words are used, and especially when they are used intentionally in violation of conventions, the speaker has *harmed* the audience by causing offense.

There is a hint of circularity, or at least arbitrariness, to this sort of response. Using dirty words is offensive because they violate conventions about what is offensive speech. But that still leaves us to ask why just these words are dirty and 'copulate,' 'poop,' etc. are not. Some criterion should support the taboo if it is to have any traction. There have been suggestions that the use of dirty words is to be discouraged because it is indicative of some further flaw in a speaker's character, such as intellectual laziness. This seems like a poor basis for *moral* blame, though. The dirty words *extend* someone's vocabulary, and we don't morally blame people for having fewer words for sex (or excrement, etc.) if their smaller vocabularies are exclusively non-dirty.

Perhaps moral blame is the wrong sort of criterion when it comes to dirty words. Some philosophers have said that our value theories should also have room for what Peter Glassen called *charientic* judgments. A charientic judgment would not imply that a person or action had one moral value or another, nor that their character or actions had some aesthetic value such as ugliness, but that they or their actions were inappropriate in an unseemly way. To say that someone was obnoxious, boorish, or brutish would be charientic judgments, for instance. Many have suggested that dirty words are *vulgar* – indicative of a low, uncultured, uneducated character and intellect – and we can read this as a charientic judgment. Mohr (2013) suggests that this took greater hold in the English-speaking world in the 18th and 19th centuries:

> Obscene words violated class norms – they were seen as the language of the lower classes, the uneducated – and accessed the deepest taboo of Augustan and Victorian society, the human body and its embarrassing desires, which had to be absolutely hidden away in swaths of fabric and disguised in euphemisms.
>
> (2013, pp. 176–177)

But this is, at best, an indirect, unreliable indication of anything. Privileged people swear when they like, and not everyone who works with their hands for a living swears indiscriminately. It only suggests a kind of gatekeeping – i.e., a set of linguistic manners that can be used to mark privileged groups from unprivileged groups.

So, the earlier point about conventions may be the last resort here. Perhaps dirty words are taboo in most contexts simply because large portions of our linguistic communities have taken them to be so, and flouting those standards is offensive because it shows disrespect for many of our partners in conversation. There is something to be said for this as an interpretation. I'm aware that it is considered impolite to show the sole of one's foot to others in many parts of western Asia. When I've run afoul of such traditions, others have courteously mentioned them to me, and I've adjusted my conduct. Imagine violating them on purpose to let the offended party know I disrespect them. Using dirty words to those offended by them might be a kind of indirect insult in this vein. Then again, *feeling* offended is not necessarily constitutive of harm (moral or otherwise), and social conventions are not above challenge or criticism.

What are prospects for the 'meep'-happy students of our thought experiment? The initial stages of the introduction seem quite plausible. Teenagers introduce new expressions and co-opt existing ones for new purposes all the time. What poses the most substantial hurdle for them would be finding an audience to reciprocate the "taboo" status of their usage. If this group is small, or isolated, or simply lacks privileged social statuses from which they can shape wider convention of standard usage, then their usage is not likely to gain traction in the long run. Readers might consider whether it would be more plausible that an existing expression could be reappropriated – *made* dirty, so to speak – by segments of a linguistic community. Working-class British speakers might have been said to have done this in the early 19th century with the word 'sod,' truncated from 'sodomy.'

RESPONSES

The array of different roles that dirty words fill and the social implications of filling them should give anyone pause before offering or accepting a simple unified theory of profanity. For a broad, accessible historical overview of this history for European languages (plus a bit on biblical ones), readers should pick up Mohr (2013); for one more narrowly focused on English, see McEnery (2006). In the present day, there is some question about whether the taboos we place on dirty words should be written into law. (Consider the ways in which some uses of profanity on broadcast television or radio are met with fines in the US, for instance.) Recent arguments for proscriptions on offensive speech more generally have followed the work of Feinberg (1983) on obscenity. Shoemaker (2000) argues that dirty words don't rise to the level of obscenity because none of the purported grounds for prohibiting them rise to the level of public reasons (those in which the public good is at stake, rather than personal inclinations) that can be used consistently in writing and applying the relevant laws.

There has also been considerable empirical research on the effects of using taboo words. Jay (2009) presents an overview of their place in contemporary psychology. Donahoo and Lai Tzuyin (2020) note the difficulty of pinning propositional content to dirty words, and instead compare them with other categories of expressions for the emotional and social content that they express. Another surprising observation has been an analgesic (pain-relieving) effect from certain utterances. This may be related to the expressive role mentioned above, as the exhilaration of shouting forbidden words packs a kick that has genuine physiological effects. Stephens and Umland (2011) found pain relief from certain strategies involving profanity, though these effects diminished with overuse. (See Van Lancker and Cummings (1999) for detail on the neurological aspects of this research.) Potts (2007) incorporates the distinctive expressive qualities of profanity into the contemporary formal semantics. For instance, this framework would suggest formal ways of accounting for emotional qualities that language users introduce to a context. Many dirty words suggest negative emotions in this way, so uttering 'the *damn* dog' instead of 'the dog' typically communicates that attitude of the speaker in context.

RECOMMENDED READINGS

MAJOR WORKS

Jay, T. 2009. "The Utility and Ubiquity of Taboo Words." *Perspectives on Psychological Science* 4 (2): 153–161.

McEnery, T. 2006. *Swearing in English.* New York: Routledge.

Mohr, M. 2013. *Holy Shit: A Brief History of Swearing.* Oxford: Oxford University Press.

Raz, G. 2009. "Principal Tells Students 'Meep' Is Off-Limits." *NPR.org*, November 14. Accessed February 17, 2022. Available from: www.npr.org/templates/story/story.php?storyId=120422662.

RESPONSES

Donahoo, S., and V. Tzuyin Lai. 2020. "The Mental Representation and Social Aspect of Expressives." *Cognition and Emotion* 34 (7): 1423–1438.

Feinberg, J. 1983. "Obscene Words and the Law." *Law and Philosophy* 2: 139–161.

Potts, C. 2007. "The Expressive Dimension." *Theoretical Linguistics* 33 (2): 165–198.

Shoemaker, D. 2000. "'Dirty Words' and the Offense Principle." *Law and Philosophy* 19 (5): 545–584.

Stephens, R., and C. Umland. 2011. "Swearing as a Response to Pain – Effect of Daily Swearing Frequency." *The Journal of Pain* 12 (12): 1274–1281.

Van Lancker, D., and J. Cummings. 1999. "Expletives: Neurolinguistic and Neurobehavioral Perspectives on Swearing." *Brain Research Reviews* 31 (1): 83–104.

PROPAGANDA

Background: When we think of the goals and strategies guiding linguistic communication, we tend to idealize them as cooperative, rational, and truth-seeking. Much of analytic philosophy of language – even its more pragmatically oriented thinkers – took this for granted. Consequently, accounts of language and speech acts are often stripped of important social and political dimensions. Propaganda subverts all three of those ideals, with important social and political implications.

What is propaganda, and how does it work? The very word has a pejorative quality to it, implying deception and manipulation. That pejorative quality also makes it a term like 'oppression' that speakers will often apply to other communities' actions and practices, but much more reluctantly to their own. Any such notion should be one that could be applied back to oneself and one's community in principle, though, and this has been a theme in many discussions of the communicative strategies we find in public discourse.

George Orwell's perennially-assigned-in-high-school-English-classes novel *Nineteen Eighty-Four* is often read in this light. Orwell depicts a dystopian future society ruled by a brutal authoritarian regime. The novel's protagonist, Winston Smith, works in the Ministry of Truth, which censors, rewrites, or destroys texts and speech that

DOI: 10.4324/9781003183167-48

suggest dissent or the very possibility of divergence from party doctrine. The tenets of party doctrine are repeated throughout the novel.

WAR IS PEACE
FREEDOM IS SLAVERY
IGNORANCE IS STRENGTH

All three appear several times, usually together, and this repetition is suggestive of brute force. Given their apparent self-contradiction, they don't offer space for rational engagement; they undermine the very possibility of it. They are not to be debated or even seriously discussed; they are to be accepted.

This sort of crude but strategic use of false or nonsensical language with political violence in its subtext does characterize some real-world practices, particularly the Stalinist Soviet Union (a clear target of Orwell's satire), and various despotic regimes of the recent past. But this may mislead us. This is propaganda at its most clumsy, unsophisticated, and obvious. Few people will change their beliefs in virtue of it, even if they feel its latent threats and comply. Propaganda's purpose, broadly put, is to influence agents when there cannot be rational persuasion, particularly when it influences its audience to support the interests of the propagandists. More canny strategies here would make themselves less apparent, to deepen their impact. To influence a community in a way that achieved some goal but did so by having speakers internalize that goal (or something in service of it) in a way that felt free and authentic would likely better serve that goal in the long run.

So, propaganda often makes appeals to values and attitudes that its audience already holds to amplify or redirect their focus. After the 2016 elections in the United States, American intelligence agencies concluded that their Russian counterparts had led an influence campaign conducted largely with ads, memes, and discussion groups on social media. This wasn't the brute force attack of Big Brother, but rather targeted use of data collected by those social media companies, ostensibly for advertising purposes. That highly personalized data made it possible to tailor messages to individuals according to their values and likely political views, and thus to antagonize voters across the political spectrum.

If you were active on social media at the time, it is likely you were served such ads at some point. Yet very few Americans would say that they were influenced by propaganda here, because they *really did* value (or hate) those things served to them. At most, many will say, they were persuaded, or further motivated to do what they would have done in any case. And of course, the 2016 election interference campaign reflected – in methods and spirit – many covert election interference campaigns conducted by American intelligence agencies over the last century, which surely only aroused existing political sentiments and ideals, which were surely already in line with American interests anyway. Surely. Few people of any nationality tend to think of the statements their governments make as propaganda when the contents of those statements intersect with their own values and interests, despite the tailoring of messages and selective use of details. Somehow, propaganda manages to be everywhere, but rarely close to home in many people's imagination. What we seem to need here is a more comprehensive philosophical answer to what constitutes propaganda.

RESPONSES

Any understanding of propaganda that we may develop will take place at the intersection of the philosophy of language, epistemology, and political philosophy. Two influential background figures on recent scholarship in this area are Noam Chomsky and Charles Mills. Chomsky and Hermann (1988) laid out the case that much of the verbiage from official American sources during the Cold War was a more subtle form of propaganda that minimized the worst effects of military and covert operations, legitimated some victims over others, and cast doubt on elections when they did not reach favored outcomes. A more enduring facet of their critique suggests that mass media sources were complicit in these efforts, rather than challenging those narratives or sustaining the sort of liberal bias that is often attributed to them. Many of the historical details of this work will be distant to younger readers, but the themes of their critique merit consideration. Charles Mills stands out as an important figure bridging the worlds of analytic epistemology and philosophy of language and philosophy of race. Mills (2007) offers a conception of *epistemic injustice* – a wrongful distortion of shared knowledge and standards of evidence in favor of some groups over others – that makes some forms of ignorance central. Mills points to the enduring aversion to discussing racism and its place in American history in public discourse.

This is rarely done explicitly by denying that history, but regularly by marginalizing discussion of some questions and details (e.g., "You're making everything race," or "Long time ago. It's time to move on."). It is possible to assist in sustaining an unjust social order by ensuring that questions that might challenge the legitimacy of dominant groups' status simply never arise, and that ignorance of such matters is all but guaranteed.

Jason Stanley's *How Propaganda Works* (2015) stands out as a major work in recent analytic philosophy at the intersection of philosophy of language and epistemology as they shape political discourse. Much of this concerns propaganda directed towards citizens by their own political institutions and elites. The distinctive danger of propaganda in liberal democracies, Stanley asserts, is that it is often not recognized as propaganda at all. He suggests two primary varieties of communicative strategies here: *supporting propaganda*, which uses some politically valued item to elicit emotion devoid of reason from part of the populace; and *undermining propaganda*, which presents itself as defending or exemplifying some ideal in the service of undermining that very idea. Supporting propaganda might include the use of extremely patriotic tropes and symbols to elicit emotional responses rather than reasons to generate support for some ideal. Stanley offers numerous examples of undermining propaganda. Citing the work of W.E.B. DuBois, he includes the framing of blatantly racist historical accounts of post-Civil War America as "scientific" and "rational" by prominent historians who made special claims to authority on those ideals.

Both supporting and undermining propaganda may be used in many contexts, but they become especially dangerous in the hands of what he calls a "flawed ideology." A flawed ideology would be a conception of the political order of a society in which certain things were valued, but which also distorted those values, drove those who held the ideology to false beliefs, and blinded them to its worst excesses. Those in the grip of a flawed ideology may thus have the "best of intentions" and little or no personal animus towards other groups, yet still form beliefs and take actions that serve to oppress others. Dominant groups will then tend to gravitate toward flawed ideologies that preserve their positions, often at the direction of demagogues. In Stanley's view, material inequalities (e.g., wide gaps in wealth, access to education, access to political institutions) will tend to exacerbate these tendencies, as dominant groups become increasingly acclimated to their privileged status and non-dominant groups have fewer avenues by which to challenge flawed ideologies. As those inequalities multiply, we should expect further demagoguery and greater use of both forms of propaganda.

Direct criticisms of Stanley's account of flawed ideologies are offered by Brennan (2017). McKinnon (2018) considers Stanley's work on recent disputes between transgender activists and their "TERF" or "gender critical" opponents. She interprets many of their public statements and appeals to ideals of female identity as propaganda in Stanley's sense. (McKinnon does not explicitly call them "undermining propaganda," but compare her critique with those points of Stanley's work.). However, McKinnon does suggest some reservations about Stanley's account. Stanley worries that less privileged members of dominant groups may be led by flawed ideologies to adopt false beliefs about their own positions – e.g., if the flawed ideology of white supremacy holds sway, working-class white citizens may come to believe propaganda blaming their dismal state on other racial groups, rather than the inequalities and structural conditions under which they live and work. McKinnon casts doubt on this as a general truth, suggesting that those who occupy disadvantaged standpoints are *more* apt to see the tensions (and the falsehoods) at the heart of their social practices.

Another response to Stanley comes from Olúfẹ́mi Táíwò (2017). Táíwò notes that Stanley's account, while involving public institutions and other social structures, remains one in which the primary focus is on individuals' beliefs and other doxastic attitudes. Táíwò suggests that social structures themselves can have propagandistic effects, regardless of any agents' beliefs, so an appropriate account must look at the practical effects of social structures, rather than just their beliefs and explicit statements between them. Whereas Stanley's account emphasizes agents and groups making overt speech acts in supporting or undermining modes, Táíwò sees as much or more potential for propaganda in framing discourse that simply excludes or omits information. This suggests a "mis-education" model in the tradition of Carter Woodson's 1933 *The Mis-Education of the Negro*. Whereas a model like Stanley's focuses on "expressed-content" propaganda (as Táíwò calls it), a mis-education model includes the possibility of "Trojan horse" propaganda that shapes public discourse by limiting what is reasonable and available to all agents, much like Mills (see above). This leaves "the potential for distortion, occlusion, or perversion of knowledge" (2017, p. 2) at every turn. "Education" here would include not only formal institutions like schools and universities, but any epistemic resources that shape the common ground of knowledge – what agents can both learn and expect to be recognized as knowledge by the rest of their community. Social structures may thus explicitly legitimate certain forms of knowledge (and agents who hold them) and delegitimize other forms, implicitly simply by leaving them out and rendering them alien to our social practices. For instance, if the standard history curriculum in high school and college courses includes little or no space for the voices and perspective of African Americans, then it renders them passive instruments of White political institutions during the era of enslavement and the passive beneficiaries of noble White sentiments in the years that follow. In either case, this set of practices leaves agents – Black, White, and otherwise – unprepared and unsuited to critique their institutions, thereby offering indirect support to their present forms. Nguyen (2018) has recently characterized this sort of epistemic insularity in concentrated media environments known as "epistemic bubbles."

A further, more general concern is whether there is a distinction to be drawn between wrongful uses of propaganda (which we might characterize as deceptive or manipulative) and rightful ones (which we might insist are skillful persuasion, if a slippery sort). A seminal text on this question is Jean Ellul's *Propaganda: The Formation of Men's Attitudes* (1965). The ethical dimensions of propagandistic strategies are revisited in Marlin (2002), and Rosenberg (2007) offers a fine-grained empirical look at how different types of deliberative discourse may incorporate them or be distorted by them.

RECOMMENDED READINGS

MAJOR WORKS

Chomsky, N., and E. Hermann. 1988. *Manufactoring Consent: The Political Economy of the Mass Media.* New York: Pantheon Press.

Ellul, J. 1965. *Propaganda: The Formation of Men's Attitudes.* New York: Random House.

RESPONSES

Brennan, J. 2017. "Propaganda About Propaganda." *Critical Review* 29 (1): 34–48.

Marlin, R. 2002. *Propaganda and the Ethics of Persuasion*. Peterborough: Broadview Press.

McKinnon, R. 2018. "The Epistemology of Propaganda." *Philosophy and Phenomenological Research* 96 (2): 483–489.

Mills, C. 2007. "White Ignorance." In *Race and Epistemologies of Ignorance*, edited by S. Sullivan and N. Tuana, 13–38. Albany: SUNY Press.

Nguyen, C. 2018. "Echo Chambers and Epistemic Bubbles." *Episteme* 17 (2): 141–161.

Rosenberg, S. 2007. "Types of Discourse and the Democracy of Deliberation." In *Deliberation, Participation and Democracy: Can the People Govern?*, 130–158. New York: Palgrave Macmillan.

Stanley, J. 2015. *How Propaganda Works*. Princeton: Princeton University Press.

Táíwò, O. 2017. "Beware of Schools Bearing Gifts." *Public Affairs Quarterly* 31 (1): 1–18.

PART VII

LINGERING ISSUES ABOUT MEANING

INTRODUCTION

Admittedly, this section is a bit of a grab bag of issues that don't quite fit anywhere else in this book. What they have in common is a thorn-in-the-side quality for every account we have offered so far. No matter what approach you adopt to meaning and pragmatics, these will be head-scratchers.

Entry #36 introduces some puzzles about metaphor. It is common to distinguish between literal and figurative meaning when discussing metaphor, but there are considerable challenges to making this distinction clear for a theory of meaning. Entry #37 introduces a problem involving normative words and sentences – those that express how things should be done (or not done) or invoke some standard of correctness. Much of what we say in ethics is explicitly normative, for instance. The difficulty here is that such expressions appear to be both literal reports of some fact ('Murder is wrong') and also some form of non-literal action-guiding content (*discouraging* us from murdering or disapproving of doing so). Many people doubt that there are moral truths to report, but this is not where the problem lies. We face substantial difficulty in pinning down just what such sentences mean, despite their apparent intelligibility. Entry #38 follows a similar difficulty with vagueness in natural language. A word like 'bald' clearly applies in some cases and not in others, but any proposal for drawing

DOI: 10.4324/9781003183167-50

a boundary between those where it does and those where it doesn't appears implausible. We face a paradox with all the dire implications discussed in entries #16–20, and difficult choices to make about how to proceed.

Entries #39–40 both cover tricky issues surrounding names. In entry #39, we encounter some puzzles surrounding fictional names like 'Luke Skywalker' or 'Sherlock Holmes.' We can make apparently meaningful statements involving those names and assess their apparent truth or falsity with great confidence. Yet there is nothing for those names to signify in the actual world, and nothing (or not enough) to make them true in familiar ways. Names seem to mean something, even where there is no actual thing for them to signify; how they can do so is trickier than it first seems. Conversely, there might be multiple names for the same thing – English speakers call the major city in England 'London' while French speakers call it 'Londres.' Not everyone knows this, and someone might use both names without recognizing that they co-refer. (See also entry #5.) This presents us with a paradox concerning beliefs: one speaker's beliefs expressed with the name 'London' might not match their beliefs expressed with the name 'Londres' even though they appear to mean the same things. How meaning operates within our beliefs proves to be a challenging puzzle to unravel.

METAPHOR

Background: Much of early analytic philosophy of language presumed that there were fixed meanings for each word or sentence in a language that analysis would reveal. Metaphors throw a wrench into the works of that assumption. While they don't simply report facts, their usage is not divorced from the literal meanings of their constituent expressions. As with some other entries in this section, the pragmatic quality they take on when they use them introduces a novel, dynamic quality that is difficult to capture theoretically.

"What light through yonder window breaks? It is the east, and Juliet is the sun."

— *Romeo and Juliet, (Act 2, Scene 2)*

Like most high school students in the English-speaking world, I read these words in class at one point. And like many who did, I thought to myself, "No, she's not." Juliet is not a sphere of plasma; she is of unremarkable mass and temperature relative to other stars. She cannot successfully fake her own death, much less perform nuclear fusion at her core, generating electromagnetic radiation visible for light-years around her. Maybe this is all Romeo's fault, as he evidently lacks the

DOI: 10.4324/9781003183167-51

most basic knowledge of astrophysics. (Clearly, I wasn't much of a poet in high school.)

Shakespeare is engaging in *metaphor* here, of course. We may call the use he is making of the phrase 'the sun' *figurative*, rather than *literal*. The metaphorical phrase here should not be read quite as we ordinarily would, as designating the stellar object in our corner of the galaxy. Somehow, it says something else to us when it is used in just this way, in just this context. The play from which this is taken is a piece of fiction, all of which we read in a non-literal way, but metaphors are pervasive in our ordinary usage, too. Speakers use phrases like 'late bloomer' or 'night owl' for people and speak of a 'heart of stone' or being 'on the right track.' Some metaphors have endured so long that they have become standard meanings, such as the "mouth" of a river or the "head" of an organization. George Lakoff and other cognitive scientists have made the case that much of our ordinary language and thought rely on the same cognitive processes that give us metaphor. (See Lakoff and Johnson (1980) for a nice entry to this line of thought.)

How does a word or phrase come to serve as a metaphor, though? Aristotle claimed that it was "the application of an alien name by transference either from genus to species, or from species to genus, or from species to species, or by analogy, that is, proportion" (335BCE/1996, 3.XXI, 1457b). Very roughly, Aristotle uses "species" as we might say "type," while a genus would be a collection of such types based on commonalities. 'Vehicle' might name a genus of objects, with 'truck' and 'motorcycle' as some of its species. Thus, in each of Aristotle's proposed "transferences," we intentionally apply an expression to some type to which it does not properly apply.

We see many metaphors making this sort of swap:

(1)   Flynn is a bear in the morning.

This metaphor also makes use of the proportional feature that Aristotle mentions. To say metaphorically that someone is a "bear" is to suggest that they are brutish and hostile. People exhibit these qualities at times, though to much lesser degrees than bears do.

Implicit in this is another observation that Aristotle made: a metaphor may be more or less appropriate to its context. If Flynn is more hostile in the morning, and hostility is something that speakers readily associate with bears, the metaphor will work well. But consider:

(2)   Flynn is a cassowary in the morning.

Cassowaries are extremely dangerous birds and have killed humans in rare instances. But they are little known to speakers outside of Indonesia and Papua New Guinea, and so using them as a metaphor elsewhere will often fail because speakers won't know what inferences and analogies to make.

These descriptions of metaphor will no doubt sound plausible, even familiar, to most of us. But there is a puzzle lurking here. As the appropriateness condition would suggest, metaphors are not simply stock phrases playing a conventional expressive role. It matters what 'bear' means when we read (1), and many metaphors make use of such expressions for the first and only time. Thus, it seems natural to say that metaphors *mean* something. But, as we noted in the opening of this entry, what they mean does not appear to be their literal, conventional meaning. Flynn is not actually a bear in the morning, only to switch to human at midday and back again after midnight. If we use expressions figuratively, do they actually take on a second meaning, in addition to their conventional one? This is a tempting suggestion, but if we often use metaphors in novel and unique ways, then how would speakers determine those "second meanings?" If there were a second metaphorical meaning, it would have to be generated by speakers and their audiences spontaneously and harmoniously on the spot. Outside that context where we're speaking of Flynn, almost no one would say that 'bear' *means* 'grumpy in the morning.' But, if there are no metaphorical meanings, then how could we use metaphors to communicate in ways that we clearly do?

RESPONSES

Responses to the puzzle of metaphorical meaning – if there is such a thing – have taken differing routes, depending on the degree to which they incorporate conventional, literal meanings that might play a role in comparative interpretations, and how much they shift the work of that interpretation to context-dependent, pragmatic inferences.

Max Black (1954) offers a useful survey of common themes in classic semantic accounts of metaphor. There are *substitution* views, on which the metaphorical expression substitutes its own meaning for another, literal one. The substituted meaning is then a clue to the literal meaning it replaces, often extending one's language to cover possibilities for which no expressions are yet available. There are also *comparison* views, on which the metaphorical use of expressions does not inject a new meaning, but instead creates an "elliptical simile" in which "the metaphorical statement might be replaced by an equivalent literal comparison" (1954, p. 283). Substitution and comparison views face significant challenges. Substitution views can rarely assign more than stylistic or decorative value to metaphors, which sells many of their instances short. Comparison views invite us to consider similarities between the literal and metaphorical expressions, but there are countless such possible affinities to consider and scant means to decide when they have been exhausted or the correct one has been discovered. Black favors what he calls an *interaction* view, on which two different thoughts are activated by a single expression, and the expression's meaning emerges as a result of their interaction. For instance, the interaction might involve a mapping between the extensions of the literal meanings of the interacting terms ('Flynn' and 'bear' in (1)) to discern the features being figuratively highlighted (e.g., hostility). Those who adopt this view face an open-ended challenge of deciding which features may carry over from one to the other. The metaphorical effect comes as we "attend to both the old and new meanings together" (1954, p. 286). A companion to this view is offered by Beardsley (1962).

A contrasting view is that metaphors don't have novel meanings at all: their only meaning is the literal, conventional meaning that we would assign to those expressions in any other case. We could call this a *brute force* account of metaphor, and contemporary versions of it build on the work of Donald Davidson (1984). If I use a metaphor, then my words just have their literal meanings, which are obviously false, as competent speakers will know. Davidson argues that, rather than introducing an additional meaning, the expression's literal meaning in a metaphor is so out of place that it forces us to consider the primary subject with the secondary subject in a novel fashion. On Davidson's view, what changes in a metaphor is not the meaning, but the *use* we make of that meaning. Reimer (2001) shares the core features of Davidson's view and extends them to address various criticisms. Lepore and Stone (2010) also share Davidson's approach and bring it to bear on more recent contextualist accounts (mentioned in the paragraphs that follow).

Searle (1993) notably offered an "indirect" view of metaphor, on which one proposition is said, but another is meant. Accounting for this is a "special case of the general problem of explaining how speaker meaning and sentence or word meaning come apart" (1993, pp. 83–84). So, we don't arrive at what the speaker is saying via a literal interpretation of what is uttered, and a new sentence meaning is not generated by metaphorical use. The speaker meaning of someone's utterance of (1) instead depends on an assortment of pragmatic features, and much like Grice's plans for conversational implicatures (see entry #28), Searle's aim was to formalize this sort of pragmatic interpretation. He offers eight major principles (1993, pp. 104–108), whose details are too extensive to elaborate here, but which emphasize the themes of similarity, exaggeration, and shared assumptions discussed earlier. Searle suggests that metaphorical sentences may be given a paraphrase to unpack the speaker's meanings of their utterances in conventional sentence meanings (as I did, loosely, for (1) above). But Searle offers no method for deriving such a paraphrase and emphasizes that metaphors do something more than we can capture with the sentence's truth conditions. Someone who receives a metaphorical utterance must figure out what a speaker means from other shared meanings, and it is here that the distinctive expressive character of metaphors lies.

The context-dependence of metaphor has struck many philosophers of language as especially important, but Searle's decision to leave the truth conditions of metaphorical sentences intact while shunting the work of interpreting metaphors over to the pragmatic side of our linguistic behavior has been met with greater suspicion in recent years. Semantic contextualists have argued that variations in semantic content and truth conditions are regular features of many types of expressions and sentences, including metaphors, and that holding sentence meanings invariant and passing off the work of interpreting them in context to pragmatics becomes implausible. Metaphors, such views suggest, are just one further way in which words and sentences can mean different things across contexts. Sperber and Wilson (2008) emphasize this point in offering a "deflationary" account of metaphor. They argue that metaphors involve no special linguistic features, nor are special principles or cognitive mechanisms involved in their interpretation. On their view, communication proceeds when speakers produce evidence of their meanings (intentions and other mental states), and those who receive their utterances infer the meanings from those utterances and their shared context. The figurative/literal distinction would thus be a matter of degree, at most, and not a fundamental distinction in our accounts of meaning.

Contextualists come in other varieties, too. Stern (2000) suggests that metaphorical expressions acquire new meanings in the contexts in which they are uttered, and that this novel acquisition can be modeled along the same lines that we use to understand demonstratives. Bezuidenhout (2001) contrasts Searle's "indirect" view of metaphors, on which we say something by saying *something else*, with a "direct" view of metaphors. On her view, we don't first think of the literal reading of an expression, reject it, and then search for an alternative; we interpret a metaphorical sentence directly, employing pragmatic features, but with semantic constraints. In this way, some aspects of what is said in a metaphor are pragmatically determined in conjunction with relevant information from the non-linguistic environment. For criticisms of contextualist accounts of metaphor, see Camp (2006) and Lepore and Stone (2010). (Interested readers should also look at entries #21–24, which discuss contextualism and its critics in more depth.)

RECOMMENDED READINGS

MAJOR WORKS

Aristotle. 335BCE/1996. "Poetics." In *Aristotle: Introductory Readings (Hackett Classics)*, translated by T. Irwin and G. Fine, 288–318. Indianapolis: Hackett.

Black, M. 1954. "Metaphor." *Proceedings of the Aristotelian Society* 55: 273–294.

Davidson, D. 1984. "What Metaphors Mean." In *Inquiries into Truth and Interpretation*, 245–264. Oxford: Clarendeon Press.

Lakoff, G., and M. Johnson. 1980. "Conceptual Metaphor in Everyday Language." *Journal of Philosophy* 77: 453–486.

Sperber, D., and D. Wilson. 2008. "A Deflationary Account of Metaphors." In *The Cambridge Handbook of Metaphor and Thought*, edited by R. Gibbs, 84–105. Cambridge: Cambridge University Press.

RESPONSES

Beardsley, M. 1962. "The Metaphorical Twist." *Philosophy and Phenomenological Research* 22 (3): 293–307.

Bezuidenhout, A. 2001. "Metaphor and What Is Said: A Defense of a Direct Expression View of Metaphor." *Midwest Studies in Philosophy* 25: 156–186.

Camp, E. 2006. "Contextualism, Metaphor and What Is Said." *Mind & Language* 21 (3): 280–309.

Lepore, E., and M. Stone. 2010. "Against Metaphorical Meaning." *Topoi* 29 (2): 165–180.

Reimer, M. 2001. "Davidson on Metaphor." *Midwest Studies in Philosophy* 25: 142–155.

Searle, J. 1993. "Metaphor." In *Metaphor and Thought*, edited by A. Ortony, 83–111. Cambridge: Cambridge University Press.

Stern, J. 2000. *Metaphor in Context*. Cambridge: The MIT Press.

THE FREGE-GEACH PROBLEM

Background: Many accounts of natural languages begin with assumptions that truth and representation are fundamental properties of natural languages. They assume that linguistic behavior is fundamentally a matter of communication, that the fundamental type of information that we communicate to others is representational, and that truth-aptness is the fundamental feature of any representation (or at least one fundamental feature). But we must then take further steps to make sense of words and sentences that express normative judgments or guide action.

Consider two familiar sorts of sentences:

(1)   Grass is green.
(2)   Murder is wrong.

Both appear to be generalizations, and they share the same syntactical form. We might say that (1) is descriptive of some condition, and that it is truth-apt. That is, it might be true or false, and it is the sort of sentence for which questions of its truth are fitting. Maybe you'd want to argue that grass *isn't* green – it comes in many different colors, or some more precise color term is more appropriate. Either way, (1) is a sentence that *could* be true. Can we say the same about (2)? 'Wrong'

DOI: 10.4324/9781003183167-52

suggests a less straightforward property than 'green.' What exactly would *wrongness* be? Imagine everything that we might call "wrong" – all the actions, all the refusals to act, all the things that could be said, never said, etc. When you lump them all together, they won't seem very similar. What binds them all together is that we *evaluate* them in the same way, not that we *describe* some common feature.

So, what do normative sentences *say*? Any answer to that will be contentious. Suppose we took a straightforwardly realist position: normative properties like wrongness are real properties of objects, events, and states of affairs. If so, they would have to be very strange properties. We can't measure or observe them like physical properties. They also apparently have distinctive motivational features; knowing that an action is wrong typically entails having a strong motivation not to take it. Descriptive sentences don't have that sort of action-guiding impetus built into them; (1) doesn't ask or discourage you from doing anything. Some philosophers have thought that these worries about normative properties can be overcome, while others have found them serious enough to call the very existence of normativity into doubt. But there is another type of approach that has been taken that is of special interest to philosophers of language.

What if these problems only arise because we have taken an excessively narrow approach to what the meanings of normative expressions (like 'wrong') and sentences involving them might be saying? What if their role were not to *describe* something, but to *express* something? We might then offer a different sort of analysis of sentences like (2), and it might not be necessary to posit unusual properties in the world. And what such sentences express might include different forms of action-guidance, solving the other part of our problem. We can point to familiar sorts of sentences that express numerous things without purporting to describe:

(3)   Let's go Pens! Woooooooooo!
(4)   No parking after 4:00.
(5)   We don't use that word in this house.

Sentence (3) might be yelled at a Pittsburgh Penguins game by fans. You can yell this when the team is winning, losing, or you're simply excited. No attempt to describe the game is being made. It expresses something about your emotions and attitudes toward the team. Sentence (4) expresses a rule that prescribes something (when and where to park), and this guides the action of someone who sees such a sign. Sentence (5) may look like a description at first, but it is not. Suppose you drop an F-bomb at the Thanksgiving dinner table, and a parent or grandparent says this to you. They are not denying that the word has ever been uttered; they are expressing a norm that governs the unacceptability of that word (a very *local* norm in this case). We could say that (3)-(5) express emotion, prescribe action, and express allegiance to a norm, respectively. (For deeper looks at what to make of these, see Stevenson (1937/1963) and Hare (1952).)

Expressivists suggest that normative language expresses combinations of these features, giving voice to our attitudes. Their role would be to influence our attitudes and how we act on them, not to represent the world outside of our language. The absence of some entity or property that we could identify as wrongness does not undercut (2) because it is not an attempt to report such facts. If someone yells "Let's go Pens!" to you, it makes no sense to insist that this is false, even if you favor another team or don't care about hockey at all. Nor does it prove (5) false to note that you *did* just use that word.

If sentences like (2)-(5) don't purport to represent anything, many philosophers have said they are not truth-apt. That may not sound bad for an expressivist view. Those sentences can do the expressive work they are supposed to and weren't trying to represent anything anyway. But the problem runs much deeper. Take an argument:

(6)   If grass is green, then grass is not purple.
(7)   Grass is green.

----

(8)   Grass is not purple.

By most accounts, a deductive argument functions by establishing logical relations between sentences. Those relations establish various sorts of consequence, which can be studied formally in logic. The relations may be between groups of sentences, as (6)-(7) jointly entail (8), giving us a set of premises and a conclusion. There may also be relations within parts of a sentence, as we see in (6), which connects 'Grass is green' with 'Grass is not purple' via a logical operator of the form 'if . . . then . . .'. Most logicians would argue that the only types of sentences that can fill these spots in an argument are those that are truth-apt. Thus, sentences like (2)-(5) could not play a role in a well-formed argument. Geach (1960, 1965), building on the work of Frege, noted that this does not appear to be the case:

(9)   If murder is wrong, then we should punish murderers.
(10)   Murder is wrong.
----
(11)   We should punish murderers.

This seems to be a well-formed argument. Yet (10) and (11) express evaluation, and (9) takes two normative sentences and connects them with 'if . . . then . . .'. An expressivist can say that (10) has no truth-value, only an expressive one, but it is not apparently different from the embedded occasion of that sentence in the first half of (9). And the occasion of 'Murder is wrong' in (9) is not actually expressing commitment to something. The 'if . . . then . . .' operator allows us to embed a sentence on its left side hypothetically, without having to assert it. We could also form a conditional that says 'If murder is right, then . . .' without endorsing murder. If the occurrence in (9) is not truth-apt and merely expressive, then (9) as a whole would be ill-formed. By comparison, no sentence of the form 'if Let's go Pens! Wooooooooooo!, then . . .' will be truth-evaluable; the truth of the whole is a function of the truth of its parts, and one of its parts cannot have any truth value. This is called the Frege-Geach Problem, or the embedding problem, since we must make sense of those embedded normative sentences. Should we say that the embedded sentence in (9) has a radically different meaning from the free-standing ones in (10) and (11)? Geach and most others have taken this to be an implausible response. Should we say that all these sentences are descriptive after all? If so, we will be left to explain the action-guiding qualities that expressivists so readily embraced.

RESPONSES

For a review of recent work on the Frege-Geach problem, see Woods (2018). Geach himself took the problem to be a decisive blow against expressivist accounts (he called them "ascriptivist") of normative language. And many metaethicists have followed Geach on this point, arguing that the language we use in ethics is fundamentally descriptive.

That may be bad news for ethical and other forms of normative language. If the language we use does purport to describe normative properties, and there are serious problems with positing such properties, then what we say with that part of the language would be fundamentally in error. Others have tried to rehabilitate normative properties to either naturalize them or simply accept their non-natural status. Each of those approaches faces significant challenges, so there has been considerable interest in expressivism, despite the persistence of the Frege-Geach problem.

Mark Schroeder (2008) has argued that the first task in giving an expressivist account is to generate a suitable account of inconsistency for non-descriptive sentences. (See also Unwin (1999).) Inconsistency matters because it is central to accounts of argumentation, but is also typically defined in terms of truth. For descriptive sentences, this is simple: two sentences like 'Grass is green' and 'Grass is not green' are inconsistent because of the logical inconsistency of their descriptive contents. (They can't both be true at the same time.) But an expressivist account must explain the difference between 'Murder is wrong' and 'Murder is not wrong' in terms of different sorts of attitudes expressed by them. Schroeder suggests that we can think of expressivists' responses to this as falling into two types: those that explain this inconsistency in terms of the contents toward which we have attitudes in normative talk ("A-type") and those that explain it in terms of the attitudes themselves ("B-type"). The difference here lies in whether an account suggests that normative sentences introduce description in addition to expressing attitudes, or if everything about them should be understood in terms of attitudes.

For A-type expressivists, the attitudes we hold toward normative sentences resemble beliefs in important respects, because the contents themselves have additional normative features toward which we can have belief-like attitudes. In this vein, Horgan and Timmons (2006) have offered what they call "cognitivist expressivism" that incorporates "ought-commitments," on which moral judgments are truth-apt "despite being nondescriptive, because they possess enough of the key, generic, phenomenological, and functional features of belief" (257). Schroeder worries that this approach will lead to a methodologically implausible proliferation of different attitudes packed into these "ought commitments." His approach posits only a single type of attitude – *being for* – that accounts for inconsistency in normative sentences, suggesting a more straightforward integration with the rest of our semantic theory. (For responses to cognitivist expressivism, see Bedke (2012) and Strandberg (2015).)

For B-type expressivists, the possibility of inconsistency lies outside the semantic contents themselves. For instance, Blackburn (1984) presented a view he called *quasi-realism* that involved the *projection* of attitudes onto things in the world, rather than *receiving* something's impingement on us. We project disapproval onto certain killings in (2), on this view. He then emphasizes attitudes about our own attitudes in addressing the Frege-Geach problem. Whereas a sentence like (2) expresses disapproval of murder, a conditional like (9) expresses disapproval toward an attitude of accepting the left side of the conditional but not the right. (Thus, it disapproves of [*someone's disapproving of murder, but not of punishing murderers*].) Gibbard (2003) develops an even more extensive semantics for normative parts of the language, and pairs it with an interpretation that emphasizes "plan-laden content – judgments laden with to-be-doneness and okayness" (200). A plan in Gibbard's sense is a mental state that melds facts about the world with commitments about what to do in light of them. We could have these for both our actual circumstances and other possible ones too, and thus model which such combinations fall within such plans. Those that don't are inconsistent with our plans and the sentences that express them. The meanings of normative language emerge as expressions of allegiance to such plans. For discussions of these B-types accounts, see Unwin (1999) and Dreier (2006).

RECOMMENDED READINGS

MAJOR WORKS

Geach, P. 1960. "Ascriptivism." *Philosophical Review* 69 (2): 221–225.

Geach, P. 1965. "Assertion." *Philosophical Review* 74 (4): 449–465.

Hare, R. 1952. *The Language of Morals*. Oxford: Clarendon Press.

Woods, J. 2018. "The Frege-Geach Problem." In *The Routledge Handbook of Meta-ethics*, edited by T. McPherson and D. Plunkett, 226–242. New York: Routledge.

RESPONSES

Bedke, M. 2012. "The Ought-Is Gap: Trouble for Hybrid Semantics." *Philosophical Quarterly* 62 (249): 657–670.

Blackburn, S. 1984. *Spreading the Word*. Oxford: Oxford University Press.

Dreier, J. 2006. "Negation for Expressivists: A Collection of Problems with a Suggestion for Their Solution." *Oxford Studies in Metaethics* 1: 217–233.

Gibbard, A. 2003. *Thinking How to Live*. Cambridge: Harvard University Press.

Horgan, T., and M. Timmons. 2006. "Cognitivist Expressivism." In *Metaethics After Moore*, edited by T. Horgan and M. Timmons, 255–298. Oxford: Oxford University Press.

Schroeder, M. 2008. *Being for: Evaluating the Semantic Program of Expressivism*. Oxford: Oxford University Press.

Stevenson, C. 1937/1963. "The Emotive Meaning of Ethical Terms." In *Facts and Values: Studies in Ethical Analysis*, 10–31. New Haven: Yale University Press.

Strandberg, C. 2015. "Options for Hybrid Expressivism." *Ethical Thoery and Moral Practice* 18 (1): 91–111.

Unwin, N. 1999. "Quasi-Realism, Negation, and the Frege-Geach Problem." *Philosophical Quarterly* 49 (196): 337–352.

38

SOMETHING ON VAGUENESS

Background: One feature of the ideal conceptions of language offered by many analytic philosophers is that words have determinate meanings, and there are determinate truth values that we can assign to the sentences that include them. The classical paradoxes discussed in entries #16–20 present apparent contradictions, but these don't arise from any difficulty in interpreting the sentences themselves. Vague terms like 'bald' present us with a different problem: they clearly apply in some cases, not in others, and have a range of borderline cases that are difficult, if not impossible, to determine.

One feature of some of the terms we find in natural language is *vagueness*. This is to say that there are conditions under which they would definitely apply (or sentences asserting them would be true, if you prefer), and there are conditions under which they definitely would not, and then there are some conditions under which it would be unclear whether they applied, even if we had all the information that could be gathered. This third category is often called a set of borderline cases, in which we can see judgments going either way, and it becomes difficult if not impossible to decide.

'Bald' would seem to be a vague term. Some people have "a full head of hair," as we say, some grow very little or none, and then there are people who lie somewhere between. (We'll stick to hair on one's

DOI: 10.4324/9781003183167-53

head for now.) To decide those borderline cases, we might devise a system and stipulate a threshold. Suppose we provide a notion of "scalp coverage" in some well-defined way, expressed as a percentage of the scalp with active hair follicles, taking into account the different sizes and shapes of people's heads. That will be tricky and perhaps contentious, but let's assume it for the moment. Given this sort of measure, we would find some people with 100 percent coverage, or close to it. Someone exhibiting advanced male pattern baldness probably has around 30 percent coverage – think of someone like the actor Patrick Stewart[1] here. Somewhere between those two measures, we will find borderline cases.

One intuitive response here is to suggest a threshold by which to classify cases and let that define the term. Suppose we make our threshold 50 percent, so it is true of anyone with more than 50 percent coverage that they are not bald, and it is true of anyone with 50 percent or less that they are bald. Clear cases (like Patrick Stewart) are on one side of the line or the other, as we would expect, and every single borderline case will be, too. But this seems like an odd solution when we look closer. There would be cases in which someone was just *one hair* away from being bald. A strong breeze or a quick pass of the comb before work, and suddenly they're bald, even though they would look just the same to us. Even if we could look more closely, counting every last hair somehow, it would still be strange to change so suddenly if we're genuinely trying to capture what 'bald' means when we use the term. How could *one hair* make that sort of difference? We could set the threshold at some other degree of coverage, but that would solve nothing. Wherever we set it, it solves our borderline problem only by counting some cases and not others in a way that seems arbitrary.

Well, so what? Maybe some parts of the language are just messy. What else would you expect from a crowdsourced project conducted over thousands of years by billions of people? Our examples don't seem like they would have catastrophic consequences, and if some terms do, we could introduce more precisely defined ones. The trick is that, even if these are just the sloppy meanings of everyday language, they are still meaningful. And they will still be matters covered by whatever sort of logic we adopt. Here, concerns about vagueness intersect with a classic problem called "the Sorites paradox." It's also sometimes called "the paradox of the heap," and as you can probably guess, it depends on the vagueness of 'heap.' Imagine we had 10,000,000 grains of salt, which would be a bit more than a liter. Pour those out on a table and you have a heap of salt. Take away one grain, and you still have a heap; take away one more, and you still have a heap. We might think of this as implying a sort of rule: removing one grain never changes a heap into a non-heap. But now we're in position to see the paradox. Imagine we start with our 10,000,000-grain heap and our rule as premises:

(R)   Removing one grain never changes a heap into a non-heap.
(1)   Zero grains are not a heap.
(2)   10,000,000 grains are a heap.
(3)   If 10,000,000 grains are a heap, then 9,999,999 grains are a heap.

Sentence (3) here follows from (R) and (2). I take it that (1) will be plausible no matter how we approach these issues. And we can keep going like this:

(4)   If 9,999,999 grains are a heap, then 9,999,998 grains are a heap.
(5)   If 9,999,998 grains are a heap, then 9,999,997 grains are a heap.
. . .

We can keep going this way until we get to two final steps:

. . .
(10,000,002) If 1 grain is a heap, then zero grains are a heap.
(10,000,003) Zero grains are a heap.

Sentence (10,000,003) follows from sentences (2) through (10,000,002) in a very simple 10,000,000-step series. We're now committed to saying both that zero grains are a heap, and that they are not a heap. We can run this in the other direction, too. Start with no grains. Adding one does not give you a heap, and adding one grain to one grain does not give you a heap, and so on until you have 10,000,000 grains and are both affirming and denying that they are a heap. This is a serious consequence, as it would undermine classical logic if all this were true. We can avoid that by insisting that there is some point in this series at which we will no longer have a heap (or a person will no longer be bald, etc.), though, as we saw earlier, any attempt to do that seems arbitrary. Vague terms like these are common in natural languages, so this is not an esoteric concern for professional logicians that we can wall off from ordinary speakers. We need to say something more substantial about how vague terms operate.

RESPONSES

Some philosophers have treated vague terms as either a metaphysical or an epistemic problem. To treat it as a metaphysical issue would imply that some property in the world itself had an indeterminate nature, which vague terms somehow faithfully mirrored. Epistemic approaches would imply that there were the thresholds of the sorts we discussed earlier, but that they remain unknown to us (even though we introduced these terms). These approaches have been less popular than semantic approaches, though. (And of course, we're talking about language here, so those are the ones that would interest us, for now.)

One approach to the problem of vagueness would be to simply bite the bullet and find a way to live with the indeterminacy of the borderline cases. This is the starting point for a family of accounts known as *supervaluationism*. On such accounts, notions of "super-true" and "super-false" are introduced for the clear cases we described earlier. The borderline cases would then have a third kind of value, akin to the truth-value "gaps" of some paracomplete logics.[2] So accounting for vagueness in this way would spell an end to classical two-valued logic, but it would leave open the possibility of preserving many features of logical consequence and validity from classical logic. The 10,000,000+-step argument from our example above would remain *valid*, but we need not say that it is *sound*. That is, if all its premises were (super)true, the contradiction we derive with it would have to be (super)true, but we're not compelled to draw this conclusion, thanks to the different sort of status assigned to the borderline cases.

A supervaluationist can say that, while those borderline cases are not super-true or super-false, at least one of the premises fails to be super-true and so the contradiction does not follow, thereby deflating the threat of the paradox. This puts us in the awkward position of saying that there is some number of grains at which the pile stops being a heap (or starts, if we're going the other way), as well as compelling us to adopt a new account of truth with some very intuitively mysterious features. But supervaluationists may argue that vagueness just shows truth to be very different from our untutored intuitions and offers us a formal approach to a logic than can accommodate that. See van Fraassen (1966), Fine (1975) and Keefe (2000) for supervaluationist accounts, and Williamson (1994, Chapter 5) for objections. Analogous (though certainly distinct) efforts have been made to solve the paradox with three-valued logics (Tye 1994) and infinite-valued logics (Smith 2008).

Recently, there have been numerous contextualist accounts of vagueness. Contextualist accounts, broadly speaking, emphasize the ways in which the meanings of some sentences or classes of expressions function in ways that are sensitive to the contexts in which they occur. (See entries #21–22 for further detail.) Contextualist accounts in this vein suggest that the apparent semantic indeterminacy of vague terms is actually the shifting of the extensions of those terms according to different sorts of features of conversational contexts. We assume that a certain set of things will fall into the extension of 'bald' (or any other vague term) that remains fixed, but instead, they will have an open texture that only contextual features can make determinate. Our sense that there is a semantic indeterminacy to vague terms may thus be that, in the abstract, we don't have enough of the relevant features to determine the extensions. Åkerman (2009) surveys the landscape of contextualist accounts of vagueness in greater detail, though with a clarity and economy that will suit readers new to such accounts.

Pragmatic contextualists such as Soames (1999) and Shapiro (2006) look to the state of the conversation for their contextual features, such as assertions that have been made and accepted by speakers. For instance, if speakers' assertions have established that a given conversation concerned professional basketball players, a vague term like 'tall' might have an extension including fewer people (well over six and a half feet, let's say) than it would in a conversation concerning kindergarten students (where the tall ones are less than four feet tall). *Psychological* contextualists such as Raffman (1996) and Fara (2000) suggest that the relevant contextual features are psychological states of speakers, which ground their dispositions to make judgments about objects being in the extension or not, but which are also apt to vary from context to context. The apparent indeterminacy of vague terms would thereby be a result of failing to notice such shifts. Challenges linger for any form of contextualism about vagueness, though. For one, the sorts of contextual variation mentioned here can often be made explicit or stabilized (note my specifications of basketball players and kindergarteners above) in ways that are not available for vague terms. It falls to the contextualists to elaborate their case in a way that does not allow context-sensitivity to simply peel away from vagueness in the end.

NOTES

1. Captain Picard of *Star Trek* (for readers born before 1985), or Professor Xavier of the *X-Men* (for those born after).
2. See entry #20 for more.

RECOMMENDED READINGS

MAJOR WORKS

Fine, K. 1975. "Vagueness, Truth and Logic." *Synthèse* 30 (3–4): 265–300.

Raffman, D. 1996. "Vagueness and Context-Relativity." *Philosophical Studies* 81 (2–3): 175–192.

Tye, M. 1994. "Sorites Paradoxes and the Semantics of Vagueness." *Philosophical Perspectives* 8: 189–206.

van Fraassen, B. 1966. "Singular Terms, Truth-Value Gaps, and Free Logic." *Journal of Philosophy* 63 (7): 481–495.

RESPONSES

Åkerman, J. 2009. "Contextualist Theories of Vagueness." *Philosophy Compass* 7 (7): 470–480.

Fara, D.G. 2000. "Shifting Sands: An Interest-Relative Theory of Vagueness." *Philosophical Topics* 28 (1): 45–81.

Keefe, R. 2000. *Theories of Vagueness*. Cambridge: Cambridge University Press.

Shapiro, S. 2006. *Vagueness in Context*. Oxford: Oxford University Press.

Smith, N. 2008. *Vagueness and Degrees of Truth*. Oxford: Oxford University Press.

Soames, S. 1999. *Understanding Truth*. New York: Oxford University Press.

Williamson, T. 1994. *Vagueness (Problems of Philosophy)*. New York: Routledge.

39

MEANINGS OF FICTIONAL NAMES

Background: It has been an assumption among most analytic philosophers of language that names that don't designate anything are meaningless. Yet this fails to distinguish supposed names that are simply empty from those that are used in fiction, where they play roles in meaningful sentences. Attempts to address this apparent inconsistency are our focus here.

(1)   John Coltrane was born in North Carolina.
(2)   Pam Beesly works in Scranton.
(3)   Luke Skywalker was born on Polis Massa.

Let's call all three of these statements true for the moment. While (1) is trivia strictly for jazz enthusiasts, most readers will have watched some of the US version of *The Office* and know of Dunder-Mifflin's long-running receptionist. Unless you're especially devoted to the *Star Wars* universe, (3) may come as a surprise. (I had to look it up.) Most people would guess Tatooine, if they ventured a guess at all. And let me stress this: if they had guessed anything else, they would have been *wrong*.

The differences among these sentences are probably obvious. Whereas (1) is literally true of an actual person, both (2) and (3) are fictional statements. Pam Beesly and Luke Skywalker are the fictional

DOI: 10.4324/9781003183167-54

creations of writers and actors, and not actual people in the world. Fictional characters are often inspired by actual people, of course. George Lucas has mentioned Samurai warriors of feudal Japan as one inspiration for the Jedi knights in the Star Wars universe, including Luke Skywalker. Vlad the Impaler inspired Bram Stoker's Count Dracula, and that character has reappeared in countless works and inspired many more. But Vlad the Impaler is not Count Dracula; any statement that Vlad the Impaler *is* Dracula must be read figuratively. The character of Pam Beesly may have been inspired by an actual person, but that person is not Pam Beesly.

This leaves us with a puzzle. It appears that the fictional names in (2) and (3) have no referents, at least not of the familiar sort. By most accounts, we therefore could not interpret them, and they could not have truth values. Yet it also seems, as I said, that they are correct in some way. Had I said that Luke was born on Tatooine, I would have been wrong. For an assertion like (2) or (3), we would typically assume that a correct statement is a true one. Likewise, we would typically think of meaningful names as those with referents, and those without referents as meaningless.[1] Russell and Frege had analyzed expressions with no apparent referent, but their methods were not yet aimed at fictional terms and would not readily explain the correctness that we have noted. So, what can we do?

One intuition that people sometimes have is that fictional names can be meaningful and fictional sentences true because they refer to and describe something much more mundane: they are about our *ideas* of these characters and stories. Pam Beesly doesn't exist, but the name 'Pam Beesly' refers to my idea of that character. W.V.O. Quine (1948) considered this suggestion for 'Pegasus,' the Greek mythological creature, but he noted that this is implausible. There might be such a psychological entity as our Pam-Beesly-idea, but when someone talks about Pam Beesly, they are not making psychological claims. Suppose we identified some region of my brain responsible for thinking of Pam Beesly; would it have to move to Scranton to make (2) true, as we took it to be? Would it have to work as a receptionist? Would we have to say that the Luke Skywalker part of my brain was born in the Polis Massa region of my brain? (What does 'born' mean, in that case?) If we torture these questions long enough, it may yield some less ridiculous reading, but even then, this is not what people are typically saying when they talk about Pam Beesly or Luke Skywalker, and we're trying to account for what they are actually saying.

We could say that, since (2) and (3) are fiction, all bets are off, we can play with the details as we like, and the only constraints are what we conventionally allow each other to say about the story. It's interesting to think about "fan fiction" here, in which creators establish characters and frameworks for a fictional universe, which fans then use to create extensions of the stories on their own. I'll admit some sympathy with this, but I urge readers not to rush to glib conclusions. Writers did have free rein when creating the *Star Wars* universe, and if the right sources say that Luke Skywalker was born on Polis Massa, then they say that with all the authority we could ask for. But we're asking what it *means* for them to use those names if we have given up the pretense that they refer to familiar, everyday objects. We speak of fictional characters not only "in their world," but in critical statements that refer to them while acknowledging their fictional status:

(4)   Pam Beesly is the most manipulative character on *The Office*.

True or false, this is not an "in world" statement about that fictional universe like (2)-(3), which fictional characters in that narrative might say to one another. We make it *about* that fictional world, and apparently refer to objects *in it* to do so, even though we're not in it, and don't believe it exists.

RESPONSES

Many responses to this puzzle answer it straightforwardly: fictional names do refer to real objects, and sentences involving them are truth-apt, though the objects are very different from everyday objects. We can call theories that make this commitment *fictional realist* accounts of fictional characters. They share a sense that there is nothing unusual about the semantics of fictional names, but the entities to which they refer are not concrete entities in the actual world like a person. When, outside of philosophical circles, we say that fictional characters don't exist or aren't real, we're typically saying that they are not actual, concrete individuals like us – i.e., not flesh and blood, physical creatures like us that we could encounter. However, many philosophers contend that there are other types of objects that can exist. Abstract objects would exist in the realm of the purely conceptual, yet they would still exist as objects. Mathematical objects such as numbers are often mentioned as a possible example of this type.

Positing that such abstractions are real and exist, independent of our thoughts, is contentious, but it has been an appealing approach to many working on fictional names. Schiffer (1996) speaks of fictional characters as "language-created language-independent entities." We introduce them with the practices and conventions of storytelling, and we play at referring or taking true sentences like (2)-(3), as we're familiar with practices of fiction-telling. However, in sentences like (4), speakers do purport to say something true (or false), and so we should take commitments to the existence of fictional characters seriously. They would be abstract objects created by their authors, but just as real and designation-ready as the posits we make in science or mathematics. (Criticisms of this move to abstract objects for fictional characters are offered in Brock (2002) and Everett (2005).) This theme of creation of an abstract individual object by the act of writing runs through numerous works on fictional names, notably van Inwagen (2001) and Thomasson (1999). The emphasis on creation in these accounts highlights an important difference from other purported abstract objects: fictional characters would be *contingent* creations. Every possible world will include the number we designate with the numeral '17,' but the creation of the fictional character Luke Skywalker won't happen in a possible world where George Lucas does not write screenplays or writes other ones instead. (For critical discussion of these creation-focused accounts of abstract individual objects, see Yagisawa (2001) and Goodman (2004).) Another approach would be to treat fictional characters not as individual objects, but as roles or kinds that many different individuals could fill. A role in this sense would be a set of properties definitive of that character – e.g., Pam Beesly is a receptionist, works in Scranton, etc. The abstract object invokes only collections of properties, which will have to be included in our inventory of the world anyway. Proponents of such views include Wolterstorff (1980) and Currie (1988); Brock (2002) offers criticism of this as well.

A contrasting set of views emphasize pretense about fictional names and entities. On a pretense view, we take it that speakers generally know that an entity does not exist, but we speak and think as if it did, and play through different scenarios and conversations as if certain propositions were the case. This accords with some familiar patterns of ordinary usage of fictional names. Those who watch *The Office* or *Star Wars* generally know that they are consuming a piece of fiction and would avoid any serious claim that those characters are real people if we pressed the point philosophically. Kripke (2011) adopts a view in this vein about fictional names. On that account, we must accept the consequence that, strictly speaking, fictional names are meaningless.[2] This is not to say that they are nonsense or gibberish, but that in a final, serious, and literal analysis of fictional discourse, we could not give an interpretation that actually designates some entity to which we attribute these fictional properties. But we can carry on the conversation as if we did, and speak as if 'Pam Beesly is a receptionist' was meaningful, by mock-asserting that and other propositions (e.g., that Pam Beesly answers phones, directs visitors to offices for meetings, etc.).

Adams *et al.* (1997) take up this approach, and favoring a "direct reference" approach indebted to Kripke and John Stuart Mill, they accept that this makes sentences incorporating fictional names meaningless. This does not render them nonsensical, though. Instead, they express *incomplete* propositions, akin to '*x* is taller than Michael,' where the variable leaves a component of the proposition unspecified, and hence incomplete. This makes it impossible to fully interpret them and deem them true or false, but it does not render them *unreadable*. We may still interpret the syntax of such sentences and note relations of other meaningful parts of such sentences to the rest of the language. 'Luke Skywalker was a Jedi' and 'Luke Skywalker was born on Polis Massa' cannot be fully interpreted, but we can note that 'Luke Skywalker' is being used as a name, that it recurs, that 'born' implies birth and a lifetime, etc. Walton (1990) defends a version of pretense that also does not presume real entities to whom fictional names refer, but with less pessimistic implications for truth. Walton's account includes a more extensive proposal for how practices of make-believe operate. This account elaborates how real-world conditions may serve as "props" in games of make-believe or fiction, and the "principles of generation" by which they then establish truths within the fiction. How can there be truth without entities? Walton argues that the truth-conditions of statements about fiction don't need to include such entities, only that the statements are licensed by the fiction in question. Designation and correspondence to the facts are replaced by *fictional assertion*, whose rules determine whether the truth-conditions are met. A more critical response to pretense theories is offered by Bjurman-Pautz (2008), who doubts that pretense can account for "fictional coreference." Suppose you mention Luke Skywalker and I say, "He was a great pilot;" 'he' and 'Luke' fictionally co-refer, but we cannot say what makes this so if the terms don't refer to real entities. This does not entail a realism about fictional characters, but it may throw pretense accounts into question.

NOTES

1. This is admittedly a very broad characterization of this view that many people (including me) have questioned. Bear with me for the moment.
2. Kripke (2011) is discussed in entry #50.

RECOMMENDED READINGS

MAJOR WORKS

Kripke, S. 1973/2011. "Vacuous Names and Fictional Entities." In *Philosophical Troubles: Collected Papers*, edited by S. Kripke, vol. 1, 52–74. New York: Oxford University Press.

Quine, W. 1948. "On What There Is." *Review of Metaphysics* 2: 21–38.

van Inwagen, P. 2001. "Creatures of Fiction." In *Ontology, Identity, and Modality*, 37–56. Cambridge: Cambridge University Press.

Walton, K. 1990. *Mimesis as Make-Believe*. Cambridge: Harvard University Press.

RESPONSES

Adams, F., G. Fuller, and R. Stecker. 1997. "The Semantics of Fictional Names." *Pacific Philosophical Quarterly* 78 (2): 128–148.

Bjurman Pautz, A. 2008. "Fictional Coreference as a Problem for the Pretense Theory." *Philosophical Studies* 141 (2): 147–156.

Brock, S. 2002. "Fictionalism About Fictional Characters." *Nous* 36: 1–21.

Currie, G. 1988. "Fictional Names." *Australasian Journal of Philosophy* 66 (4): 471–488.

Everett, A. 2005. "Against Fictional Realism." *Journal of Philosophy* 102 (12): 624–649.

Goodman, J. 2004. "A Defense of Creationism in Fiction." *Grazer Philosophische Studien* 67 (1): 131–155.

Schiffer, S. 1996. "Language-Created Language-Independent Entities." *Philosophical Topics* 24 (1): 149–167.

Thomasson, A. 1999. *Fiction and Metaphysics.* Cambridge: Cambridge University Press.

Wolterstorff, N. 1980. *Works and Worlds of Art.* Oxford: Oxford University Press.

Yagisawa, T. 2001. "Against Creationism in Fiction." *Philosophical Perspectives* 15: 153–172.

'LONDRES EST JOLIE . . .'

Background: In entries #46–47, we look at arguments from Saul Kripke and Hilary Putnam that push back against Frege's views on sense. There, they argue that proper names and natural kind terms don't have clusters of descriptions associated with them by which we may articulate their meanings. Instead, they simply designate their referents. Fregeans often point to contexts in which we ascribe belief to refute this view. Kripke's 1979 puzzle attempts to turn such cases against the Fregean view.

A widely held view among philosophers of language, typically attributed to John Stuart Mill, is that the semantic content of a name consists solely in its reference to its bearer. On this "Millian" view, names play no other linguistic function, and in particular they don't describe their bearer in any significant way. In entry #5, we considered Frege's arguments against the Millian view, in favor of assigning his notion of the *sense* of a name, which determines its referent. A further class of cases that Frege took to support his view are sentences that express propositions involving the ascription of beliefs to speakers. To illustrate this point, note that the first two of

DOI: 10.4324/9781003183167-55

the following sentences can apparently be true in a case where the third is false:

(1)   Farrokh Bulsara is Freddie Mercury.
(2)   Abby believes that Freddie Mercury sings well.
(3)   Abby believes that Farrokh Bulsara sings well.

How could this be so? Presumably, Abby is unaware of (1). If so, she may not know who the name 'Farrokh Bulsara' designates, and thus has never formed any beliefs involving that name. Or maybe she has never heard her friend Farrokh sing and doesn't know that he performs under another name. Frege's view was roughly that a belief is directed toward the sense of expressions involved in it, not directly to its reference. Since 'Farrokh Bulsara' and 'Freddie Mercury' have different senses, beliefs that we express by including them will have different senses, and thus we may hold different attitudes toward them. Hence, Abby may believe the embedded sentence ('Freddie Mercury sings well') in (2), but not the one in (3). If Mill were right, Frege argued, there would be no way of accounting for this difference, since both names designate the same person. The names in (2) and (3) designate the same thing, so what Abby believes in each case should be the same. They're not, so Mill must have been wrong.

Frege's argument convinced many philosophers of language, but by no means all. Saul Kripke argued that Frege's views, or at least the prevailing interpretations of them by the mid-20th century, entailed implausible consequences for modal contexts. (These are discussed in detail in entry #46.) Kripke's response was to adopt a view much more like Mill's, though that was a tough sell in belief contexts because of the argument discussed above. In "A Puzzle About Belief" (1979/2011), Kripke offers a new puzzle to throw Frege's conclusions about belief contexts into doubt and revive prospects for a Millian solution to it.

To get this puzzle going, we first assume two principles:

(D)   If a normal English speaker, on reflection, sincerely assents to 'p,' then he believes that p. (137)
(T)   If a sentence of one language expresses a truth in that language, then any translation of it into any other language also expresses a truth (in that other language). (139)

We call the first '(D)', as in 'disquotational;' to say what the content of a belief is, we simply remove the quotes placed around the mention of a sentence ('p'). And '(T)' is for 'translation.' We will assume these without argument for the time being. Both are either assumed in Frege's argument about belief contexts, or elsewhere in his work.

Imagine we have Pierre, a French speaker who grows up in France. In school, he reads of a city that the French call 'Londres,' which is full of beautiful architecture, great art, and other delights. He forms a belief, and he expresses that belief via his assent to the French sentence, '*Londres est jolie.*' 'Londres' is the French name for London, of course, and so with (D), (T), and what little French we remember from high school, we conclude:

(4)   Pierre believes that London is pretty.

Now, suppose Pierre takes a job with a British firm. With just enough English to get by, he moves to the UK and finds a place to live. But Pierre can only afford a run-down apartment in a squalid corner of the ugliest part of London, and he comes to have a dismal view of the city as a whole. He learns most of what he knows of London from his neighbors, who call the city 'London' and not 'Londres,' so no one explains to Pierre that these are two names for the same city. Pierre will thus readily assent to the English sentence:

(5)   London is not pretty.

But he does not assent to the English sentence:

(6)   London is pretty.

And so, with (D) and Pierre's assent to (5), we conclude:

(7)   Pierre believes that London is not pretty.

Thus, (4) and (7) attribute contradictory beliefs to Pierre despite appropriate starting points and apparently reasonable principles, giving us a puzzle to resolve. The original puzzle from Frege left room for Abby to have a belief about Freddie Mercury, but not one about Farrokh Bulsara. But in Kripke's puzzle, Pierre really does hold both beliefs, and they really do appear to contradict one another.

Are there simple ways to throw the puzzle out? The relevance of both (4) and (6) depends on a translation from French, and there are sometimes worries about the faithfulness of translation, but this is a *very* elementary translation. Can we say that Pierre has changed one of his beliefs, or lost one somehow? Pierre won't say that he has. A striking feature of Kripke's paper is how many different possible solutions he considers and refutes, and I won't attempt to cover them all here. But one is especially pertinent to Frege's original argument. Suppose a Fregean said:

Pierre has different senses for 'London' and 'Londres,' so the beliefs have different senses. It is the senses of these sentences that are believed, so there is no contradiction, and no puzzle.

There is something temptingly commonsensical about this — that there is something that we "get" when we know the meaning of a word, and that different words may differ in this respect, despite designating the same things. Frege put this in terms of cognitive significance, and it's an appealing diagnosis for both Abby's and Pierre's cases. Kripke argues that this would make communication impossible, if it were true. Each of us will associate somewhat different sets of descriptions with any given name, and our utterances to one another would be perpetually mismatched. Few words, if any, would mean the same when used by different people, and so there would be no hope of mutual understanding or belief. Language must first serve as a "common currency" among speakers, despite any additional idiosyncrasies that we attach to our words.

RESPONSES

The net effect of Kripke's puzzle is not to show that we must adopt a Millian account of names, nor that there is a Millian account that will satisfactorily characterize belief contexts. But problems involving belief contexts had been seen as a definitive blow against Millian accounts, and now we have a puzzle instead. Responses range from defenses of Fregean assumptions to extensions that favor Millian accounts to attempts to defuse the puzzle altogether as a non-starter. Kripke closes his paper on a note suggesting an openness to the unsolvability of the puzzle: there may be no fact of the matter about the truth or falsity of any of the belief ascriptions involved. Kripke had been open to the prospect of a "gappy" theory of truth (see entry #20) on which some sentences have no truth value, despite the appearance of truth-aptness. This would be developed by Soames into a view of "partially-defined predicates" that don't assign truth values to all their possible objects. Powell (2012) develops a strategy with this to allow us to *reject* either (4) or (7) while *denying* neither of them. Chalmers (2002) takes a more radical and Frege-friendly approach known as "two-dimensional semantics." He suggests that the intension of a thought captures the ways in which the world may have an impact on its truth-value, and these intensions may be split into *epistemic* and *subjunctive* categories. Roughly, epistemic intensions are tied to the ways in which a person thinks about a word's referent, while the subjunctive intension is tied to the under-lying nature of it across possible worlds. Thus, epistemic intensions capture some of the spirit of Frege's sense distinction, and Pierre's apparent contradiction can be chalked up to mismatched epistemic intensions, despite common subjunctive ones. (See Sandgren (2019) for criticism of Chalmers's approach.)

Numerous responses have focused on beliefs and belief reports more specifically. Some of these have attempted to defuse the paradox by adjusting what is ascribed in such reports. Bach (1997) argues that belief reports don't actually report beliefs; instead, they describe them. As descriptions may differ, so our "belief reports" may differ, because they express incomplete propositions, even though the propositions believed may still be given a Millian interpretation. Kvart (1986) took a similar view of belief reports as "paraphrasing" beliefs but resists a Millian interpretation of belief contents. McMichael (1987) suggests that there are two types of belief reports: *de re* and *sub nominae* ('under a name'). *De re* reports will permit the substitution of co-designat-ing names, as Kripke and other Millians suggest, but not *sub nomi-nae* reports like Pierre's, which heads off the paradox. Brown (1992) takes some belief states themselves to be "partial" – roughly, they are mediated by other objects of belief, rather than directly on a proposition. Thus, Pierre may have inconsistent beliefs, but in an excusable way if his partial states have no apparent conflicts. Others have offered solutions that would let us overrule Pierre's reports of his belief in various ways. Marcus (1981) modifies the disquotation principle to include a requirement that the assented proposition must itself be possible. This allows us to ascribe incompatible beliefs to Pierre, even if he would not assent to them. Owens (1995) adopts an "anti-individualist" stance on which attitude ascriptions will be sensitive to conditions external to the psychological states of a speaker. Hence, we may assign beliefs to Pierre, even if he does not recognize them, but this does not entail a commitment to Millianism. For a response to Owens, see Frances (1998).

Other responses have taken the puzzle to have mistaken assumptions and dismiss it out of hand. Salmon (1986), while also a Millian, notes that the compelling versions of the puzzle require a stronger "biconditional" version of the disquotation principle, which he finds implausible. Taschek (1988) doubts that Fregeans should even be troubled by the puzzle, as it turns entirely on substitutions of co-designating names without an additional semantic feature that affects cognitive significance – i.e., a Fregean sense. With those in hand, the substitutions of 'London' and 'Londres' would leave the embedded sentences with different senses, and thus their inconsistency is no great surprise. Hanna (2001) argues that Kripke's translation principle conceals an equivocation between different understandings of linguistic competence, and that we can discount the language in which speakers formulate their beliefs in stating what proposition they believe. Moore (1999) argues that Kripke's disquotation principle does not reflect ways in which shifts in the context of conversation may undermine such ascriptions of belief. What we assent to in some contexts we would reject in others, so a general disquotational principle obscures our actual beliefs.

RECOMMENDED READINGS

MAJOR WORK

Kripke, S. 1979/2011. "A Puzzle About Belief." In *Philosophical Troubles: Collected Papers*, vol. 1, 125–161. Oxford: Oxford University Press.

RESPONSES

Bach, K. 1997. "Do Belief Reports Report Beliefs?" *Pacific Philosophical Quarterly* 78 (3): 215–241.

Brown, C. 1992. "Direct and Indirect Belief." *Philosophy and Phenomenological Research* 52 (2): 289–316.

Chalmers, D. 2002. "The Components of Content." In *Philosophy of Mind: Classical and Contemporary Readings*, edited by D. Chalmers, 608–633. Oxford: Oxford University Press.

Frances, B. 1998. "Arguing for Frege's Fundamental Principle." *Mind and Language* 12: 341–346.

Hanna, P. 2001. "Linguistic Competence and Kripke's Puzzle." *Philosophia* 28 (1–4): 171–189.

Kvart, I. 1986. "Kripke's Belief Puzzle." *Midwest Studies in Philosophy* 10: 287–325.

Marcus, R.B. 1981. "A Proposed Solution to a Puzzle About Belief." *Midwest Studies in Philosophy* 6: 501–510.

McMichael, A. 1987. "Kripke's Puzzle and Belief 'Under' a Name." *Canadian Journal of Philosophy* 17 (1): 105–125.

Moore, J. 1999. "Misdisquotation and Substitutivity: When Not to Infer Belief from Assent." *Mind* 108 (430): 335–365.

Owens, J. 1995. "Pierre and the Fundamental Assumption." *Mind and Language* 10: 250–273.

Powell, L. 2012. "How to Refrain from Answering Kripke's Puzzle." *Philosophical Studies* 161 (2): 287–308.

Salmon, N. 1986. *Frege's Puzzle.* Atascadero: Ridgeview Press.

Sandgren, A. 2019. "Puzzling Pierre and Intentional Identity." *Erkenntnis* 84 (4): 861–875.

Taschek, W. 1988. "Would a Fregean Be Puzzled by Pierre?" *Mind* 97 (385): 99–104.

PART VIII

NATURALISM AND EXTERNALISM

INTRODUCTION

Each entry in this section presents a problem or puzzle about how natural language relates to the theoretical approaches we take in the sciences and how we fit into the natural world. Entry #41 introduces the "poverty of the stimulus" argument, which calls into question whether humans could acquire the natural languages we speak from scratch. If not, the argument goes, then our capacity to do so must be hardwired into us and our linguistic abilities are more properly thought of as biological functions. Entry #42 builds on this "hard-wiring" claim by considering cases of apes who purportedly acquire the use of sign language. If we find that they hit hard limits to their acquisition, then our biological differences would seem to play a role, lending support to the views in entry #41. Entry #43 looks at the role that specific processing centers in the brain play in language production and interpretation, and entry #45 poses questions about whether natural selection could be the reason that humans developed such sophisticated linguistic abilities. Entry #44 introduces the Turing test (also known as the "imitation game"), a famous thought experiment from computer scientist Alan Turing that invites us to ask whether a computer that could convincingly converse with us should count as thinking in the same sense that we do. If so, thought and language

DOI: 10.4324/9781003183167-57

might be another part of the natural world for scientists to study, but not specifically biological phenomena.

Entries #46–50 all address puzzles and thought experiments posed by the work of Saul Kripke and Hilary Putnam, whose work on designation has been widely influential and hotly debated over the last 50 years. Both of them challenge Frege's account of sense (see entry #5) for names and what are called "natural kind terms." A kind term designates the whole of some type of thing; natural kinds would be types of things that exist naturally, without regard for our beliefs or social practices. Natural kind terms would designate natural kinds. So 'shortstop' would be a kind term, but not a natural kind term. Had humans never existed and never invented baseball, that type would never have been constructed. However, the kind terms in the sciences like 'oxygen' or 'hemoglobin' might be natural kind terms, if our theories are correct. Most importantly, Frege claimed that every meaningful expression has a sense that determines its reference, but Putnam and Kripke argued that names and natural kind terms have their designation fixed directly to what they designate without the need for a sense to mediate that relation. This is a form of semantic externalism. It treats meanings for some words and sentences as necessarily involving something external to our thoughts and practices. We look at thought experiments from Kripke in entry #46 and Putnam in entry #48 to motivate this view. Entry #47 includes a thought experiment that fills in some gaps in the views expressed by Kripke and Putnam. Entry #49 poses a puzzle about how we should interpret sentences involving natural kind terms for kinds that don't exist. They seem meaningful, yet have nothing to designate, contrary to semantic externalism. (Compare with entry #39.) Entry #50 looks at a thought experiment once posed to Kripke: could there be unicorns? That is, even though there have never been any, and we come to know this term from fiction, could there one day come to be creatures that matched the descriptions of them and which we rightly called 'unicorns?' Surprisingly, Kripke says no, and that any sentence involving the word 'unicorn' is, strictly speaking, meaningless.

THE POVERTY OF THE STIMULUS

Background: The development of analytic philosophy of language during the 20th century ran concurrently with important work in computer science, linguistics, and cognitive psychology. These projects shared an emphasis on logical analysis and information processing. The "cognitive revolution," as this would be known, treated speakers' linguistic abilities as computational phenomena – i.e., machines processing information in a formal symbolic system (what we typically call a "program"). One of the most pressing questions for such accounts, and for anyone with an interest in natural languages, is how speakers acquire their first language.

How does someone acquire their first language? This is a question that is difficult to answer empirically. We can't interview infants, and we have few memories of this period in our own lives. More importantly, our knowledge of our first language is typically implicit and unfamiliar to us. Most speakers of natural languages can explicitly describe few of the grammatical structures of those languages, even though they can produce and interpret sentences in those languages very well. Just in reading the sentence before this one, you correctly interpreted a determiner (a quantifier, more specifically) before the head of the noun phrase modifying its reference class and picked up its anaphoric link to the pronoun in the sentence's dependent clause.

DOI: 10.4324/9781003183167-58

Unless you've taken some linguistics classes, you also probably don't know what any of that grammatical terminology means and couldn't have described things that way yourself. You have an implicit command of English grammar that allows you to take a finite vocabulary and generate and interpret an indefinitely large number of new sentences. How did you acquire that?

One kind of answer is an empirical-acquisition approach. This would imply that you were born with a blank slate – no words, no concepts, nothing – but experiences started flooding in, you noticed patterns in them, and your linguistic competence grew out of this. You might imagine being young, and an adult pointing to things, saying a word, and your repeating it back to them. That might get you some nouns to work with, and from there you would need to notice more abstract, formal properties of well-formed sentences to develop your grammatical knowledge. We can call these abstractions the "principles of your grammar." As I noted earlier, you would be *aware* of very little, if any, of this. Yet your linguistic competence would grow along with your experience.

As familiar as the prosaic details of this approach might sound, it faces some serious difficulties. Linguist Noam Chomsky countered empirical-acquisition accounts with what has come to be called the argument from the poverty of the stimulus (APS)[1]. He noted that the grammars of natural languages have a richness and complexity that only extensive scientific study reveals to us. Infants simply don't produce anything else of such complexity on their own. It would astound us if a three-year-old figured out differential calculus on their own, yet almost every child becomes competent in some natural language grammar at a young age. How could they choose such a complex system of principles from so many possibilities, even if they could formulate them? They have adults to help them, but there is a pitfall there, too. Most of the linguistic output to which infants are exposed is of fairly poor quality, if we're concerned with its grammar. Even linguistically competent adults misplace verbs, stop mid-sentence when they get distracted, and make countless other mistakes. Yet infants acquire increasingly complex grammatical structures, use them fluently, and start producing new sentences in ways they have not yet been shown. They also readily discard information that does not serve a grammatical role without being instructed to do so – e.g., they disregard the fact that some people speak with higher-pitched voices, while others speak at lower pitches. And this accelerated-yet-systematic character of their acquisition is also broad in surprising ways. Note that I have avoided the words 'say' and 'utterance' here, which are suggestive of spoken language. Singelton and Newport (2004) describe the ways in which children born deaf and taught American Sign Language with inconsistent input will develop linguistic competence with signs just as quickly as speaking children, and even surpass the competence of their teachers at a young age.

None of this would be possible, Chomsky argued, if all infants were doing was imitating the features of the adults around them. Chomsky offered different versions of this argument over time, and his "Knowledge of Language as a Focus of Inquiry" (1986, Chapter 1) is the most direct and fully realized of them. A concise version of this argument can be drawn from Laurence and Margolis (2011, p. 221):

1. An indefinite number of alternative sets of principles are consistent with the regularities found in the primary linguistic data.
2. The correct set of principles needn't be (and typically isn't) in any pre-theoretic sense simpler or more natural than the alternatives.
3. The data that would be needed for choosing among the sets of principles are in many cases not the sort of data that are available to an empiricist learner in the child's epistemic situation.
4. So, if children were empiricist learners, they couldn't reliably arrive at the correct grammar for their language.
5. Children do reliably arrive at the correct grammar for their language.

---

6. Therefore, children aren't empiricist learners.

This is a bold argument that would have swept away large portions of developmental psychology, linguistics, and philosophy of language when Chomsky first proposed it. It has been far more controversial in light of Chomsky's own response. If children do arrive at the correct grammar, yet cannot acquire it empirically, then he argued that they must already possess a form of the grammar when they are born. We can call these *nativist* views, in contrast with empiricist accounts. Knowledge of grammar would thus exist as a collection of mechanisms hardwired into the developmental course of our brains and activated with minimal external stimulus, he asserted. This should be no more surprising than that we're hardwired to develop other organs with complex structures destined to perform certain functions. To make that case is not to assert that infants are born speaking or signing some natural language. It is to say that the underlying mechanisms that allow us to produce and interpret sentences in a natural language are innate in us, waiting to be activated and developed by even the dismal evidence sets that children receive.[2]

RESPONSES

To determine whether a system that did not have a grammar innately could acquire it, cognitive scientists and neuropsychologists would later turn to a different sort of computation. By the 1980s, computer scientists had turned their attention to the potential of large networks of processors to perform tasks, rather than building faster processors. This lent itself to a different means of computation: a *connectionist* model, on which tasks were completed by large, densely interconnected networks of simple nodes passing (or inhibiting) signals between them. Rather than a single central processor performing the work, the whole of the network could be said to be completing it in a distributed fashion. Distributed processing systems don't have a central set of instructions – a program – by which they conduct their work. Instead, each part of the system has a minimal set of instructions for interacting with its neighbors and managing its connections, and the work of the system arises out of patterns in these interactions. Rather than writing programs, developers would write the minimal instructions for each node to be flexible and revisable; when a task was completed successfully, the nodes would strengthen their existing connections, and if the system failed, they would revise them to make other outcomes more likely. In some respects, the architecture of such networks more closely resembles the architecture of a brain, with each node resembling a neuron. These models can be seen as the forerunners of contemporary work on neural networks and machine learning.

Connectionist approaches were successful at mirroring features of the early stages of language acquisition in infants. In one study, Elman *et al.* (1996) developed a network that not only learned to create past tense forms of verbs as human infants do, but also began to make *the same specific types of mistakes* that human infants do. No one programmed a grammar into such networks, yet there were the results. Fodor and Pylyshyn (1988) were early critics of this approach, arguing that any model of human language acquisition needed to be both systematic and productive. That is, humans acquire language in ways that assign systematic roles to subsentential lexical items – e.g., recognizing nouns and verbs, and assigning different roles to each. Those capacities are productive in that once they emerge, we produce and interpret large numbers of new grammatically similar sentences with ease, e.g., once you learn how to produce and interpret 'Flynn loves Liz,' you grasp how to produce and interpret 'Liz loves Flynn.' Connectionist models were doomed to either lack these features or achieve them simply by stabilizing into forms that effectively encoded a universal grammar. Smolensky (1991) argued against this, elaborating the possibility of what he called "distributed representations" that were sensitive to linguistic structures without reverting to a computational architecture that nativists demand. Early successes of this approach are discussed in Elman *et al.* (1996), and a sustained general defense of it is found in Bechtel (1993). It would be fair to say that most contemporary anti-nativist accounts incorporate some elements of connectionism, or some descendent of such views.

Fiona Cowie (1999, Chap. 8–11) has argued against recent revisions of the APS, distinguishing those with an empirical basis from those that are purely logical. She argues that the empiricist versions underestimate the psychological abilities that infants bring to the task, and so we may reject them out of hand. Logical versions of the argument (notably Fodor's; see entry #13) characterize language acquisition as the development of a theory, but misconstrue the nature of theory construction to better fit computational views. This can leave us feeling as if there were no alternatives to nativism, but we should reject that assumption, as well. Laurence and Margolis (2001) offer extended critiques of Cowie's views. Clark and Lappin (2010) examine the empirical cases that might be made for the APS in even greater detail than Cowie and examine several different nativist-friendly computational models of learning to assess their viability in support of the

APS. They argue that the nativist-friendly models yield dismal results, while recent probabilistic and machine-learning models have shown promising results that don't require the innate knowledge of universal grammatical features suggested by the APS.

Tomasello (2003) opposes nativism and asserts that much of the plausibility of the APS rests on an impoverished understanding of the cognitive development of infants at the time the original arguments were made. Infants bring a much wider array of cognitive and social skills (though non-linguistic ones) to the period of their acquisition than was previously thought. Their skills at reading the intentions of others, to share and direct the attention of others, and discerning patterns in their environments greatly enrich their acquisition process. In place of nativism, he proposes a grammar, in which many different types of usage of linguistic items and structures form "an inventory of constructions" (2003, p. 6) with some that bear greater similarity to many others as a core, and more idiosyncratic items at the periphery. (Thus, the core would superficially resemble the rigid, rule-based grammar of nativism, explaining that view's initial plausibility.)

NOTES

1 It's also called the "POS" by others, including some authors in the Recommended Readings.
2 Nativism was also vigorously defended by Jerry Fodor. His argument differs from the APS, though it ends with a similar conclusion. See entries #12–13 for details, and see Sterelny (1989) for objections.

RECOMMENDED READINGS

MAJOR WORKS

Chomsky, N. 1986. *Knowledge of Language, Its Nature, Origian and Use*. New York: Praeger.

Elman, J., E. Bates, M. Johnson, A. Karmiloff-Smith, D. Parisi, and K. Plinkett. 1996. *Rethinking Innateness: A Connectionist Perspective on Development*. Cambridge: Bradford Books, The MIT Press.

Fodor, J., and Z. Pylyshyn. 1988. "Connectionism and Cognitive Architecture." *Cognition* 28: 3–71.

RESPONSES

Bechtel, W. 1993. "The Case for Connectionism." *Philosophical Studies* 71 (2): 119–154.

Clark, A., and S. Lappin. 2010. *Linguistic Nativism and the Poverty of Stimulus.* Malden: Wiley-Blackwell.

Cowie, F. 1999. *What's Within: Nativism Reconsidered.* New York: Oxford University Press.

Laurence, S., and E. Margolis. 2001. "The Poberty of the Stimulus Argument." *The British Journal for the Philosophy of Science* 52 (2): 217–276.

Singelton, J., and E. Newport. 2004. "When Learners Surpass Their Models: The Acquisition of American Sign Language from Inconsistent Input." *Cognitive Psychology* 49 (4): 370–407.

Smolensky, P. 1991. "Connectionism, Constituency and the Language of Thought." In *Meaning in Mind: Fodor and His Critics*, edited by B. Loewer and G. Rey, 201–227. Cambridge: Blackwell.

Sterelny, K. 1989. "Fodor's Nativism." *Philosophical Studies* 55: 119–141.

Tomasello, M. 2003. *Constructing a Language: A Usage-Based Theory of Language Acquisition.* Cambridge: Harvard University Press.

'IF I COULD TALK TO THE ANIMALS . . .'

Background: In entry #41, we considered the possibility that there was a strong biological basis for our linguistic competence. That would suggest that our capacity for acquiring a first language in childhood was the natural course of development for a set of faculties hardwired into our biology. This might lead us to wonder whether our linguistic competence is a uniquely human biological feature, and whether other species might learn to speak languages like ours.

Humans appear to be unique among the planet's species in using languages as conceptually rich and grammatically complex as ours. Yet many other animals do seem to lead lives with behavioral complexities and apparent purpose that is reminiscent of our own. That no other species *speaks* as most humans do comes as no surprise: other species simply don't have key physiological features of human vocal tracts. But there are other means by which we can communicate with a language. *Manual* communication – the use of one's hands in signing to others – is a mode of communication in a natural language on a par with speaking. While other species cannot vocalize as humans can, some – other apes, in particular – have manual dexterity that compares much more favorably. We might wonder whether it would

DOI: 10.4324/9781003183167-59

be possible for apes closely related to humans to learn a language in which they could sign their thoughts and communicate with us.

During the 1970s, this suggestion found traction with numerous psychologists around the United States. A great deal of this attention centered on a series of studies done with a chimpanzee named Washoe, and a further series done with a gorilla named Koko. (See Patterson (1978) and Gardner and Gardner (1971) for these studies.) In both cases, researchers worked with the apes over several years and claimed that apes had mastered hundreds of signs that they used spontaneously in novel ways, exhibiting some rudimentary concatenations of signs that paralleled the early stages of deaf humans' acquisition of signs. Penny Patterson, Koko's caretaker and an animal psychologist, claimed that Koko had mastered over 1,000 words in a modified version of American Sign Language. This included two-sign combinations with adjectives modifying nouns ('hot potato'), possessives ('Koko purse'), negations ('me can't'), and even some three-sign combinations that suggested deeper syntactical structures ('Give me drink'). Patterson describes extended, purpose-driven exchanges like the following:

(Koko leads her companion to the refrigerator.)
K: You me there (indicating the refrigerator).
B: What want?
K: Eat drink.
B: Eat or drink, which?
K: Glass drink.
B: That? (Gets out juice.)
K: That.
(Patterson 1978, p. 89)

Koko has become a cultural touchstone over the years. Most people could not name a prominent primatologist or animal psychologist other than Jane Goodall, but many more know Koko's story and take it as affirmation of non-human animals being conscious and potentially communicative.

Responses to these accounts began to emerge in the late 1970s. One of the most striking came from Herbert Terrace. He had defended behaviorist models of language acquisition against Noam Chomsky's challenges and undertook what came to be called "Project

Nim." In this study, efforts were made to teach a chimpanzee named Nim Chimpsky American Sign Language. Terrace's study was strictly controlled and rigorously analyzed; the results were disappointing. His team found that while Nim could repeatedly and spontaneously use numerous signs, he only reliably used them in one- and two-word combinations. Longer strings of signs were not syntactic or semantic elaborations of shorter ones, so any resemblance to human infants was superficial. Nim also used signs to get food or other items, but never to state or describe things without such goals. Nim appeared to be merely producing gestures to gain rewards but stopping well short of using the gestures in a linguistic manner. (See Terrace (1979) and Terrace *et al.* (1979) for more.)

Terrace had initiated the project expecting different results but followed the data where they led. Data would prove to be a sticking point for studies on Koko and Washoe, as well. Terrace noted that the meager successes Nim produced depended on generous interpretations from the researchers, often picking the most promising combinations from much longer strings of apparent signs. The Gardners' and Patterson's accounts were short on direct data that would address this criticism; most accounts of Koko and Washoe's signing were narrative summaries lacking crucial details. Seidenberg and Petitto (1979) argued that none of the earlier studies showed what they purported. Data that might support their conclusions had never been published, and what data had been made public were frequently taken to imply linguistic conclusions they did not sufficiently support. By the late 1970s, there had also been extensive research on language acquisition in deaf children that the ape studies never considered, and which reflected unfavorably on any claim that the apes were learning ASL as humans would. (Neither the Gardners nor Patterson had expertise in deaf communication.) None of this proves that no ape (or other non-human animal) could ever acquire a language of course, but critics argued that the results simply don't support the view that they could.

RESPONSES

To most Western philosophers, the very idea that non-human animals might have the same linguistic and intellectual capacities that humans do was not at all plausible. Where a statement has been made (often simply by presumption), our rationality has been taken to separate us from other animals. Whatever sounds and gestures other animals might make, this line of thought suggests, they don't do so in ways that reflect or express rational beliefs, intentions, or any other sort of thought. A contemporary argument in this vein is offered by Davidson (1982), who contends that animals with no natural linguistic abilities cannot have propositional attitudes. To take an attitude towards a proposition (such as belief in it) requires a concern for objective truth, and this requires a degree of reflection on our own attitudes that would prompt us to change them if they conflicted with the facts. Non-linguistic animals change their behavior, but do so only when directly prompted, rather than by the self-criticism and self-correction that typifies rational agents. This sort of reflection on beliefs is possible only for animals with sophisticated linguistic capacities to articulate different beliefs' contents, so non-linguistic animals are ruled out in principle. Jacobson (2010) replies to this argument, contending that there are forms of normativity available to non-reflective creatures. They value the objects and states in which they find themselves, turning their attention to them accordingly, and can be surprised when their expectations fail. These suffice to mirror the relevant features of Davidson's account without requiring reflection, and hence without requiring linguistic abilities.

Arguments like Davidson's seem less obviously true to many contemporary philosophers of language. It seems anthropocentric, or at least arbitrarily restrictive, to set the bar so high for beliefs and the capacity for language. It may seem excessive to hold other species to the standards of grammatical complexity that human languages exhibit; perhaps they have languages with which they communicate, but much simpler ones. There are activities common across many species that nonetheless look different in their details and degrees of complexity, but which are still rightly treated as the same type of activity. But there is a risk in being too generous in theoretical interpretation here, too. If any kind of causal interaction that influences other organisms counts as linguistic, then we will find ourselves with implausible consequences. When I trim the tops of the basil plants in my garden, I'm causally influencing their development, but I'm not *saying* to them, "Grow wide, not tall," and they are not *interpreting* me as such.

To be a candidate for linguistic interaction, two organisms must engage in a recognition of common possibilities among each other's mental states, which linguistic performances may affect. Language users must therefore be able to project internal states like their own onto other organisms and use linguistic items to influence those states in others. I report my beliefs to you in order to get you to adopt them, as well; I report my desires in order to get you to believe that I have them and perhaps to form your own desire to help with mine. Psychologists refer to this capacity for positing and recognizing others' internal states as "theory of mind," or "mindreading." This can be treated as an empirical question; where we find a species has this capacity, we have greater reason to treat their behavior as linguistic, even if it is less complex than our own.

Framing the issue in these terms owes a debt to Premack and Woodruff (1978). (Primate communication is a consideration in their work, though they don't engage directly with the more contentious "signing ape" studies.) The conclusions they draw are modest, and they acknowledge that they cannot yet state definitively whether the primates they studied do form a theory of mind. Their caution reflects a longstanding dispute in psychology and the philosophy of mind. We have historically had no means of observing and measuring mental states as we do physical phenomena. Advanced technology like fMRI machines offer us increasingly fine-grained looks at the activity of the brain, but even then, we must hypothesize and infer how those physical states might constitute mental states or give rise to them.

Philosophers and psychologists have disputed how liberally we should postulate such states and apes' potential for a theory of mind has been a focus of such disagreements. Animals that had the capacity to ascribe mental states to others would need a rich array of concepts, self-reflective capacities to recognize salient features of their own mental states, and some rational capacity to infer from observations of others' behavior that they were likely to be in the same state. Povinelli has opposed ascribing a theory of mind to non-human animals on these grounds. On his view, we have no experimental approaches that could entitle us to such a conclusion. When we observe behavior in animals that might strike us as their "mindreading," we can always offer an equally plausible "behavior-reading" hypothesis. (This is sometimes known as "Povinelli's problem.") Suppose my cat has a contentious relationship with another neighborhood cat. Whenever the other cat approaches a window where he's sitting, my cat raises his hackles and starts hissing. There is a mindreading hypothesis here: my cat has some internal state by which he ascribes an internal state to the other cat that is very aggressive. But there is also a plausible hypothesis that appeals only to behavior: my cat recognizes the other cat, and when he does, his pulse habitually rises, adrenaline surges, he reflexively puffs his tail, and hisses. The latter hypothesis assumes less but explains just as much. (See Povinelli and Vonk (2003) for a statement of these views.)

Skepticism in this vein about theory of mind for non-human apes had been the predominant view since the deflating criticism of ape-signing studies in the late 1970s. That has shifted since the first decade of this century, however. Two particularly important figures in this transition have been Michael Tomasello and Josip Call, whose earlier work had suggested that humans might be alone in our "mindreading" capacities, but later reversed their views. Studies to which they both contributed suggested that chimpanzees were proficient in not only perceiving objects in their environments, but in ascribing those perceptual states to other chimps. These shifts in their views are articulated and motivated in Tomasello and Call (2006). Povinelli and Vonk (2006) responds directly to many of those challenges to their more austere views. An extensive historical review and critique of this entire debate is offered in Fitzpatrick (2009).

RECOMMENDED READINGS

MAJOR WORKS

Gardner, B., and R. Gardner. 1971. "Two-Way Communication with an Infant Chimpanzee." In *Behavior of Nonhuman Primates*, edited by A. Schrier and F. Stolnitz, vol. 4, 117–184. New York: Academic Press.

Patterson, F. 1978. "The Gestures of a Gorilla: Language Acquisition in Another Pongid." *Brain and Language* 5: 72–97.

Premack, D., and G. Woodruff. 1978. "Does the Chimpanzee Have a Theory of Mind?" *Behavioral and Brain Sciences* 1: 515–526.

Seidenberg, M., and L. Petitto. 1979. "Signing Behavior in Apes: A Critical Review." *Cognition* 7: 177–215.

Terrace, H. 1979. *Nim.* New York: Knopf.

RESPONSES

Davidson, D. 1982. "Rational Animals." *Dialectica* 36 (4): 317–328.

Fitzpatrick, S. 2009. "The Primate Mindreading Controversy: A Case Study in Simplicity and Methodology in Animal Psychology." In *The Philosophy of Animal Minds*, edited by R. Lurz, 258–277. Cambridge: Cambridge University Press.

Jacobson, H. 2010. "Normativity Without Reflectivity: On the Beliefs and Desire of Non-Reflective Creatures." *Philosophical Psychology* 23 (1): 75–93.

Povinelli, D., and J. Vonk. 2003. "Chimpanzee Minds: Suspiciously Human?" *Trends in Cognitive Science* 7 (4): 157–160.

Povinelli, D., and J. Vonk. 2006. "We Don't Need a Microscope to Explore the Chimpanzee's Mind." In *Rational Animals?*, edited by S. Hurley and M. Nudds, 385–412. Oxford: Oxford University Press.

Tomasello, M., and J. Call. 2006. "Do Chimpanzees Know What Others See – Or Only What They Are Looking at?" In *Rational Animals?*, edited by S. Hurley and M. Nudds, 371–384. Oxford: Oxford University Press.

43

BROCA'S AREA

Background: Entries #41–42 introduced new themes in the relation between our language and our biology. Our species may be unique on this planet in using languages for communication, as even the best animal cognition studies show little to no evidence of grammatical complexity behind gestures and calls from others. However, this appears to be a contingent result of our evolutionary descent, not a logical or metaphysical necessity. Thus, it has seemed natural for many philosophers and scientists to ask how our brains generate our linguistic behavior.

Several entries in this book have considered human linguistic abilities in a naturalistic vein; that is, they have taken them to be one further part of the natural world, and fit subjects for scientific study now and in the future. Quite often, the most pressing questions we have about language are not matters to which we could apply current methods, but philosophers and scientists taking naturalistic approaches will insist that this will change over time. Philosophy's role is to analyze and reframe our understanding of language and cognition to clear a path for future scientific study. Discussions in this vein often shift from more general questions about evolution and cognition to questions about neuroscience: how does a brain like ours produce and interpret speech?

DOI: 10.4324/9781003183167-60

This is a broad question that would require many specific types of investigation, but one important consideration in attempting to address this is the degree to which any such cognitive ability is *localized* in some region of the brain or the central nervous system. This sort of discovery often appears in badly oversimplified terms in scientific journalism – e.g., "The amygdala is where emotions are expressed!" Clickbait headlines aside, it is an empirical question to what degree our understanding of cognition is fruitfully structured with this sort of localization, and there is considerable evidence that some features of cognition do have such structural regularities. A landmark study by neurologist Paul Broca (1861) correlated damage in a region of the dominant hemisphere of the brain (the left in Broca's patients) with impediments in speech production. This region came to be known as "Broca's area." Roughly, it is located between your ear and temple within the skull and is about an inch in diameter. Damage to Broca's area has been associated with what is now known as expressive aphasia, in which speakers struggle to produce speech fluidly. In severe cases, speakers may struggle to produce even single words or phrases, and their speech will lack most syntactical and grammatical structures. (For a review of the history and contemporary clinical consensus view on Broca's aphasia, see Saffran (2000).) Note that the correlation here is a negative one: *damage* to Broca's area was correlated with *diminished* linguistic function. Broca could not yet point to normal functioning of a region of the brain and identify it with successful linguistic performance. Still, this strongly suggested a starting point for future research, and there has been intense interest in it in the intervening years.

In 2021, amid dismal medical news about COVID-19, there were reports of an exciting development in neuroprosthetics. Moses *et al.* (2021) reports on the development of a prosthetic device consisting of a multielectrode array placed underneath a patient's dura matter (inside the skull, but not quite directly touching the brain). The array tracks electrical activity across regions of the brain known to be crucial to speech production in most people. Data from the array are then fed to software that learns to recognize patterns in the electrical activity and correlates them with the patient's efforts to produce a word. The system then uses predictive algorithms to anticipate what the patient might say, in order to accelerate the conversion of the activity in their brain to words and sentences on a screen or a text-to-speech program.

This offers great promise for patients who have linguistic competence but have lost the ability to produce speech due to injury. Note that this device does not employ a detailed model of the pathways in Broca's area in advance which it imposes upon the observational data. This reflects existing limits on our knowledge of the brain. We don't have such a model, and a neuron-by-neuron model of even a small region of the brain would require a daunting degree of computational power, even given the best contemporary resources.

All of this points to a thought experiment in the philosophy of mind that we may adapt slightly. Imagine for a moment that we come to have a substantially more developed model of the neurological terrain of the brain by which we produce speech. We might then identify being a producer of certain kinds of speech with having a brain or central nervous system (CNS) in state F, where F is a sufficiently specific description of the brain or CNS-state. For now, imagine that this is done with technology akin to contemporary fMRI scanners, but with much greater resolution. Note that this is not to say that the brain states cause or are merely correlated with our speech production and interpretation – those brain processes would *just be* the faculties, churning away at their tasks. A consequence of that assumption is that, if there were such an area or process, then only it could produce language as we know it. Identifying a brain state or process with our linguistic abilities here is akin to identifying water with H_2O. Consequently, a world without oxygen would be a world without water.

Such a discovery would certainly be a win for neuroscience, and Broca's work suggests where we should look for it. It would also explain the rather obvious point that we don't find other species using natural languages; put them in the supercharged-fMRI machine, and you undoubtedly won't find the same things going on. But now, imagine a series of possibilities. Suppose Earth is visited by a highly intelligent alien species who prepared for their visit by studying our languages via radio signals, and they converse fluently with us in English. Then, we ask them to get into our supercharged-fMRI machine. To our surprise, they don't have a corresponding area of their central nervous system. Maybe their brains look nothing like ours and perform tasks in radically different ways. In that case, they have no Broca's area and should not have linguistic faculties like ours. It's tempting to waive off this thought experiment and say that we're being too generous with our imagination, but this misses the point of the experiment. Even if we have not met such aliens, why should we say that it is *impossible* for them to exist? If this is possible, then the explanatory significance of Broca's area is much more complicated. (For a rigorous examination of this line of objection to reducing linguistic competence and other psychological states to neural or physical ones, see Fodor (1974) and entry #44.)

RESPONSES

Our thought experiment makes colorful use of extraterrestrials and does so to make a logical and explanatory point. For neuroscientists, the question at hand is more purely empirical: what do we *actually find* brains doing? Here, we need not appeal to aliens to complicate matters. A naïve conception of the brain as a fixed set of structures with regions devoted exclusively to specific tasks conflicts with research that shows regions continually interacting with one another, as well as the profound plasticity of the brain and central nervous system. Neuroscientists often observe adjustments and structural changes to regions of the brain when damage occurs to replace the damaged regions, or the expansion of some regions when some function it serves is emphasized for an extended period. For instance, Allen *et al.* (2013) compared specific neuroanatomical regions among native deaf signers, hearing signers, and hearing non-signers to affirm an increased volume of parts of Broca's area in deaf signers (suggested by earlier studies) and correlated it with an increased volume of the visual cortex. This would at least suggest that deaf signers' brains reorganize to enhance the integration of visual regions of their brains with linguistic regions, facilitating visual recognition of signs. Weiller *et al.* (1995) found that, in some patients with aphasia after a stroke, rather than repairing or reconstituting Broca's area in their left (dominant) hemisphere, there was a reorganization of structures in the right (non-dominant) hemisphere associated with speech to support some return of function. But Karbe *et al.* (1998) later reined this hypothesis in, finding that right-hemisphere reorganization was less effective in reclaiming speech functions than typical reconstitutions of Broca's area in the left hemisphere, and that it was found primarily in patients with more severe initial post-stroke damage.

Many of the more radical claims about plasticity have been scaled back by researchers in the early part of the 21st century. In a comprehensive review of recent findings, Wilson and Schneck (2021) found some evidence for reorganization of language regions in the right (non-dominant) hemisphere after a stroke (as mentioned in Kalbe *et al.*, above), but not for the recruitment of other regions in the dominant hemisphere or for radical reorganization of the network of regions involved in speech production, or recruitment of more general-purpose regions. But this has prompted many attempts to model what happens in Broca's area to contribute to speech production. Above all, the assumption that Broca's area is an all-encompassing home of our language faculties, or even the sole seat of a major feature such as syntax, has been set aside in favor of more complex, interconnected roles. We'll sample just a few proposals here.

Grodzinsky (2000) suggests that much less of our linguistic ability is localized in Broca's area than originally assumed, and that the processing necessary for speech production is distributed over a wider set of dominant-hemisphere sites. What does occur in Broca's area, in his view, are several higher-level syntactic-processing tasks that appear prominently in surface grammar (hence, their impairment in cases of damage to Broca's area). Thompson-Schill (2005) suggests a role of *selecting* information from competing information sources within the brain when activating representations in working memory. Disruption of that selection process (as we would expect with damage to the region) while attempting to produce speech would leave speakers impaired at tasks such as word retrieval, one of the key symptoms of expressive aphasia. Hagoort (2005) doubts that Broca's Area is an area devoted exclusively to linguistic functioning, even one as narrow as Grodzinsky suggests (pp. 162–163). Instead, he suggests that its location at the confluence of other regions sensitive to various types of information makes it a prime candidate for "binding" or unifying those different types of representational structures into larger units like sentences. Tremblay and Dick (2016) go so far as to call Broca's area and models that place it at the center of linguistic production "dead." They argue that it has never been well-defined (cf. Hagoort pp. 159–160), and is a relic of earlier neuroanatomical models, while its putative role owes too much to cognitive models that treat the brain as a collection of isolated modules, even as evidence now suggests a more distributed set of highly connected structures are responsible.

RECOMMENDED READINGS

MAJOR WORKS

Broca, P. 1861. "Remarks on the Seat of the Faculty of Articulated Language, Following an Observation of Aphemia (Loss of Speech)." *Bulletin de la Société Anatomique* 6: 330–357. Available from: http://psychclassics.yorku.ca/Broca/aphemie-e.htm.

Fodor, J. 1974. "Special Sciences." *Synthèse* 28 (2): 97–115.

RESPONSES

Allen, J., K. Emmorey, J. Bruss, and H. Damasio. 2013. "Neuroanatomical Differences in Visual, Motor, and Language Cortices Between Congenitally Deaf Signers, Hearing Signers, and Hearing Non-Signers." *Frontiers in Neuroanatomy* 7: 1–10.

Grodzinsky, Y. 2000. "The Neurology of Syntax: Langauge Use Without Broca's Area." *Behavioral and Brains Sciences* 23 (1): 1–21.

Hagoort, P. 2005. "Broca's Area as the Unification Space for Language." In *Twenty-First Century Psycholinguistics: Four Cornerstones*, edited by A. Cutler, 157–172. Mahwah, NJ: Lawrence Erlbuam.

Karbe, H., A. Thiel, G. Weber-Luxemberger, K. Herholz, J. Kessler, and W. Heiss. 1998. "Brain Plasticity in Poststroke Aphasia: What Is the Contribution of the Right Hemisphere?" *Brain and Language* 64: 215–230.

Moses, D., S. Metzger, J. Liu, G. Anumanchipalli, J. Makin, P. Sun, J. Chartier, *et al.* 2021. "Neuroprosthesis for Decoding Speech in a Paralyzed Person with Anarthria." *New England Journal of Medicine* 385: 217–227.

Saffran, E. 2000. "Aphasias and the Relationship of Language and Brain." *Seminars in Neurology* 20: 409–418.

Thompson-Schill, S. 2005. "Dissecting the Language Organ: A New Look at the Role of Broca's Area in Language Processing." In *Twenty-First Century Psycholinguistics: Four Cornerstones*, edited by A. Cutler, 173–190. Mahwah, NJ: Lawrence Erlbaum.

Tremblay, P., and A Dick. 2016. "Broca and Wernicke Are Dead, or Moving Past the Classic Model of Language Neurobiology." *Brain and Language* 162: 60–71.

Weiller, C., C. Isensee, M. Rijntjes, W. Huber, S. Müller, D. Bier, K. Dutschka, R. Woods, J. Noth, and H. Diener. 1995. "Recovery from Wernicke's Aphasia: A Positron Emission Tomographic Study." *Annals of Neurology* 37: 723–732.

Wilson, S., and S. Schneck. 2021. "Neuroplasticity in Post-Stroke Aphasia: A Systematic Review and Meta-Analysis of Functional Imaging Studies of Reorganization of Language Processing." *Neurobiology of Language* 2 (1): 22–82.

44

'HELLO WORLD!'

Background: In entries #41–43, we looked at puzzles and thought exper-iments that prompted us to think about natural languages as subjects of scientific study. Most philosophy of language has treated natural languages as ideal, abstract structures fit for logical analysis; entries #41–43 all sug-gested that attention to our biology might be essential to understanding our capacity to use languages. In this entry, we take a turn in just the opposite direction, to consider whether there could be languages in wholly non-bio-logical systems.

Machines "talk" to us a lot these days. From digital assistants to voice-activated phone menus to the predictive text generated by search engine windows, software responds to some of our linguistic behaviors in order to generate appropriate responses. How much, if any, of this "talking" should count as genuine language use? We can create machines that mimic intelligent behavior in narrow ways with relative ease. Electric eyes open doors as people approach them, but not because such systems recognize objects *as people* or *want* then to come inside. The voice-activated phone system at your pharmacy plays recordings of voices that we interpret as offering options to refill prescriptions, speak to a pharmacist, etc., but they are running simple algorithms that activate other components of the system, not

DOI: 10.4324/9781003183167-61

understanding that 'amoxicillin' *refers* to an antibiotic or *inferring* that a doctor's office should be called. It is a point of philosophical interest whether this gap is temporary, soon to be bridged as technology improves, or if non-biological systems cannot become language users in principle.

One type of answer to this question grew from the work of mathematician Alan Turing. Turing is perhaps the single most important contributor to modern computer science, having shown that all effectively computable problems could be solved by a mechanical device known as a "Turing machine." A Turing machine specifies how a machine would perform certain logical operations to solve mathematical problems, so we could think of it as a computer with a single, fixed program. (A "universal Turing machine" could instantiate all such sets of instructions and is thus more like our contemporary notion of a computer.) Turing anticipated great things from his machines; he expected that more sophisticated versions of them would become *thinking machines*, with all the relevant capacities that we have. Most of us would still distinguish between work done by human intelligence and that done by computers. The simple, step-by-step binary calculations of a Turing machine seem too blind to the content that they model to compare with our own. But Turing believed that the differences between us and the machines were matters of degree and complexity, not of kind. No one would mistake mid-20th century computers for thinkers, but he anticipated much greater things in the future.

To motivate this view that machines might one day think and speak, Turing (1950) offered a thought experiment. He called this the "imitation game," though it has come to be known as the "Turing test." Suppose you have two people, A and B, who are placed in separate rooms, and you, the "interrogator," are tasked with discovering something about their identities. Turing suggests that one might be a man, another a woman, and you must determine who is who. Various cis-gendered clues, such as vocal tone, would make this too easy, so let's suppose that only typed messages are exchanged. The interrogator may ask them questions; A and B win the game by imitating each other and fooling the interrogator. Now, suppose that, instead of two people, we have one human and one advanced Turing machine that can generate well-formed sentences in your language. How would you decide who was the human and who was the machine? You could ask directly, but everyone in this game is trying to deceive you, and is free to lie and subvert expectations with their answers. Suppose we put our ingenuity to work on this, searching for questions that would make the machine reveal itself. Imagine that some machines managed to beat most people, most of the time. Turing's view was that machines that could consistently do this were not just modeling intelligence; they *were* intelligent, thinking machines.

"Passing the Turing test" became a benchmark for the advancement of information technology. Writing in 1950, Turing anticipated that in 50 years' time, we would have digital computers with 10^9 bits of memory that could play the imitation game and beat average interrogators for five minutes about 70% of the time. As hardware predictions go, that's actually quite good – better quality home computers had that much memory in 2000, and some in research institutions had dramatically more. How have computers done at the imitation game? Early efforts on this go all the way back to the 1960s and the development of "chatbots." Weizenbaum (1966) describes a program called ELIZA that imitates interactions with a therapist. There are dozens of ELIZA emulators online today. Here's a fairly typical exchange that I had with one:

M: Hello. I'm Michael.
E: Did you come to me because you are Michael?
M: No, I came to you to talk about language.
E: You're not really talking about me, are you?
M: I'm certainly trying.
E: Do you enjoy being certainly trying?
M: It's pretty annoying in this case.
E: Say, do you have any psychological problems?

It's easy to see what ELIZA is doing here. The program has a set of stock responses that it uses to start or redirect conversation, and in other cases, it selects words or phrases from my responses to insert into another set of stock responses. Note how "certainly trying" is plucked from my third response and put into a question in the next line. Winograd (1972) describes SHRDLU, a much more sophisticated program that exchanges commands and answers questions about a simple model of a small physical world ("blocks world") with objects that it can manipulate. SHRDLU could process text inputs in much more sophisticated ways than ELIZA. For instance, it could both track pronouns across conversations and recognize when it had lost track of them. While these "chatbots" will seem crude to contemporary readers, they paved the way for much more sophisticated systems that we now regularly employ.

RESPONSES

Let's return to the philosophical question: should we call this *thinking* and genuine language use? Computers manipulate symbols all the time, but no one would suggest that in doing so they are *thinking* about math, or how we're doing against the zombies in a video game, or the content of this essay. Why should we expect faster computation generate something qualitatively different like thinking and using a language? Two more thought experiments speak to this point.

Searle (1980) imagines being wrangled into an experiment by scientists working in Chinese, a language that he doesn't speak. They place him in a room with two large slots in one of its walls. He is also given a stack of cards with shapes he doesn't recognize, and a book of instructions that tells him how to swap some of his cards for others. The scientists then open one of the slots and hand him a card; he scans through the instruction book and finds that shape; the instructions point to another shape on one of his cards; he finds that card and passes it through the second slot when the scientists open it. Suppose that the shapes on the cards are Chinese characters, and that the cards handed to Searle express questions, while the cards he returns express appropriate answers. What is this conversation about? Presumably the scientists know, but surely not Searle. But this is just what digital computers do, albeit with much larger tokens. They manipulate symbols of which they have no intrinsic grasp according to rules that they follow automatically. At most, he thinks, this is a simulation of thinking and speaking, but no more the real thing than a meteorological model of a hurricane run on a computer is a hurricane. (This is often called the "Chinese room" thought experiment. For replies, see Boden (1990), Churchland and Churchland (1990), Haugeland (2002) and Rey (2002).)

A second, roughly contemporaneous thought experiment comes to us from Ned Block (1981, §2, p. 19ff). Block argued that it would be possible to create an unintelligent machine (by any reasonable estimate) that could pass the Turing test. Suppose we take the letters of English and any punctuation we regularly expect to use, which gives us about 40 characters. We can imagine writing out every possible string of those up to some finite number of characters. For now, let's just talk about the strings up to 200 characters long. One of our 40 characters will mark a blank space, so any string shorter than 200 characters will be accounted for by adding additional blank spaces as needed. A couple strings might look like this:

(1)   HKSDJFHKSD FK.UH,EKFU;'!,HSKDUFKEF KWF
        ASUDHF . . .
(2)   IS PITTSBURGH WEST OF PHILADELPHIA?

(Typesetting won't allow us to show 200 characters per line, so just imagine that those strings carry on that long off the side of the page.)

There will be a lot of these – around 10^{320} possible strings. If one is reading in English, a large majority of those strings will just be gibberish, like (1), but a subset of them will be interpretable as English sentences, like (2). Suppose we sort through all the possible strings to find the *sensible* ones, like (2). Block then imagines a machine that accepts strings of characters as inputs up to some finite length. And for each sensible string that it accepts as an input, the machine outputs a sensible string that responds to it, selected by the engineers who build the machine. Thus, for (2), the machine might return:

(3)   YES, IT'S ABOUT 300 MILES TO THE WEST.

For every sensible thing you say or ask it, it will give you a sensible response that an intelligent being might give. But it's hard to accept that such a machine is intelligent.

What if the machines were not blindly pairing up sentences in this way? What if their interaction were unprogrammed, spontaneous, and sensitive to changes in their environments in ways that more closely resembled language use by intelligent humans? The promise of such success has emerged in the last decade in natural language processing with advances in techniques known as *machine learning*. In the briefest of terms, machine learning proceeds by building programs that build their own models in cycles of trial, error, and revision. Machine learning processes in computational linguistics are formed by creating an initial program that can note patterns among data points, identifying items of semantic or syntactical importance, and searching for relations among them by rounds of statistical analysis. The results in recent years have been surprisingly novel, nimble, and sensitive to fine-grained details in ways that defy some of the assumptions at work in Searle's and Block's thought experiments. Recent public successes of such systems would include Watson, a system develop by a team of IBM researchers that appeared on an episode of *Jeopardy!* and dominated two human former champions. (See Ferrucci *et al.* (2010).) Such successes remain narrowly focused on specific fields and questions, rather than indicative of a general artificial intelligence, but they are too considerable to shrug off as old tricks in new guises. Machine learning and computational linguistics in general are demanding fields, but avid readers might start with Clark *et al.* (2010) and Manning and Schütze (1999). (See also the Responses section of entry #41 for more on machine learning models.)

RECOMMENDED READINGS

MAJOR WORKS

Searle, J. 1980. "Minds, Brains and Programs." *Behavioral and Brain Sciences* 3: 417–457.

Turing, A. 1950. "Computing Machinery and Intelligence." *Mind* 59 (236): 433–460.

RESPONSES

Block, N. 1981. "Psychologism and Behaviorism." *The Philosophical Review* 90 (1): 5–43.

Boden, M. 1990. "Escaping from the Chinese Room." In *The Philosophy of Artificial Intelligence*, 89–104. New York: Oxford University Press.

Churchland, P., and P. Churchland. 1990. "Could a Machine Think?" *Scientific American* 32–37, January.

Clark, A., C. Fox, and S. Lappin. 2010. *The Handbook of Computational Linguistics and Natural Language Processing*. Oxford: Wiley-Blackwell.

Ferrucci, D., E. Brown, J. Chu-Carroll, J. Fan, D. Gondek, A. Kalyanpur, S. Lally, *et al.* 2010. "Building Watson: An Overview of the DeepQA Project." *AI Magazine* 31 (3): 59–79.

Haugeland, J. 2002. "Syntax, Semantics, Physics." In *Views into the Chinese Room*, edited by J. Preston and M. Bishop, 379–392. New York: Oxford University Press.

Manning, C., and H. Schütze. 1999. *Foundations of Statistical Natural Language Processing*. Cambridge, MA: The MIT Press.

Rey, G. 2002. "Searle's Misunderstandings of Functionalism and Strong AI." In *Views on the Chinese Room: New Essays on Searle and Aritificial Intelligence*, edited by J. Preston and M. Bishop, 201–225. New York: Oxford University Press.

Weizenbaum, J. 1966. "Eliza-A Computer Program for the Study of Natural Language Communication Between Man and Machine." *Communicatons of the Association for Computing Machinery* 9 (1): 36–45.

Winograd, T. 1972. "Understanding Natural Language." *Cognitive Psychology* 3 (1): 1–191.

NATURAL LANGUAGE
AND EVOLUTION

Background: The naturalistic outlooks of entries #41–43 suggested that human capacities for linguistic behavior stem from a distinctly biological set of traits. That same naturalistic perspective would then suggest that we should ask how and why such traits took shape over the course of our evolutionary descent. Whether those traits develop as adaptations to address specific needs or as by-products of a more general expansion of our cognitive abilities is our focus here.

There is a puzzle at the heart of humans' language abilities that has gripped evolutionary biologists, linguists, and naturalistically inclined philosophers of language. As we saw in entry #42, there is apparently a significant gap between our linguistic abilities and any parallel psychological and communicative abilities we find in other species. While the cries and gestures of other animals may convey something about their internal states to one another, they lack the syntactic complexity and a slew of grammatical features that all human languages exhibit. In entry #43, we saw that there are apparently structures within human brains that are especially important to producing and interpreting speech (or manual communication via signs). Even if we as a species are unique on this planet in these respects, this would not imply that no other species could ever exhibit such abilities.

DOI: 10.4324/9781003183167-62

Still, what should strike us here is how large this apparent gap between us and other creatures is. The comparison may seem unfair, though. Perhaps the gap is only a matter of the *degree* of complexity in our languages vs. other species' languages. That would suggest that typical human linguistic abilities were a distinctive feature of our species, but no more mysterious or singular than blue whales' great size or the speed of a hummingbird's wings. Giving this suggestion a fair shake led Terrance Deacon (1997, p. 39ff.) to consider a thought experiment. What might we consider a maximally simple language, trying to be as general and species-neutral as we can in doing so, and how often do we find it among other species? To do so, we shouldn't restrict ourselves to speech, as many other means of communication are at least as viable. But we also should not count all interactions where one party influences another; the molecular motion in the atmosphere is not *communicating* with the mercury in a thermometer, *telling* it to rise. The minimal conditions, Deacon suggests, are (1) some degree of symbolic reference (words standing for something, rather than simply reacting to its presence) and (2) some combinatorial rules for generating strings of those symbols. These two should provide a "system for representing synthetic logical relationships among these symbols" (41).

Some might say that this would not be enough for a language, but any less would surely be too little. Languages must have some symbolic and grammatical structure if they are to be more than mere reactive behaviors among organisms. And this maximally simple fragment of a language might be very minimal, indeed. It would be enough to have only a handful of words, and only a few grammatical rules. A "simple language" like this would be simpler than the one human children exhibit for the first few years of their lives, but it would still have distinctively linguistic features.

So much for defining our simple languages. But even if we set this lower bar for our fellow organisms, we don't find them exhibiting these features. While members of other species may react in complex ways, sensitive to features of their environments and needs, as we saw in entry #42, they hit a wall when it comes to any regular, purposive recombination of those responses that would suggest grammatical knowledge. And, while many other species will behave in ways that associate sounds or gestures with certain conditions, we don't find them doing so in distinctly symbolic ways – e.g., Koko the gorilla's trainers could get her to use signs to react to things in her presence that she wanted immediately, but she struggled to use them consistently or productively otherwise.

If we take it that our abilities developed naturally, right alongside other species in similar environmental conditions, then the question becomes why such a categorical difference should ever emerge. Many linguists and philosophers have followed a path suggested by Noam Chomsky, who held that the human language faculty is a "module" or "organ" within our brains. That is, it is a system within us that develops to play certain specific functions, which develops according to an innately specified set of biological instructions. A language "organ" would not have identifiable physical boundaries like our kidneys or liver do, but it would serve the distinctive function of producing and interpreting speech, much like the kidneys filter waste, or the liver produces bile. And much like those organs, it would develop in specific ways strictly for those purposes. (Chomsky made the case for this many times over the years; see his (1980) for a succinct but comprehensive case.)

It might be tempting to say that it is *obvious* why we would develop our linguistic abilities: they offer us a significant advantage when it comes to survival and reproductive success. Being able to talk to one another in such sophisticated ways allows us to avoid threats and cooperate effectively in gathering resources, which give us more security and better opportunities to reproduce and have offspring that go on to similar success. Pinker and Bloom (1990) argued for this sort of Darwinian adaptationist approach. The complexity of the functions they perform could not emerge by sheer accident, and only natural selection for those faculties could explain their universal appearance across the whole of our species. While there is great diversity in the surface grammar of natural languages, Pinker and Bloom suggest that this is not reflective of deeper differences in "mental grammars." Natural languages in all their varieties transmit propositional structures between speakers, and only selection for a linguistic module within us would explain this universality and uniformity.

Readers should note carefully what is asserted here, and what is contentious about it. To say that some feature of an organism is an adaptation in the present sense is to say that it is fixed and inherited. Such an adaptation might be flexible and responsive to an environment, but it is still inherited by offspring from their biological ancestors. To argue that the language faculty itself is an adaptation fixed by natural selection suggests that a specific, complex set of traits, fixed in roughly their present form, were focal points of natural selection over the last 300,000 years. Yet the principles of the "universal grammar" seem to be highly abstract and arbitrary. If so, then they should not have the kind of functional significance that an adaptation must have to predominate in natural selection. Humans in prehistorical societies surely drew some functional benefits from being able to communicate with each other – e.g., success securing food and avoiding predators. But did they really need our highly complex grammar with considerable resource costs (bigger brains to sustain, time to acquire) for this? Despite his commitments to the innateness of universal grammar, even Chomsky resisted the claim that it was an adaptive trait of this sort. Pinker and Bloom insist that the abstract, arbitrary character of the principles in our language faculty is no obstacle. The arbitrariness doesn't matter, they argue, so long as all the speakers are adopting the *same* linguistic principles. What started as arbitrary constraints are eventually selected for and innately specified. For recent developments of these accounts, see Hauser *et al.* (2002) and Pinker and Jackendoff (2005). Gontier (2012) reviews the field with a more strictly philosophical eye (specifically, the explanatory and epistemological dimensions of the debate.)

RESPONSES

The modular, adaptationist view defended by Pinker and Bloom has met with resistance in recent years. While general opposition to natural selection is rare in scientific inquiry, many scientists and philosophers of language are hesitant to rush to adaptationist explanations, given how flexible our faculties are and how widely the features of natural languages vary. Not *every* complex behavioral trait must be an *adaptive* trait, we should note, even if we make natural selection central to our explanatory strategies in biology.

A growing number of evolutionary linguists, psychologists, and anthropologists have included culture among the elements in language's origins in humans. Whereas adaptationist accounts would place our knowledge of grammar within each person, cultural co-evolution accounts would distribute some of the work of developing and sustaining that knowledge to our interactions with fellow speakers.

Tomasello's (2008) work in evolutionary anthropology makes the case that our divergence from our simian ancestors and cousins was an expansion of our social capacities. As we developed greater capacities for shared intentionality, a "common ground" of shared knowledge, skills, and intersubjective states – pathways to the communicative interactions we have in natural languages – emerged. The crucial evolutionary leap was not simply greater cognitive abilities, in Tomasello's view, but distinctively *social* ones that allowed us to participate in shared cultures. Laland (2017) suggests that the most important capacities that developed in humans to allow them to use language were not enhanced capacities to calculate or learn, but rather new capacities to *teach* one another. Behavior that was not simply mimicked but taught allowed for cultural transmission of all forms of knowledge. Much of what modular approaches would need to locate in each speaker's brain would thus be sustained by cultures, instead.

Christiansen and Chater (2008) argue that adaptationist approaches face several insoluble explanatory challenges. The human population has dispersed over the last 130,000 years; we would expect divergent populations to adapt to different local conditions with many local grammars, not a universal one. (We do see this sort of local adaptation with other traits.) Natural languages change more rapidly than modules could evolve, and we may wonder why adaptations would fix the most abstract properties of language, while leaving so much variation in their superficial ones. Instead, they argue that natural languages and human brains *co-evolved* over time. This would imply that there is no universal grammar built into our biology, but that the capacities our brains develop are well-suited to acquiring and using natural languages. (Deacon (1997), whose thought experiment appears earlier in this entry, proposed such a view.) There would be no linguistic module, fixed in its form, and serving only linguistic functions. Rather, linguistic abilities would be the product of many different cognitive capacities that served many different functions, supported by an array of cultural processes. Natural languages have evolved to suit our cognitive architecture, even though no part of that architecture has evolved specifically and exclusively to produce language. As Christiansen and Chater put it, "Language is easy for us to learn and use, not because our brains embody knowledge of language, but because language has adapted to our brains" (2008, p. 490). Critical responses to Christiansen and Chater can be found in Catania (2008) and Piatelli-Palmarini *et al.* (2008).

A more radical version of the idea that languages and human brains co-evolved without selection for a linguistic module is offered by Nicholas Ritt (2004). Ritt emphasizes that natural languages are much like biological species that need to propagate themselves, lest they disappear. He proposes a "replicator-based" perspective on language, on which constituents of language are *memes* – mental patterns, realizable in many different possible physical systems, and readily transferable between them – that use speakers as hosts. This treats languages as processes taking place in the brains of speakers, but the processes themselves are not uniquely dedicated to producing language. Instead, languages may be thought of as "replicator teams" or collections of information structures that colonize existing cognitive processes to replicate themselves over the course of many generations. Ritt's view suggests that we don't have a language so much as *it has us*.

RECOMMENDED READINGS

MAJOR WORKS

Chomsky, N. 1980. "On the Biological Basis of Language Capacities." In *Rules and Representations*, 185–216. New York: Columbia University Press, Blackwell.

Deacon, T. 1997. *The Symbolic Species: The Co-Evolution of Language and the Brain*. New York: W.W. Norton, Penguin.

Pinker, S., and P. Bloom. 1990. "Natural Language and Natural Selection." *Behavioral and Brain Sciences* 13: 707–727.

Tomasello, M. 2008. *Origins of Human Communication*. Cambridge, MA: The MIT Press.

RESPONSES

Catania, A. 2008. "Brain and Behavior: Which Way Does the Shaping Go?" *Behavioral and Brain Sciences* 31 (5): 516–517.

Christiansen, M., and N. Chater. 2008. "Language as Shaped by the Brain." *Behavioral and Brain Sciences* 31 (5): 489–509.

Gontier, N. 2012. "Selectionist Approaches in Evolutionary Linguistics: An Epistemological Analysis." *International Studies in the Philosophy of Science* 26 (1): 67–95.

Hauser, M., N. Chomsky, and W.T. Fitch. 2002. "The Language Faculty: What Is It, Who Has It, and How Did It Evolve?" *Science* 298: 1569–1579.

Laland, K. 2017. *Darwin's Unfinished Symphony: How Culture Made the Human Mind*. Princeton: Princeton University Press.

Piattelli-Palmarini, M., R. Hancock, and T. Bever. 2008. "Language and Ergonomic Perfection." *Behavioral and Brain Sciences* 31 (5): 530–531.

Pinker, S., and R. Jackendoff. 2005. "The Faculty of Language: What's Special About It?" *Cognition* 95: 201–236.

Ritt, N. 2004. *Selfish Sounds and Linguistic Revolution: A Darwinian Approach to Language Change*. Cambridge: Cambridge University Press.

46

WHAT IF SHAKESPEARE DIDN'T WRITE *HAMLET*?

Background: Frege's work led many philosophers of language to accounts of proper names on which most or all of those expressions have a sense that determines their reference. This supplanted earlier accounts on which the meanings of proper names were understood entirely in terms of their reference. In the 1970s, a new theory of reference emerged, spearheaded by Saul Kripke and Hilary Putnam. Their views hark back to purely desig-nation-based accounts of names popular before 1900 but may also revive some classical problems along the way.

If someone asked you what your name means, how would you answer? One answer that might come to mind is deceptively simple: you might just say, "Me," perhaps while pointing to yourself. Maybe that would feel too simple, though. Remembering your Frege, you might imagine that your name would need to have a sense and recall that these were sometimes spelled out in illustrations with further descriptions. Any single description might be too broad or apply to too many people to give us a sense of just who your name names. You might instead think that, to spell out the sense of your name, you could give a *cluster* of descriptions. While no single description would be enough to single you out, a relatively short list of them might very well do so.

DOI: 10.4324/9781003183167-63

To illustrate how this might work, imagine we did this with the name of someone famous, much of whose history is familiar to us. Suppose we ask what the name 'William Shakespeare' means. If you remember your high school English class, you might give a cluster of descriptions that included 'born in Stratford-upon-Avon, wrote *Hamlet*, married Anne Hathaway . . .' Let's assume that there comes to be some canonical version of this cluster and that our linguistic community strongly associates those descriptions with that name. In a Fregean spirit, we might say that this was the sense of the name, and we would expect it to lead us to its reference. We can't catch up with Shakespeare in person, but we can follow the descriptions through historical records to focus on one person in the past who was the bearer of the name. We could do similar things with someone who was around at present, and similar things for names of things other than people. We could call this a *descriptivist* account of the meaning and reference of proper names.

There are some difficulties with this view as it's been stated. These were famously noted by Saul Kripke (1980). For one, it would seem to make those clusters of descriptions (or some significant subset of them) necessarily true of the bearer of the name. If a name's meaning is that cluster of descriptions, then anything to which it applies must have them, and anything that lacks them does not bear that name. In this way, names would resemble analytic truths: if 'bachelor' just means 'unmarried, eligible male,' then it would be a necessary truth that bachelors are unmarried. If meaning of 'William Shakespeare' were a cluster of descriptions including, 'author of Hamlet,' it would *necessarily* be the case that he wrote Hamlet, that anything that did not write *Hamlet* was not Shakespeare, and we would know this necessary truth with *a priori* assurance.

That's just who William Shakespeare *is*, one might say. But surely William Shakespeare might have lived a life in which he did not write *Hamlet*. Since the mid-19th century, there have been fringe theorists who asserted that he wrote few or none of the works attributed to him. Those claims are almost certainly false, but they are not *logically* or *necessarily* false. We could imagine a scenario in which William Shakespeare needs a play and calls in a favor from Ben Jonson. This would be strange, but not impossible. There's no reason to stop there, either. We could imagine Shakespeare subcontracting all his works from other writers; his marriage to Anne Hathaway could have been a fraud to keep up appearances; perhaps he was born in Liverpool, but thought Stratford sounded more impressive.

In principle, we could imagine there being a person named 'William Shakespeare,' but of whom none of the descriptions in that cluster are actually true. Even more puzzlingly, we could turn this scenario on its head. Suppose we have a person named 'William Shakespeare,' of whom none of this cluster of descriptions is true, while at the same time, there is another person with another name, of whom all these descriptions *are true*. Would it then follow that this other person *was* William Shakespeare? That person might have been born in Stratford, written *Hamlet*, etc., but does that make that person William Shakespeare? Suppose that person was known to their friends and family as 'Patrick Flynn;' would it make sense to walk up to that person after their many literary achievements and say, "No, no. You're not Patrick Flynn. You're William Shakespeare." (If this doesn't seem sufficiently bizarre, imagine someone coming and doing so to you with another name, insisting, "No, we checked the cluster. You're Hamilton Esterhaus."[1])

Some expressions do work this way. 'The tallest person in the room' could be unpacked as a cluster of descriptions plus a little context-sensitive reckoning, and we could then use that as a recipe for singling someone out in such a setting. This might come as a surprise to that person, unlike their name, and it would apply to different people in different circumstances. Proper names seem to work in just the opposite way, though. While many different things could happen in the course of a person's life or an object's history, the name will only apply to that thing. And it will apply to that thing in different "possible worlds," as philosophers like to say. That is, even if we were to run through all the different combinations of possibilities that could make up a complete history of the universe, and we were to imagine every different possible configuration of properties that the bearer of a name could have in those possible worlds, the name we use for that thing would still refer to that thing.

Proper names, Kripke argued, are *rigid* designators. They will refer to one and the same thing in every possible world where they refer to anything at all. *Non-rigid* designators like "the tallest person in the room" might refer to different things in different contexts, or to different things in other possible worlds. In some other possible world, something might be known by a different name – perhaps my parents could have named me Padraic Michael Wolf instead of Michael Padraic Wolf. But that is not to say that my name does not designate me rigidly. We can still speak of me in that other possible world using my name, and say, "Michael Padraic Wolf is known by a different name in some other possible world."

You might reasonably wonder *how* a proper name can do all this. With the "cluster" model suggested earlier, we at least had a recipe for determining what the referent would be. If those properties we associate with a person (or whatever is named) are only contingently assigned, then we're approaching a view of names articulated by John Stuart Mill, who said that names serve "the double purpose of a mark to recall to ourselves the likeness of a former thought, and a sign to make it known to others" (1849/1975, p. 29). A "mark" would suggest that names are simply labels, offering no more semantic content than to point to their bearers. This lets us avoid the strange implications of making names clusters of descriptions that I described earlier, but there still must be some means of fixing their reference, and it must be public if we're to share it as speakers in the same linguistic community.

Kripke's solution was to suggest that each proper name had an introduction to the language in which the bearer of a name was "baptized" with it, so to speak. In the early hours of my life, my parents informed the relevant authorities that their child (me) would have my name. Maybe they pointed to me in the nursery; maybe that wasn't necessary. But such actions on speakers' parts fix the reference of proper names, Kripke said, and other speakers may then use those names, leaning on the work done at their introduction. Obviously, there is much to be said about the conditions that make such introductions legitimate and binding for speakers. If my parents had pointed at the wrong baby in the nursery and spoken my name, the nurses weren't going to say, "Too late. That other one's named Michael now." And many of these examples have centered on names for persons, but again, we could imagine similar introductions for anything we could name.

At roughly the same time, Hilary Putnam was thinking along similar lines on related subjects. His work converges with Kripke's on important claims about natural kind terms. Kind terms designate kinds of objects and properties; natural kinds are those that would putatively exist as a matter of the laws of nature, rather than as artifacts or conventions in our social practices. Thus, 'oxygen' might be a natural kind term, while 'professor' would not, even if it designates a kind.

Putnam noted that scientific inquiry has given us rapidly evolving conceptions of natural kinds. In 1700, European scientists investigating water would have told you that it was a continuous, uniform substance; by 1800, consensus was emerging that it was a compound of two types of atoms. The familiar 'H_2O' microstructural formula would take hold in the 1860s, and physical chemists today would tell us that the glass of water before us is a swirling miasma of different molecules (H_2O, OH^-, H_3O^+ and more) with roughly twice as many hydrogen atoms as oxygen atoms. If we imagine that the kind term 'water' is a cluster of descriptions, we would have wholly different clusters in 1700 and 2000, yet we're purportedly talking about the same things with the same word. Natural kind terms must also be rigid designators, Kripke and Putnam suggested, and function like proper names in many respects. Our paleolithic ancestors must have stood before a lake or stream and dubbed the stuff therein with some progenitor of our word 'water.' We have gone on to offer sophisticated theoretical descriptions of it, and some of these have even worked their way into the everyday "stereotype" of water that non-experts have, as Putnam put it. But he and Kripke argue that these have not become part of the meaning of the word 'water,' and they are not what fixes its reference.

RESPONSES

The works from Kripke (1980) and Putnam (1973) described here have been among the most widely read and discussed works in the philosophy of language in the last 50 years. They are also broad in scope, touching on themes in metaphysics, epistemology, science, logic, and a host of other theoretical issues in related fields. For now, I will emphasize some sources that inform or anticipate these arguments, and some of the most prominent (and representative) criticisms that were made to them.

To get a better sense of the historical antecedents of these arguments, readers will want to check Book 1, Chapter 2 of Mill (1849/1975), as well as the entries on Russell and Frege from earlier in this volume. Many of Kripke's views were anticipated by parts of Donnellan (1966) and Marcus (1961). The "cluster" concept of names that Kripke discusses is defended by Searle (1958), one of few directly cited authors in *Naming and Necessity*. Evans (1973) and Soames (2002) refine and extend the accounts of naming and rigid designation in ways that have proven influential. More sharply critical responses can be found in Dummett (1973) and Devitt (1989). The extension of rigid designation to natural kind terms suggested by both Kripke and Putnam has been both influential and contentious in equal measure.

NOTE

1. The suggestion being that 'Hamilton Esterhaus' is an unfamiliar name to you. In rare cases, this might happen – e.g., a mix-up at birth. Even in those rare cases, it's not a set of descriptions about what someone did with their life that determines who they are and what their proper name is.

RECOMMENDED READINGS

MAJOR WORKS

Kripke, S. 1980. *Naming and Necessity*. Oxford: Basil Blackwell.

Mill, J.S. 1849/1975. "Book I: Of Names and Propositions." In *A System of Logic (Collected Works of John Stuart Mill, vol. 7)*, edited by J. Robson. London: Routledge and Kegan Paul.

Putnam, H. 1973. "Meaning and Reference." *Journal of Philosophy* 70: 699–711.

RESPONSES

Devitt, M. 1989. "Against Direct Reference." *Midwest Studies in Philosophy* 14: 206–240.

Donnellan, K. 1966. "Reference and Definite Description." *The Philosophical Review* 75 (3): 281–304.

Dummett, M. 1973. "Note on an Attempted Refutation of Frege." In *Frege: Philosophy of Language*, 110–151. New York: Harper and Row.

Evans, G. 1973. "The Causal Theory of Names." *Aristotelian Society: Supplementary Volume* 47: 187–208.

Marcus, R.B. 1961. "Modalities and Intensional Languages." *Synthèse* 13 (4): 303–322.

Searle, J. 1958. "Proper Names." *Mind* 67 (266): 166–173.

Soames, S. 2002. *Beyond Rigidity: The Unfinished Agenda of Naming and Necessity*. Cambridge, MA: The MIT Press.

47

REFERENCE AND CHAINS OF COMMUNICATION

Background: In entry #46, we saw arguments that suggested a direct form of reference for some classes of expressions – specifically, proper names and natural kind terms. Those arguments assumed that reference for proper names and natural kind terms was fixed by a "baptism" in which the expressions were introduced as designators for their referents. How this fixing informs subsequent use and is transferred between speakers in communication with one another remains to be explained.

As we saw in entry #46, many philosophers of language have taken up what came to be known as a "causal" theory of reference. On such views, the references of proper names and natural kind terms have their reference fixed by speakers who causally interact with the referent itself. This contrasts with descriptivist views, on which a proper name or natural kind term has some amount of descriptive content that determines its referent. If descriptivism were true, then every proper name and natural kind term would include a recipe for finding its referent. Causal theorists pointed out that the ways we might describe a referent could turn out to be mistaken or could be different under other possible circumstances. We should think of the reference as fixed first, with any descriptions of the referent to be discovered later, rather than presumed in the introduction of the

DOI: 10.4324/9781003183167-64

expression. (Shakespeare would still have been Shakespeare, even if he had never written *Hamlet*, etc.)

This leaves the causal theorist of reference with a new problem, however. Suppose the reference of a proper name or natural kind term is fixed, as they suggest it is. Even if there were such fixings, how would any given speaker's use of that expression include that designation? Compare two terms here – one with descriptive content, and one that causal theorists say has none. The expression 'computer scientist' has descriptive content that we could typically spell out in the form of a definition. Someone who is a computer scientist studies the properties of information-processing systems, typically by developing theoretical models of their structures. Contrast this with a proper name like 'Flynn Wolf.' This is my brother's name, as you might guess. He is familiar to me, to our family, friends, his coworkers, and his neighbors. But to almost anyone else who might read this text, he will be completely *un*known. Whereas you might understand the meaning of 'computer scientist' and be able to decide whether it applied to any given person you met, how would the name 'Flynn Wolf' retain its reference when *you* use it if it has no such descriptive content? You won't have causally interacted directly with him (for all but a few exceptions among readers of this text), so how does that name have any meaning when you use it?

Here is another concern that any account should address. For many proper names, more than one version of the name will be in use – written, spoken, or signed in just the same ways, but referring to different things, just the same. If you'd like an example, consider me, Michael Wolf. Over the years, I have crossed paths with numerous other people named 'Michael Wolf.' One such person cleaned out my bank account, thanks to my bank sending that person my new debit card. (And I got to meet that person in court. Fun!) A woman once called me at 4:00 a.m., told me a rambling story of one of her teeth cracking, and insisted that I perform an emergency root canal. (Local surgeon Dr. Michael Wolf, DDS, was considerably more qualified for this.) Presumably, there is some fact of the matter about who my bank or that woman was referring to in saying or writing 'Michael Wolf,' and in both cases, it was not me. What could indicate that difference, or determine on whom the reference was fixed? If we assume that the proper names of things and natural kind terms are fixed on something by their introduction to the language, how would this feature of their content become available to speakers who were not present for its introduction?

RESPONSES

For the causal theorist, the general answer is straightforward. A proper name or natural kind term has its reference fixed at its introduction. After this, there will be a "chain of communication" among speakers of the language, which will consist of many "reference-preserving causal links" among speakers, as Kripke (1980) put it. Think of the initial introduction and fixing of the reference as an anchor, and many linguistic exchanges between speakers as links in a chain attached to that anchor. The links could take many forms: his parents speaking to officials when he was named, records being kept as he attended schools, etc. Each of those passes the name along to others, linking back to that introduction through some number of linguistic exchanges. Someone like me will have a close connection with few steps back to the introduction of my name. For you, reading this book after it passes through editors and publishers, there will be more steps involved, and each one of those steps inherits its reference-fixing from previous links in the chain.

By convention, we will typically accept others' use of names that are unfamiliar to us and challenge them only in unusual cases. I pass the name 'Flynn Wolf' on to you, and you accept it, deferring to my authority to use it; it was passed to me by my parents, who presumably have authority over fixing it when it was introduced. And we will all be in the same sort of dependent position when it comes to names for more historically distant people and things. We can also see how to address the second concern introduced above. While there may be multiple people named 'Michael Wolf,' any given one of those names will occur as part of its own chain of communication. We may be confused in some cases, but that can be resolved.

Putnam (1975) concurred with many of these details in Kripke's account, though his work emphasized chains of communication for natural kind terms. These terms added further nuance to the chains of communication in that their purport to naturalness – an independence of the kinds they designate from our beliefs and practices – demands a different sort of authority than proper names. If my parents name me 'Michael Wolf,' then they do so with a final, dispute-ending authority, and we defer to them.[1] But, if I find a sample of a white, crystalline substance at the end of my driveway and insist that it is calcium carbonate after glancing at it, I'm not able to say with final authority that this is the composition of the substance. (Calcium chloride, used to de-ice roads, would be much more likely.) This is the sort of question about which we attempt to develop scientific responses, and a term like 'calcium carbonate' will be integrated into an array of methods, tests, and practices that offer results, to which we defer. I can be wrong, and indeed a whole community of speakers can be wrong, about what the substance at the end of my driveway is.

Consider this in light of the introduction of a natural kind term. On Putnam's view, our ancestors introduced terms like 'water' and fixed their reference by indicating something with which they had directly causally interacted. Contemporary scientists continue to do this. After that initial reference-fixing, speakers enter a mutual agreement to tie what they say with such expressions back to the thing our ancestors indicated. But what makes for the "sort of thing" invoked here is a matter that we leave to scientific inquiry. Even if our ancestors thought water a substance with no internal structure, research has revealed it to have one (H_2O). We should defer to those results in forming our beliefs and making claims. This has great benefits for ordinary speakers: they don't have to know any of this! Once the kind term is introduced, speakers can simply follow the patterns of usage laid out by earlier speakers in the chain. If they have no substantive knowledge of modern chemistry (as many don't), or if past speakers held incorrect beliefs about water (as many did), they can still refer to the things designated at its introduction, and the kind term can have the same meaning for all of us. We have what Putnam called "a division of epistemic labor," whereby ordinary speakers introduce natural kind terms and preserve their designation through chains of communication, while the work of discovering essential features of natural kinds passes on to scientific experts. (See Goldberg (2007) for elaboration of this point.) The work of those experts may then gradually work its way back into the usage and understanding of everyday speakers.

Putnam's account was embraced by scientific realists in the 1970s and 1980s, who used it to rebut challenges from anti-realists who doubted that scientific theories designated real entities or made objectively true claims. More recently, Putnam's account has been subject to two new lines of criticism. First, Thomas Kuhn (1990) has been critical of scientific realism in general, and crucial aspects of Putnam's account of the preservation of reference by an initial fixing, to which subsequent uses are then later anchored. Highlighting the historical development of some of Putnam's examples, he aims to show that these chains of communication won't suffice to ground essentialism or realism about natural kinds. Second, both Kripke and Putnam make their case for a causal theory of reference by appealing to thought experiments and the intuitions of their audience about linguistic practices. But they and their audience are almost exclusively English speakers in the West. Mallon *et al.* (2009) make an empirical case that disputes these thought experiments and intuitions. In cross-cultural studies, stark disparities emerge between different cultural and linguistic groups about what entities names designate in the cases Kripke and Putnam suggest, even when consistent chains of communication are assumed. Mallon *et al.* presented groups of test subjects in the US and mainland China with a variation on our earlier thought experiment, in which the cluster for 'Gödel' includes 'proved the incompleteness theorem' (which Gödel did do), but it turns out someone else proved the theorem. American readers were significantly more likely to give a causal-historical answer like Kripke's, while Chinese subjects decisively favored descriptivist answers. (Thus, taking someone else as Gödel, despite conventional use of the name.)

Two other lines of critique merit readers' attention. Since the 1970s, there have been numerous criticisms of the simple, straightforward selection of a natural kind for reference-fixing that Kripke and Putnam presume. Any putative reference-fixing would need to select *just one* natural kind for speakers to designate, even though earlier speakers lacked theoretical resources for doing so. The conditions of any possible introduction are consistent with fixing on multiple different kinds and entities (were our ancestors selecting H_2O, the particular lake to which they pointed, etc.?). Just what they were picking out is something we tend to read backwards from a more privileged epistemic position. The literature on this objection is reviewed and rebutted to some degree in Chapter 5 of Gomez-Torrente (2019). Additionally, there have been criticisms about the sufficiency of the causal dimension of Kripke's and Putnam's accounts of reference and calls for them to be expanded or enriched in various ways. Jackman (1999) argues that deference to future speakers is an indispensable feature of any plausible reading of the core arguments. While that should not trouble us, Jackman argues, it does complicate the simple backward-looking picture of reference being preserved by speakers' utterances causing others' beliefs and utterances in familiar ways. Wolf (2006) argues that causal terms are insufficient to account for rigidity, and that there are normative and inferential dimensions that must be included (and which cut against orthodox versions of the theory).

NOTE

1. They might change my name later, or I might change it myself when I become an adult. These would just be further nuances to the structure of this authority.

RECOMMENDED READINGS

MAJOR WORKS

Kripke, S. 1980. *Naming and Necessity*. Oxford: Basil Blackwell.
Putnam, H. 1975. "The Meaning of 'Meaning'." In *Philosophical Papers, vol. 2: Mind, Language and Reality*, edited by H. Putnam, 215–271. Cambridge: Cambridge University Press.

RESPONSES

Goldberg, S. 2007. *Anti-Individualism: Mind and Language, Knowledge and Justification*. Cambridge: Cambridge University Press.
Gomez-Torrente, M. 2019. *Roads to Reference: An Essay on Reference Fixing in Natural Language*. Oxford: Oxford University Press.
Jackman, H. 1999. "We Live Forwards but Understand Backwards: Linguistic Practices and Future Behavior." *Pacific Philosophical Quarterly* 80: 157–177.
Kuhn, T. 1990. "Dubbing and Redubbing: The Vulnerability of Rigid Designation." In *Scientific Theories: Minnesota Studies in the Philosophy of Science*, edited by W. Savage, vol. 14, 298–318. Minneapolis, MN: University of Minnesota Press.
Mallon, R., E. Machery, S. Nichols, and S. Stich. 2009. "Against Arguments from Reference." *Philosophy and Phenomenological Research* 79 (2): 332–356.
Wolf, M. 2006. "Rigid Designation and Anaphoric Theories of Reference." *Philosophical Studies* 130 (2): 351–375.

48

ADVENTURES ON TWIN EARTH

Background: In entry #46, we read about the recent development of what have been called "causal" theories of reference and "direct" theories of reference. Unlike Fregean accounts, they suggest the reference of some expressions is determined directly, by causal contact with the referent, rather than indirectly, via their sense. Kripke's primary concern had been the reference of proper names. Hilary Putnam argued for a similar view about natural kind terms, based largely on his Twin Earth thought experiment.

A natural kind term is one that purports to designate a kind of thing that exists independently of our attitudes and practices. 'Oxygen' might be a natural kind term, as well as 'gold' (the metal), and 'tiger.' I say "might be" because my best reasons for saying that they are is that they figure prominently in well-supported scientific theories. Those theories might change, though it would be astonishing if some of them did. Many of them appear in laws and other generalizations that have a lawlike necessity to them.

What could be the source of that necessity? A common answer for much of the 20th century in Western philosophy was that necessary truths could only be established by the analysis of meanings of words. It might be a necessary truth that no bachelors are married, but only because of the meaning of 'bachelor.' The necessity of a statement

DOI: 10.4324/9781003183167-65

like 'Oxygen has eight protons in its nucleus' is tricky on that sort of view, though. It does not seem that 'oxygen' *means* 'eight protons in the nucleus;' 'oxygen' was introduced to modern chemistry in 1777, but its nuclear structure was first postulated about a century and a half later. Natural kind terms have an open-ended quality to them, assuming those kinds exist independently of what we say and think of them. We might use those terms to describe or explain something, even if we continue to discover new things about them over time.

That open-ended quality ran into another assumption prevalent in 20th century philosophy of language: that meanings *supervene* on the psychological states of speakers. To say that one thing (like meanings) supervenes on another (like psychological states) is to say that there could not be a change in the supervening properties without a change in the properties that they supervene on. You would look to the underlying properties to determine the supervening properties. In plain terms, if we wanted to know what words meant, we would look to what sorts of thoughts people were typically having when they said them. Putnam noticed a point of tension here. In 1700, when people used the word 'water,' speakers would have had one set of thoughts in mind when they wrote or said that, and it might have included some of the incorrect chemistry of the day. When people use the word 'water' now, they have different thoughts. Did 'water' not mean the same thing in 1700 that it does now?

To motivate a different approach to natural kind terms, Putnam (1975) offered a thought experiment. Suppose that, in our interstellar travels, we find a planet that looks much like ours to the naked eye. There are similar-looking plants and animals, and even creatures that look like us and speak a language with a grammar identical to ours. It is so much like Earth that we call it Twin Earth. Suppose we visit Twin Earth, talking with the Twin Earthlings as much as we can, and we find that they have a word 'water' in their vocabulary. When we ask them what that is, they tell us, "The clear stuff that we drink, which is found in lakes and streams." These all sound like the kinds of things that an ordinary speaker of our language, here on Earth, would think of when that word was used. After a long visit, we take some samples of Twin Earth stuff home for a closer look and wish our Twin Earth friends well. But when we get back to Earth, we find something surprising. The samples that we took from the lakes and streams on Twin Earth don't contain H_2O; they contain some other chemical compound, which Putnam calls "XYZ." So, should we say, "There is water on Twin Earth"?

Putnam's answer was that we should not. Twin Earthlings have a word that sounds like ours, but it means something different. That is no more surprising than two Earth languages having similar-sounding words. But this is more striking because we Earthlings and the Twin Earthlings are generally thinking the same things when we use these words – "the clear stuff that we drink, which is found in lakes and streams." But that does not tell us what the word means, Putnam argues. What that word refers to cannot be determined wholly by speakers' thoughts. Even on Earth, we can be deceived about whether or not something is water at first, so we look to the chemists for answers. This failure of psychological states to settle the matter led Putnam to a bold conclusion: "Meanings just ain't in the head!"

But where (or what) would they be otherwise? Putnam argued for a view much like Kripke's. (See entry #46 for more.). A natural kind term like 'water' would be introduced by demonstration or ostension. That is, our ancestors pointed at a sample of water and introduced some word for it. Our word descends from that event, and while it surely sounds different, it refers to just the same stuff. Putnam's view was that such an introduction purported to pick out a type of stuff with some set of essential features. That essence determined which things were in the term's extension and which were not, even if our ancestors were not in a position to say so. Critically for this thought experiment, essences would be real features of the non-linguistic world; they would not be meanings that we introduce, and they would not be "in our heads." However, they are a bold, controversial commitment to make when we're doing metaphysics.

Scientific research on these questions constitutes our most refined, advanced attempts to uncover those essences and discover those necessary truths about natural kinds. Few people study science at a level that makes those details available to them, but this does not prevent others from using the word. We benefit from a "division of epistemic labor," with ordinary speakers handing more demanding theoretical questions off to experts and deferring to their results when they seem secure. (Most of us can recite 'Water is H_2O' from high school chemistry class.) This deference made the meaning of the word rest on something that extends beyond any set of thoughts that a particular person could have. We thus call it a form of semantic *externalism*. This became one of the most popular – and most contentious – new views in the philosophy of language over the last 50 years.

RESPONSES

This thought experiment has been one of the most widely read and discussed in the philosophy of language in the last 50 years. This is in part because of its clarity and simplicity, but also due to the scope of different questions and fields to which it pertains. It has been of interest not just to philosophers of language, but also to philosophers of mind, metaphysics, philosophy of science, and ethics. And while some thought experiments, such as skeptical scenarios, would have uniform implications in a great many fields (lacking knowledge in general would undermine many different views), Putnam's Twin Earth case is striking in that it has distinctive implications for these different fields.

One of the most contentious features of Putnam's case is its endorsement of essentialism. While Western philosophy has had many essentialists, and many philosophers are essentialists on some matters, there has also been a history of hesitation about such views. D.H. Mellor was scathing in making an argument about the failure to deduce essentialist commitments from the Twin Earth cases: "[Kripke's and Putnam's] premises are false, their arguments invalid, and the plausibility of their conclusions specious" (1977, p. 135). Since essences are metaphysical entities, external to our linguistic practices, they don't determine anything linguistic simply by existing, Mellor objects. The senses of kind terms, in particular, are not fixed by essences, so if we were to visit Twin Earth and find XYZ there, we should conclude that 'water' designates more than one microstructure (contrary to Putnam's view). Nathan Salmon (1981) similarly argued that the essentialism in Putnam's view was entailed by the views on meaning and reference that he was promoting. That is, it presumes the important metaphysical thesis, rather than showing essentialism is true or that his account is plausible independent of that assumption. Haukioja (2015) favors Putnam's views, while still admitting that deducing essentialist commitments from it is suspicious. Instead, he denies Salmon's view that an independent case for essentialism is needed. Natural kind terms are, as he puts it, "actuality-dependent:" objects in their actual extension figure in determining their extensions in other possible worlds. Which terms have actuality-dependence is an empirical matter of our linguistic dispositions, and these point us in essentialist directions for our natural kind terms.

The Twin Earth case also had an immediate effect on philosophers of science, initiating a wave of interest in scientific realism. Boyd (1983) suggested that scientific realism made four claims about scientific theories: (1) they have theoretical terms that refer to real entities and properties; (2) they succeed in making true claims; (3) they operate cumulatively, adding new truths and rarely needing to abandon earlier ones; and (4) they develop progressively, increasing their explanatory power and instrumental applications over time. History is full of failed theories, so scientific realists tend to emphasize that they are speaking only of "mature" theories that have a hold on things as they are. Boyd seized on the Twin Earth case to suggest that, in mature theories, speakers latch onto referents with essences that could be uncovered by inquiry. Even if 18th century speakers gave 'water' the wrong cluster of theoretical descriptions, the reference of that term can carry through from earlier speakers to the present as our theory develops. Same stuff, new theory. However, this interpretation has come under greater scrutiny recently. Few theoretical kinds in physics – and almost none in fields like biology or psychology – exist as simple combinations of properties that co-occur without exception. Thus, Häggqvist and Wikforss (2018) argue that Putnam's view is plausible only on a strong reading of essentialism about physical microstructures, which is itself implausible as a general account of science. Most theoretical kinds will require cluster of descriptions instead. Bishop and Stich (1998) challenge Boyd's strategy on the grounds that those who deploy it invariably either adopt an implausibly substantive notion of reference without argument or defend a weaker notion of reference that won't support the sorts of conclusions about truth and ontology that Boyd suggests.

Finally, the Twin Earth case has also appeared in debates about moral realism in ethics. Ethicists often find themselves struggling with accounts of how moral properties might be placed and explained as part of the world. If I see someone torturing an animal, I will judge it morally wrong. I see the physical force being used, hear its cries, but where in all this is the *wrongness*? Moral realists like Brink (1989) suggested that Kripke and Putnam's views on reference could help. The mysterious, ephemeral *not-to-be-doneness* of wrong actions could be shunted off to the meanings of moral terms, rather than placed in the world. Yet the extension of 'wrong' or other moral terms could be picked out from a sample by speakers just as they would pick water out from a lake or stream. Horgan and Timmons (1992) later offered an influential critique of this approach to moral realism by turning the tables and using a Putnam-style Twin Earth case to show that moral terms don't function like natural kind terms.

RECOMMENDED READINGS

MAJOR WORKS

Mellor, D. 1977. "Natural Kinds." *British Journal for the Philosophy of Science* 28 (4): 299–312.

Putnam, H. 1975. "The Meaning of 'Meaning'." In *Philosophical Papers, vol. 2: Mind, Language and Reality*, edited by H. Putnam, 215–271. Cambridge: Cambridge University Press.

Salmon, N. 1981. *Reference and Essence*. Princeton: Princeton University Press.

RESPONSES

Bishop, M., and S. Stich. 1998. "The Flight to Reference, or How Not to Make Progress in the Philosophy of Science." *Philosophy of Science* 65 (1): 33–49.

Boyd, R. 1983. "On the Current Status of Scientific Realism." *Erkenntnis* 19 (1): 45–90.

Brink, D.O. 1989. *Moral Realism and the Foundations of Ethics*. Cambridge: Cambridge University Press.

Geirsson, H. 2005. "Moral Twin Earth and Semantic Moral Realism." *Erkenntnis* 62 (3): 353–378.

Häggqvist, S., and Å Wikforss. 2018. "Natural Kinds and Natural Kind Terms: Myth and Reality." *British Journal for the Philosophy of Science* 69 (4): 911–933.

Haukioja, J. 2015. "On Deriving Essentialism from the Theory of Reference." *Philosophical Studies* 172 (8): 2141–2151.

Horgan, T., and M. Timmons. 1992. "Troubles on Moral Twin Earth: Moral Queerness Revived." *Synthèse* 92 (2): 221–260.

49

EMPTY KIND TERMS

Background: The causal theory of reference described in this set of entries also ushered in a more general view that came to be known as "semantic externalism." Externalists say that at least some of the meanings of words in our languages necessarily depend on the existence of objects and conditions external to speakers' thoughts. Internalists argue that meanings depend solely on conditions internal to speakers' thoughts. Causal theories of reference are squarely in the externalist camp here. In this section, we consider the implications for these views when we have "empty" kinds, with which causal contact is not possible.

Putnam introduced his account of natural kind terms with his Twin Earth thought experiment. Suppose we were to find another planet during our interstellar travels, and this planet seemed (at first look) like a perfect copy of Earth. Call this planet "Twin Earth." Twin Earth has lakes and streams full of a clear, potable liquid that the locals call 'water.' We take a few samples home with us and find to our surprise that Twin Earth has no H_2O in its lakes and streams. Some other (improbably similar) stuff is there instead, which we can call "XYZ." Putnam argued that Twin Earth has no water on it, as 'water' in our language has its reference fixed here on Earth with stuff that turns out to be H_2O. Its meaning depends on these external conditions in

DOI: 10.4324/9781003183167-66

which it was introduced. So, the Twin Earthers are using a word that sounds like ours, but means something else, much like familiar cases of words in actual different languages (e.g., 'nine' in English, which sounds just like the German word 'nein' for 'no').

Paul Boghossian (1997) has had considerable reservations about externalism and responded with a thought experiment of his own. Imagine a planet on which there is no H_2O, nor any XYZ. We can call this place "Dry Earth." But suppose that Dry Earth speakers have a word – 'water' – and that they say things with it that seem similar to things we might say. We might say that their word is meaningless because its extension (the set of things to which it correctly applies) is empty. That would be too hasty, however. We have plenty of meaningful words that don't happen to apply to anything, Boghossian notes. There are no unicorns, but 'unicorn' remains a meaningful word. What we must ask is what concept, if any, should an externalist say would be expressed when Dry Earth speakers say 'water?' The same one we have on Earth? The one from Twin Earth? Both? Neither?

Boghossian invokes a distinction among kind terms between those that are *atomic* and those that are *compound*. This distinction relates to the nature of their meaning, not something from chemistry. Atomic terms would have no internal conceptual components, only their designation and the causal route by which they entered the language. In Putnam's and Kripke's accounts, 'water' would be an atomic term. Compound terms would be analyzable into other conceptual components; so, 'H_2O' would be a compound term that we could analyze into theoretical concepts for different kinds of atoms, plus the concepts involved in molecular structures. Bear in mind how these differ as types of meanings. Atomic terms simply designate kinds with which we interact; compound terms function like clusters of descriptions, although our interaction with the world guides us in deciding what belongs in the cluster.

With these distinctions in hand, a possible solution presents itself: maybe the Dry Earth speakers have a compound concept that they express with 'water.' Perhaps it's 'potable, liquid in lakes and streams at such-and-such temperatures . . .' That's not as sophisticated as the compound concept that Earth's scientists could provide, and it would not mean the same as 'water' on Earth where the term is atomic. But at least the word would not be meaningless for Dry Earth speakers. A speaker could have that concept even if it happened to have an empty extension. Yet, as tempting as this answer is, Boghossian thinks it won't work. If the Dry Earthers' term 'water' is as functionally similar as we have suggested, then it would appear that we have one term that is somehow compound when Dry Earthers use it and atomic when we use it. Given how different the content of atomic and compound terms must be, this would not be possible. (Imagine someone saying, "This is true by definition of water when I say it, but not when you do . . .")

Fair enough, the externalist might say, the Dry Earthers must be using an atomic concept. But this will present us with a different problem. Are the Dry Earthers using Earth speakers' atomic concept (which has the same extension as H_2O), or Twin Earth speakers' atomic concept (which has the same extension as XYZ)? Dry Earthers have no way of interacting with either of these substances, so Boghossian argues that there can be no fact of the matter about which atomic concept they are using. In that case, there cannot be any concept in play at all. This should be an intolerable conclusion for the externalist, Boghossian suggests. We can clearly have "empty" kind terms that are still meaningful, yet the conditions that Kripke, Putnam, and other externalists would seem to make that impossible. The only reasonable conclusion, Boghossian asserts, is that the semantic externalism that Kripke and Putnam proposed must be false.

RESPONSES

Much of this debate is animated by disputes over the privileged status of self-knowledge and first-person access. In some papers discussed here, the approach Boghossian critiques is called "anti-individualistic" semantics. (Boghossian's 1998 paper was primarily about this subject.) For most Western philosophers of the last 500 years, it has been assumed that we have a direct access to the content of our own thoughts that is incorrigible and perhaps infallible. Suppose you have a painful sensation and have the thought, "I'm in pain right now." It would seem that no one could correct you on this point. You have a type of access to your own experiences unlike the access you have to other things, or that anyone has to you. But there are two ways we might call this into question: we might doubt that *you are in pain*, or we might doubt that *it is pain that you are in*. The first of these is a strange doubt to raise, but the second is less so. Inspired in part by

Putnam, Tyler Burge (1979) noted that the content of many beliefs depends on matters external to the scope of our thoughts. Suppose that someone said that they believed a particular glass was full of water, but we examined it more closely and found it to be pure ethanol. If someone said, "But when I say 'water,' I mean 'clear, potable liquid,' so I really was thinking that it was water, and I was right," then that should strike us as a cheap reply. The meaning of that word, semantic externalists will say, necessarily depends on objects and conditions external to speakers' thoughts. This person may have taken themselves to be thinking about water, but they were not, even if the sounds in their internal monologue were just like those for our word 'water.'

So, you could be wrong about the content of your own thoughts in certain ways. Burge doubted that this imperiled privileged access, but McKinsey (1991) was much more pessimistic about reconciling externalism with privileged access and seemed fine with letting privileged access go. McKinsey argued that, if externalism is true, then I know *a priori* that, if I have the concept of water, then water must exist. (It must exist for us to have interacted with it to introduce the term.) If privileged access is true, then I can know a priori that I have the concept of water. If both are true, then I can know a priori that water exists. But this conclusion is absurd, McKinsey argues. We cannot know that kinds of physical stuff exist just by thinking about our own thinking – we must investigate the physical stuff! McKinsey takes this as a point against Burge's efforts to make externalism compatible with privileged access. Brueckner (1992) replies to McKinsey in Burge's defense, and further replies emphasizing self-knowledge and Boghossian's Dry Earth thought experiment can be found in Haukioja (2006) and Parent (2015).

Returning to the subject of natural kind terms themselves, what are the options in responding to Boghossian for those who insist empty kind terms can be meaningful despite their lack of a sample to which speakers may anchor them? Korman (2006) and Goldberg (2006) are two responses worthy of consideration here.

Korman's objection to Boghossian begins with a sense that the thought experiment turns on too robust (and hence, implausible) a conception of the importance of reference and causal interaction with objects and properties in the world. Korman argues that for the externalist, the central lesson of the Twin Earth case is the provisional character they assign to natural kind terms. We introduce the terms and wait to see whether our interaction with the world uncovers a unity to their extensions; it may or it may not. In Putnam's example, the extension of 'jade' turns out to be disuniform. It comes in two chemical forms: *jadeite* ($NaAlSi_2O_6$) and *nephrite* ($Ca_2(Mg, Fe)_5Si_8O_{22}(OH)_2$), which look similar to the naked eye. The application conditions for natural kind terms can be stated in the form of default conditionals: 'if water turns out to be compositionally uniform . . .' and 'if water turns out to be compositionally . . .' will be the most familiar types. If the kind is uniform, then the concept applies only to samples of that kind; if the kind is disuniform, then the concept applies to any sample that is superficially water-like (e.g., potable, lakes, streams, etc.). The default conditional for an empty kind would apply to all and only samples that the kind was *believed* to have. Thus, he argues, there may be conditions that distinguish a kind term even when its extension is empty.

Goldberg (2006) offers a similar strategy in terms of satisfaction conditions for Dry Earth speakers' 'water.' The key move is to draw those satisfaction conditions from the mental states and speech of Dry Earth speakers without requiring that their choices of satisfaction conditions be causally determined for them by their environments. That might sound contrary to the spirit of externalism, but Goldberg insists that it is not. We have natural kind terms for items that we have never causally interacted with, such as "super-heavy" elements at the upper end of the periodic table. Chemists can speak of "unbihexium" (element 126), even though we have yet to discover or synthesize any of it, and there has likely never been any in our universe. We can have satisfaction conditions for concepts that are never actually satisfied, but which would still be satisfied only by something external to our thoughts and social practices. Goldberg argues that this would still be a form of externalism and would allow us to individuate concepts and have meaningful expressions, even if the extensions of those concepts were empty.

Besson (2012) reviews a number of approaches (including several of the papers discussed here) and suggests four strategic options: (1) 'water' means the same on Earth and Dry Earth; (2) 'water' is meaningful on Dry Earth, but has a meaning different from ours; (3) 'water' is meaningful on Dry Earth, but is not a natural kind term; and (4) 'water' is meaningless on Dry Earth. She argues that externalists should not accept (1) but lack the resources to pursue (2) successfully. Pursuing (3), it is tempting for the externalist to say that Dry Earth speakers simply don't have a natural kind term in their word 'water' because it is semantically complex (they must construct it speculatively from other theoretical descriptions). But Besson argues that this does not provide sufficient grounds to discount it being a natural kind term when we compare it with actual cases in which we disqualify kind terms for their "motley" character. She ends on a "skeptical note," doubting that externalists have the resources to assign meanings to empty kind terms after all.

RECOMMENDED READINGS

MAJOR WORKS

Besson, C. 2012. "Empty Kind Terms and Dry-Earth." *Erkenntnis* 76 (3): 403–425.

Boghossian, P. 1997. "What the Externalist Can Know A Priori." *Proceedings of the Aristotelian Society* 97 (2): 161–175.

Burge, T. 1979. "Individualism and the Mental." *Midwest Studies in Philosophy* 4: 73–122.

RESPONSES

Brueckner, A. 1992. "What an Anti-Individualist Knows A Priori." *Analysis* 52: 111–118.

Goldberg, S. 2006. "An Anti-Individualistic Semantics for 'Empty' Kind Terms." *Grazer Philosophische Studien* 70 (1): 147–168.

Haukioja, J. 2006. "Semantic Externalism and A Priori Self-Knowledge." *Ratio* 19 (2): 149–159.

Korman, D. 2006. "What Externalists Should Say About Dry Earth." *Journal of Philosophy* 103 (10): 503–520.

McKinsey, M. 1991. "Anti-Individualism and Privileged Access." *Analysis* 51: 9–16.

Parent, T. 2015. "Self-Knowledge About Empty Concepts." *Analytic Philosophy* 56 (2): 158–168.

COULD THERE EVER BE
'UNICORNS?'

Background: In entry #39, we saw how difficult it can be to say what a fictional name means, and how sentences including them might be true or false. Semantic externalists drew a sharp line at times between expressions that had their meaning fixed by our causal interaction with the world and those fixed by our social practices and agreements with each other. The case of fictional entities that emerge after we imagine them tests the plausibility of that line.

Could there ever have been unicorns in the world? Could there be some in the future? For the moment, I will take it that there have never been any in the actual world that we inhabit, and here I'm using 'world' in the broad sense of the entire universe, throughout its history, and do not mean simply the planet Earth. I would think that most people's first response to this would be, ". . . Yes," perhaps delivered with an incredulous stare. Unicorns would just be white horses with a single large horn protruding from their foreheads. Nothing about that seems logically or physically troublesome – much less impossible. We have horses, we have animals with comparable horns or bony structures on their heads (rhinos, mountain goats, moose, etc.), so it's just a contingent fact that our world contains no unicorns, right?

DOI: 10.4324/9781003183167-67

Let me try to motivate a little doubt with a story. When I was a student, there was a fellow student at my university a couple years behind me. Let's call him "Carl."[1] At one point, we both aspired to be professors. The thing is, Carl was not very good at philosophy, but something in it *spoke* to him, so he worked on becoming a professor. He went about it very strangely, though. He bought himself several sets of clothes in tweedy fabrics and wore jackets with leather patches on the elbows. He started smoking a pipe, sitting in a central spot on campus, and asking random pedestrians obscure questions. It was as if he was going to a Halloween party dressed as a philosophy professor from the early 20th century. None of our professors or other philosophy majors looked or acted like this, and all of it was slightly ridiculous. Carl was adding professor-like attributes to himself (albeit outdated ones), but he was not a professor, and he was not becoming a professor. Being that sort of thing has a history and a set of social practices behind it, and whatever we may think of those, Carl was not actually taking the relevant steps. For that sort of thing, how you *become* one matters greatly to whether you are one. Carl was superficially professor-like, but not actually a professor.

Could something be superficially unicorn-like, but not a unicorn? In some cases, surely. If I slather a brown horse in white paint and strap a plastic horn to its head, any resemblance to a unicorn is entirely superficial. What if mad scientists start getting crazy with the CRISPR editing and engineer white horses with horned heads? What if, in some other possible world, a horned head added to the fitness of some hooved organisms, and the frequency of this trait increased so much that naturally occurring unicorn-presenting populations developed? At least *those* would be unicorns and not just superficially unicorn-like creatures, right?

As you might guess, not all philosophers would agree. The concern here lies in how 'unicorn' (or the ancestor of that term in earlier languages) enters our lexicon. The earliest extant unicorn-like images appear in artifacts of the Indus Valley civilization in what is now northwestern India; that suggests that words for them were in use as much as 5000 years ago. Even then, their occurrence seems to be symbolic or mythical, and it requires a generous interpretation to read the contemporary concept back into them. Those accounts worked their way west into ancient Persia, and eventually were introduced to the ancient Greeks, who misinterpreted the accounts as natural histories of real-but-rare animals from distant places. By the late Middle Ages and Renaissance in Europe, unicorns had regained their mythical, symbolic status, and it's from these later sources that our contemporary use of the term derives.

Those later sources were not even pretending to be natural histories, however. The authors and artists who created the works from which we inherit this expression were not attempting to refer to actual entities with which they had interacted any more than the creators of the *Star Wars* franchise or the Marvel Cinematic Universe are trying to describe actual people. Those characters may resemble actual people, but we should not identify them with one another in a strict, logical sense. While Howard Hughes may have inspired the original version of Tony Stark in *Iron Man*, it would be a mistake to think that Howard Hughes *is* Tony Stark. Tony Stark does not exist in the actual world, at least not as a human being. There is no bringing that fictional person "up and out" of the pages of a book or "out from behind" a screen. If someone made billions of dollars developing and selling weapons to anyone who would buy them, but gave it all up to fly around in a red and yellow iron suit, that person still would not be Tony Stark. They would be superficially Tony-Stark-like, much like Carl was superficially professor-like.

By the same line of reasoning, some have argued that there could be no unicorns, properly speaking. The world might contain some superficially unicorn-like creatures, but they would not *be* unicorns. Kripke states:

> [W]e could find out that unicorns actually existed, but to find this out, we would not just have to find out that certain animals have the properties mentioned in the myth. We would have to discover a real connection between the species and the myth – at least in the case of a species that is highly biologically unspecified.
>
> (1973/2011, p. 65)

The bad news is not over for unicornophiles, according to Kripke. We must fix our reference and any grip we have on the meaning of 'unicorn' by whatever "real connection" it has to the world in the language and the circumstances we actually occupy. And in the actual world, our connection is not to some actual part of the world, but to a set of myths – to a form of fiction.

> [G]iven that there are no unicorns, we cannot say that unicorns might have existed or would have existed under certain circumstances. Statements about unicorns, like statements about Sherlock Holmes, just pretend to express propositions.
>
> (1973/2011, p. 67)

This harkens back to other work about fictional names, empty kind terms, and empty names in general. For those who make truth and reference the foundations of their accounts of meaning, these "empty" expressions pose an enduring problem. How can they be meaningful expressions, or contribute to the proposition a sentence expresses, if they signify nothing? In the second quote here, we see a brief hint of Kripke's answer: such statements are meaningless, strictly speaking, but they pretend to say something, and we entertain what they might have said without accepting it. Unlike complete nonsense, they bear enough similarity to familiar things and meaningful expressions that we can extrapolate how we might interpret statements like 'Unicorns once ran across the dales of Yorkshire.' It's fun to read stories about Sherlock Holmes, or tales of knights and unicorns, and they excite our imaginations in pleasing ways. But in the strict terms of a semantic theory, they don't say something that could be true or false in a literal sense, so Kripke says that they are not meaningful.

RESPONSES

The original version of the Kripke paper quoted at some length above was originally delivered at a conference at the University of Connecticut in March of 1973. While a printed version of that paper did not appear until 2011, transcripts of the discussion that followed presentation of the paper were published soon after in the journal *Synthèse*. (This is included as "Second General Discussion Session" in the readings below, under the various commenters' names.) Comments without a paper were unusual at the time, as they would be now, but this has the benefit of offering readers on-the-spot insights from some of the most important philosophers of language at the time, along with Kripke's on-the-spot responses to many of their questions.

An early critic of Kripke's denial that members of a fictional kind could ever exist was Michael Dummett. He noted that there were three possible arguments that Kripke might make. First, they might be metaphysically impossible because 'unicorn' is a species term that must be introduced via causal contact with members of the species; but no creature ever existed to fix the term's reference appropriately; hence, they could not exist. Second, they might be metaphysically impossible because species involve some measure of common descent among their members (and hence species terms depend on this descent); if there were in fact never any unicorns, there could never have been such common descent. Third, they might be metaphysically impossible because any creature's being a unicorn is dependent on the existence of creatures that we now identify as unicorns. There are none, so there is no condition any creature *could* satisfy to be one.

Dummett argues that all three arguments fail. The first argument presumes a version of linguistic practices concerning biological terms and their origins that does not accord with our own. Biological species are particularly ill-suited to essentialism, as every population that we might interact with is rife with variations (hence, no essential properties), and the frequency of traits within it are constantly shifting. Species terms will thus not be fixed to stable properties in the ways chemical terms might be. His rejection of the latter two arguments depends on challenges to the account of modal logic on which Kripke's argument rests. (They defy brief summary, so I will simply point readers to Dummett's piece for the time being.) Reimer (1997) extends these arguments in a direction largely sympathetic to Kripke. She asserts that Dummett is wrong not because his metaphysics or logic are misguided, but because Kripke is best understood as making a much more modest semantic claim: that there are no counterfactual situations *properly describable* as ones in which there would have been unicorns. She interprets Kripke as taking the view that species terms are indexical; in the actual world, where we fix that term, there's nothing on which to fix it. We thus cannot take a term that we have fixed (as we do other natural kind terms) and use it to speak of objects in other possible worlds.

One point from Dummett's response to Kripke here that should be noted regardless of the outcome of that exchange is that the theory of reference for natural kind terms that Kripke and Putnam offered in the early 1970s was much better suited to chemical and physical terms and underestimated the subtle but profound differences between them and the terms of biology. Members of a species share a lineage of descent, as mentioned above; chemical kinds can be newly created (in the hearts of stars, or in well-funded laboratories) without any ancestors of their kind. Chemical and physical kinds have essential microstructural properties that define them (e.g., the one oxygen and two hydrogen atoms in an H_2O molecule, the arrangement of carbon atoms in a benzene ring, etc.); biological species are rife with variations, and their internal similarities often fail to differentiate from members of other species. For readers interested in this area, an enlightening review of the history of appeals to natural kinds is offered in Hacking (1991), and the complexities and difficulties of likening biological kinds to those in chemistry and physics is provided in Dupré (1981). Efforts to revise the Kripke/Putnam account specifically for biological kinds are also included in Stanford and Kitcher (2000).

NOTE

1.   This is not his real name, obviously.

RECOMMENDED READINGS

MAJOR WORKS

Dummett, M. 1993. "Could There Be Unicorns?" In *The Seas of Language*, 328–348. Oxford: Clarendon Press.

Kripke, S. 1973/2011. "Vacuous Names and Fictional Entities." In *Philosophical Troubles: Collected Papers*, vol. 1, 52–74. Oxford: Oxford University Press.

RESPONSES

Dupré, J. 1981. "Natural Kinds and Biological Taxa." *Philosophical Review* 90: 66–90.

Hacking, I. 1991. "A Tradition of Natural Kinds." *Philosophical Studies* 61: 109–126.

Harman, G., W. Quine, S. Kripke, M. Dummett, D. Lewis, and B. Partee. 1974. "Second General Discussion Session." *Synthèse* 27: 509–521.

Reimer, M. 1997. "Could There Have Been Unicorns?" *International Journal of Philosophical Studies* 5 (1): 35–51.

Stanford, P., and P. Kitcher. 2000. "Refining the Causal Theory of Reference for Natural Kind Terms." *Philosophical Studies* 97: 99–129.

INDEX

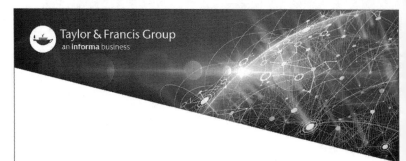